KEN SMITH

COLLECTED POEMS

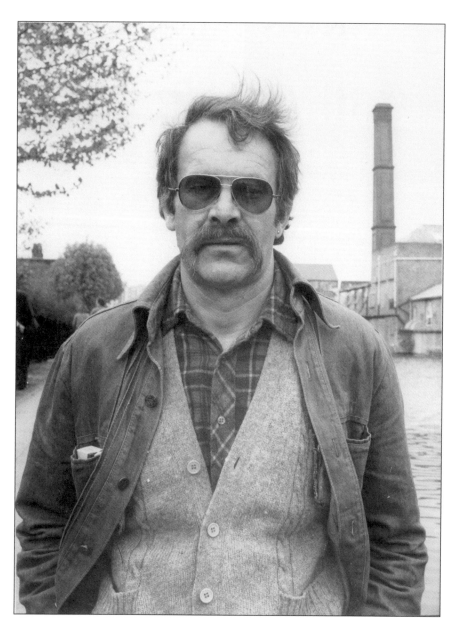

Ken Smith, London, 1982

KEN SMITH

Collected Poems

BLOODAXE BOOKS

ISBN: 978 1 78037 432 1

First published 2018 by
Bloodaxe Books Ltd,
Eastburn,
South Park,
Hexham,
Northumberland NE46 1BS.

www.bloodaxebooks.com
For further information about Bloodaxe titles
please visit our website or write to
the above address for a catalogue.

Supported using public funding by
**ARTS COUNCIL
ENGLAND**

Cover design: Neil Astley & Pamela Robertson-Pearce.

Printed in Great Britain by Bell & Bain Limited, Glasgow, Scotland, on
acid-free paper sourced from mills with FSC chain of custody certification.

ACKNOWLEDGEMENTS

This edition includes all the poems from Ken Smith's two previous retrospectives, *The Poet Reclining: Selected Poems 1962-1980* (Bloodaxe Books, 1982) and *Shed: Poems 1980-2001* (Bloodaxe Books, 2002), the latter including all the poetry which he wished to keep in print from that period. More poems have been included from his first collection, *The Pity* (Jonathan Cape, 1967), as well as all the poems from his second book-length collection, *Work, distances / poems* (Swallow Press, Chicago, 1972), in their original order but with later revised texts or revised titles taken from *The Poet Reclining* in some cases, and with some other poems from the same period added where they appear in the selection he made for *The Poet Reclining*. The final section is of poems written after *Shed* from the posthumously published *You Again: last poems & other words* (Bloodaxe Books, 2004). *Collected Poems* does not include the prose of *A Book of Chinese Whispers* (Bloodaxe Books, 1987), which remains separately available. More details of original publication are given in the bibliography on page 635.

CONTENTS

The stone poems (1971)

Death Songs/Death Dances

The Eli Poems

* These poems were not included in *Work, distances* but are from the
same period and were printed with them in *The Poet Reclining*.

from THE POET RECLINING: SELECTED POEMS 1962-1980 (1982)

Tristan Crazy (1978)

Fun City Winter (1977)

Apocrypha from the Western Kingdom

The clearing

Fox Running (1980)

The Poet Reclining

from **BURNED BOOKS** (1981)

from **ABEL BAKER CHARLIE DELTA** (1981)

TERRA (1986)

WORMWOOD (1987)

TENDER TO THE QUEEN OF SPAIN (1993)

WILD ROOT (1998)

APPENDICES

ROGER GARFITT

Ken Smith: *The Poet Reclining*

(LIFE & WORK, 1: 1938-1986)

Kenneth John Smith was born on 4 December 1938 in Rudston, a village in the North Riding of Yorkshire, the son of a farm labourer, John Patrick Smith (1904-71) and Millicent (Milly) Emma (*née* Sitch) Smith (1911-90). Harsh conditions and an unyielding temper ensured that his father never kept a job for long. The first of the wanderer figures that haunt Smith's poetry were his own family, moving on at the end of harvest:

> a darker blur on the stubble,
> a fragment in time gone, we left
> not a mark, not: a footprint.

The isolation of this life meant that he grew up 'talking to myself and inventing mates', which is where 'the habit of inventing people and dialogue, stories and fictions' began.

Solitude intensified when he moved to the city at the age of 13. The horizon shrank, the world became small and hostile. His conversation with himself became silent and turned to writing. His father had saved enough to buy a grocer's shop in Hull, an independence with which he rapidly became embittered. He prospered and bought a second shop, which Smith ran when he left school. But there were continual violent arguments, in which Smith had to defend his mother. It was a situation Smith was locked into until, at the age of 19, conscription released him.

In the Air Force he became a typist, and assuaged his boredom by reading widely and completing his university entrance qualifications. He was demobilised in the spring of 1960, returning to Hull, where he married Ann Minnis, a secretary, on 1 August. In the autumn they moved to Leeds where he read English at the university.

Leeds had become an important literary centre. The school of English included Wilson Knight, Douglas Jefferson and Geoffrey Hill, who was then teaching contemporary poetry. Jon Silkin had just completed two years as Gregory Fellow in Poetry and was now an English undergraduate himself. His successors as Gregory Fellow were William Price Turner and Peter Redgrove. Literary activity centred on the weekly magazine *Poetry and Audience*, of which Smith became assistant editor. Through *Poetry and Audience* he met Silkin, and in 1963 he became a co-editor of *Stand*, an association that lasted until 1969.

For a few months after graduating with a B.A. in 1963 he edited, reviewed, and wrote full-time. But his daughter Nicole had been born in 1961 and the pressure of supporting a family soon forced him into teaching, first at a school in Dewsbury (1963-64), then at Dewsbury and Batley Technical and Art College (1964-65). His son Danny was born in 1965 and his daughter Kate in 1966. In 1965 he moved south, to teach complementary studies at Exeter College of Art. The teaching proved complementary for him too. His own education had been literary and linear: from the art students he learned to think laterally, by image and association, and acquired a much sharper visual sense. It was a development that was to prove crucial to his poetry.

His first pamphlet, *Eleven Poems*, was published by Northern House in 1964 and his first collection, *The Pity*, by Jonathan Cape in 1967. *The Pity* was very well reviewed. P.J. Kavanagh wrote in the *Guardian*, 'Anyone who despairs of contemporary verse should be led by the hand to this book.' The most arresting poem is the title-poem, which incorporates the lines Mao Tse-tung wrote in prison when his pregnant wife was garroted in the next cell:

> I cut my hands on the cords at the strangling-post
> but no blood spilled from my veins;
> instead of blood I watched and saw the pity run out of me.

Writing in Mao's voice, Smith gives a restrained and sensitive account of that moment of inner revolution when 'Compassion... takes the hawk's wing, diving.'

In one sense Smith's poetry was released as soon as he was free from study. He wrote 'The pity' and 'Family group' in the week that he graduated. In another sense the poems still felt like studies, the results of conscious writing strategies. Despite the achievement of *The Pity*, he felt the need to break his habits of mind, to break free from his cultural inheritance: 'Part of being English is that we entertain really only a few footholds on the imagination.'

In 1969 he moved to America, where he took up a post as writer in residence at Slippery Rock State College in Pennsylvania. Once outside England he felt free 'to take much bigger risks...to follow out ridiculous ideas...I could invent much more, push a particular image in ways that in English poetry would be regarded as luxurious.' He learned from the work of American poets: James Wright, Robert Bly, David Ignatow, William Stafford, and the Alaskan poems of John Haines.

He learned still more, perhaps, from oral and primitive poetry, in which there was a revival of interest in America at that time.

His second collection, *Work, distances/poems* (Swallow Press, Chicago, 1972), includes 'Ghost songs', 'Ghost dances', and an adaptation, 'From the Nahua': but particular borrowings are important only as indications of a deeper influence on his poetic language that persisted on his return to England. When he walks beside a playing field in Exeter and writes of

> accepting my birthday.
>
> How the shadows move in
> at such news and are strange
> in the light. This feather
> left for his marker my brother
>
> the crow had dropped by the goalpost
> seems a dead man's finger
> keeping his page
> in the unfinished biography,

he is re-entering, if only for the space of a metaphor, a universe that is a unity, where the poet can discern his own myth taking shape in correspondences, reflections, foreshadowings. Poetry ceases to be what it so often is in England, an art of framed observations: it becomes the spelling out of a selfhood, 'a language to speak to myself'. The practice of the poet becomes a matter

> of silence
> and waiting, how to forget,
> how sleep, to see and not notice
> the moment the mind
> takes to its channel, its
> leaping and threading and listening,
> the business of dreams, visions,
> and distant barely perceptible sounds
> – how they effect
> what is brought to the world's gate.

One sequence is literally 'the business of dreams'. 'The Eli poems' sprang, as Smith describes in a prose passage, 'the door', from insistent dreams of a landscape through which two figures moved, Eli, a lodging-house keeper, and Kate, a mill girl he had got with child. The first poem, 'Eli's poem', was dreamed complete as a poem on a page in a book and typed out immediately on waking. The final poem, 'Half songs, 1790', came from a waking dream a year later, a daylight glimpse of Kate that was like 'a going and a showing at the same time'.

More often Smith works from a kind of personal archaeology. The sequence *The clearing* came from exploring an actual clearing (set in 'Minnesota perhaps' but in fact in Massachusetts) and sifting through the settler's abandoned house. Once again a prose passage, '*Concerning the clearing*', gives the genesis of the poems. Into this reconstructed history, the sense of 'poverty rising out of the ground', he weaves elements of his own mythology. The hawk of 'Hawk vision', who in a moment of liberation 'diving / somehow upward' vanished, now returns 'hungry, / weary, wrong-muscled, / grey bird of my death'. The fusion of personal myth with documentary material is Smith's way of relating his own life to the unity of lives, of reaffirming that he is 'a cry among cries'.

'Tales of Urias the shape-shifter', an intermittent sequence, began to take shape in Yorkshire beside Colden Water, a moorland stream that became a mill stream in the Industrial Revolution. One root of the poem is a local belief, recorded by Elizabeth Gaskell, that 'there were little people, there were spirits here...until the machinery came'. Another root is Smith's own sense of

> something very surly and crushed that for the sake of a metaphor...for the sake of a fiction you could say was the spirit of that water...My sense of the world is not much in common with my time...The universe is articulate, it is trying to speak, we are one of the agencies by which it speaks,
>
> > part of how the world thinks
> > so through us the blank
> > stuff of space knows itself.
>
> But we're not the only agency.

Here again Smith's poetry forms part of an older tradition. 'The kingdom' of which he writes is the kingdom of William Blake's grain of sand, of Thomas Traherne's Orient and immortal wheat. 'The other world' appears when we give proper attention to this world:

> Describing the buds of the sycamore
> coming out boxed each 4 to unfold
> is to be in the other world
> listening in this one.

Three years at Slippery Rock were followed by a year as poet in residence to the College of the Holy Cross and Clark University in Worcester, Massachusetts. *Work, distances/poems*, which had been rejected by three English publishers, was well-received in America. Ralph J. Mills, writing in the *Chicago Sun-Times*, welcomed Smith as 'a poet of formidable range and strength'. Smith returned to England in 1973 but continued to travel extensively in America and to have his work published in America. He continued to be better-known in America until Bloodaxe's publication in 1982 of *The Poet Reclining: Selected Poems 1962-1980* re-established his reputation in Britain. *The Poet Reclining* is a testament to Smith's integrity and endurance. A major imaginative enterprise 'in the American grain', it had to be sustained against the grain of contemporary English poetry.

There is no stylistic or thematic division between *Work, distances* and *The Poet Reclining* as there is between *Work, distances* and *The Pity*, and the above discussion of Smith's work ranges freely between them. But ten years separate the two volumes, ten years in which Smith became virtually an underground poet in Britain. He received an Arts Council Bursary in 1975 and from 1977 to 1979 he was the founder editor of *South West Review*. But his own work surfaced only in pamphlets. From 1976 to 1978 he was Yorkshire Arts Fellow at Leeds University, commuting from Exeter, where his wife Ann held a secretarial post. Immediately after the Leeds Fellowship was over, the marriage broke up.

Smith moved to London and into the experiences of his long poem *Fox Running* (1980), a brilliant recreation of a man under stress encountering the city. Rapid, compulsive rhythms create flicker pictures of the Underground and the seedier districts, in which Fox glimpses his double, the shadow he could so easily become:

> Faces
> mentioning defeat saying
> bankruptcy desertion failure redundancy
> lost bottle. Their light
> that had gone or never lit
> or they burned now on the lamp oil
> of necessity the pure oil
> of ageing euphoria.

All that separates them is the survival instinct, whatever it is in Fox that 'speaks / from the lengthening floor / of his blood his conviction / *not me not me jack*'. Smith finished up as a live-in barman in an Irish pub in Kilburn. As a poet he survived, in the words of Jeff Nuttall's *Guardian* review, by 'taking heartbreak in both hands and using it like bricks and mortar to build art...*Fox Running* is an astonishing leap in compositional scope'.

Through the University of Antioch in London Smith met the American writer Judi Benson and made a new home with her and her son Todd. From 1979 to 1981 he was writer in residence at Kingston Polytechnic, and they moved to East Ham.

The Poet Reclining was widely acclaimed, even critics like Peter Porter, who would be hostile to the element of projective verse in

Smith's poetics, being forced into 'a new respect for his powers'. His subsequent collection *Terra* (1986) included the sequences *Hawkwood* and *The London Poems*. *Hawkwood* is based on the figure of Sir John Hawkwood, a 14th-century condottiere, whose career enabled Smith 'to write about war and aggression and masculinity … under this metaphor of the wanderer'. The poems are like 'late night work Hawkwood might have done…a closed book I'm opening'. *The London Poems* are all short, 12-line poems, 'sonnets without the concluding couplet', his interest being partly formal, to see how much he could pack into three four-line stanzas.

Terra was followed by *A Book of Chinese Whispers* (1987), a collection of prose pieces. Smith's prose is closely akin to his poetry. Some ideas simply develop into prose: 'the stories are really very convoluted metaphors'. Because there was a limited market for experimental fiction, the prose pieces had only appeared in five pamphlets. *A Book of Chinese Whispers* collected these together with more recent prose, adding another dimension to the work of a poet who sees his development as a long 'learning to let be…to let a set of images or patterns or obsessions form itself into shape'.

[1985/2004]

JON GLOVER

Ken Smith: *Terra* to *Shed*

(LIFE & WORK, 2: 1986-2003)

Ken Smith's reputation was established and his readership widened by *The Poet Reclining* in 1982. To some extent his achievement paralleled the expansion and influence of Bloodaxe. His journeys were both inwards and outwards. His poems were intimately related to self-discovery as he placed himself in stranger and more demanding situations.

Terra (1986), *A Book of Chinese Whispers* and *Wormwood* (both 1987) were all published while Ken was writer-in-residence at Wormwood Scrubs prison between 1985 and 1987. These were followed in 1989 by a major prose account of prison life, *Inside Time* (with Dave Wait). He continued to travel and gather his intensely felt observations into prose and poetry, including *Berlin* (1990), on the fall of the Berlin Wall, and the poems of *The heart, the border* (1990), as well as several poem sequences for BBC radio. He travelled widely in the US, Europe and Latin America, visiting Hungary, Slovakia, Ukraine and Romania for his BBC projects, which merged poetry and speech with music and sounds recorded on location.

Later books included the collections *Tender to the Queen of Spain* (1993) and *Wild Root* (1998), as well as *Shed: Poems 1980-2001* (2002), which received wide praise from poets and reviewers in poetry magazines but not a single review in a national newspaper. Having the most significant book of his life ignored by the national press hurt him deeply, and disappointed all those admirers of his work who regarded *Shed* as one of the most important books of poetry from the second half of the 20th century. Four collections reprinted in *Shed* were Poetry Book Society Recommendations and *Wild Root* was the PBS Choice, while *Terra* was shortlisted for the Whitbread Poetry Award and *Wild Root* for the T.S. Eliot Prize. He received America's highly prestigious Lannan Award in 1997, and a Cholmondeley Award in 1998.

He continued to speak for victims of oppression, and the collaboration required for radio work was a vital counterbalance to his intense individuality. He edited, with Judi Benson, *Klaonica: poems for Bosnia* (1993), and with Matthew Sweeney, *Beyond Bedlam* (1997), a book of poems by mentally ill people. A book (with CD) of his BBC-commissioned poems from Hungary, *Wire through the Heart*, was published – in English – by Ister in Budapest in 2001.

Unlike some poets whose work is sparse, Ken Smith simply lived to write, and he was at the height of his powers when he brought Legionnaire's Disease back to London after a visit to Cuba. After four months in intensive care, he caught an infection while recovering in hospital, and died on 27 June 2003.

Like many poets of his generation, Ken Smith formed a creative symbiotic relationship with America – its landscape, history and language. While he lived for many years in London's East End, he could, perhaps, talk about the city experience only after the freedom and distances of the US and its people. His poetry offers a special insight into the world in which we now live. Highly personal yet accessible and involving, it provides a record of journeys that seem at first to be strange, distressing and unique. But many readers will continue to join him as though finding vital common ground for the first time.

Ken Smith was a great poet. He was a writer of personal experience who often reflected a sense of loss as he talked through the urban landscape. But he was also a fine poet of the visual and the present. His poems had to be heard, seen and felt, and they live on now as the visual, tactile and audible worlds of a wonderfully rich imagination. His last retrospective collection, *Shed*, published in 2002, confirmed the immense power of his poetry.

[2003]

COLLECTED POEMS

FROM

THE PITY

(1967)

Fossil

Made stone, cleft, shape and shell of a thing
past being dead, presses your finger:
a reptile once lithe in the hot sea; dead.
A simplicity still wanting pain, where skin
and nerve coiled, turning itself on itself,
dying. Not skeletal even, the dead's condition:
a pressed black stone.
Inside, white crystals, jammed, hard.

Not far from the beginning, the begetting seed
borne in it is a finished thing changed.
It suggests itself – solid, voiceless.
You keep it on your mantelpiece;
a broken thing, shaping your hand.

Grass

Grass erupts slowly, locking the soil in frail roots.
Without these tenoned fingers earth would be as sea,
drifting, unsure. It is a sort of knowledge,
gripping together, confirming that hill's shape.

Do not forget the grass; that trodden softness
could only be an innocence that insists, comes back,
season by growing season. It cannot stop itself.
Though you kill it, grass does not seem to die.

Rocks, morticed in themselves, do not require it,
nor does its colour clutch the spaces of the desert.
Its absence is death's sign, brooding its own mystery.
Grass exists. All life revolves around its rooted blade.

And yet grass does not care. Accepting without flower,
it seeds on plains or in cracked rocks, indifferent
to a touch that sears the granite. Grass
moves on, impotent in will, a rooted apathy
exposed to hoof and fire. It cannot stop itself.
Grass waits the mower's knife, the ditcher's spade.

Means

I walk the robing corridors of trains, touching
steel and glass, sure of their shape. Clutching
the sides of things, suspended by motionless objects
in motion, I am a man believing in things fingers
touch. Touch tells me most. I reject
a reflected existence in metal that lingers
beside me; it is tricked into being by light,
like an aping shadow. Yet I accept that slow
procession of fields beyond glass, this night
reaching over stooked corn, the sun's dead glow.
Watching the side rail slide into darkness, pale
windows tighten to mirrors. They borrow frail
shapes from the lit and peopled compartment.
Means become ends. I turn from this game of bent
lights and return, trusting the corn to hold still.

Both harvests

Guns twitch the gloved ears of the rabbit,
that ripened with the corn. Summer
was burrowed, with the young peering
over green shoots. Now they move
under red corn. But blades are set
and honed. A tractor roves the scythed
edges. These men who stook and bend,
bend and stook, have their business
with grain. Those who come after,
come to kill, gun under shoulder.
A rabbit is a grey thing running,
stopped, hung in air, dead. Some
hide under bound sheaves. Some panic
into the mower and are savaged, blood,
bone, and pelt. Set blades are determined.
Rabbits die running, not like standing grain
cut clean. The field is clear, its straw
lined and ordered: it will be bread

and bedding for safe cattle. The rabbit
need not fear the winter. Shot corpses
brace under fur, are shared out evenly.

Family group

He also was a stormy day: a squat mountain man
smelling of sheep and the high pasture, stumping
through pinewoods, hunched and small, feeling
the weather on him. Work angled him.
Fingers were crooked with frost, stiffened.

Ploughing he would fix his eye on the hawthorn,
walking firm-booted, concerned for the furrow.
Horse and man in motion together, deliberate,
one foot put before the other, treading cut clay.
He would not see the bird perched on the plough.
He would not chase the plover limping over stubble.

He was my father who brought in wood and lit
the hissing lamp. And he would sit, quiet
as moor before the fire. She drew him
slowly out of silence. She had a coat
made from a blanket and wore boys' shoes.
She was small and had red hands, firm-boned,
and her hair was greying. The house was stone
and slate. It was her house, his home,
and their family, and they quarrelled often.

She churned butter, baked, and scrubbed floors,
and for forty years he laboured the raw earth
and rough weather. In winter we made mats
from rags with pegs. We guarded ourselves
and were close. We were poor and poorer banking
each pound saved. Each year passed slowly.

Now he lives in the glass world of his shop,
and time is grudged. Ham and tinned meat
and vegetables are his breathing day.

He works harder and is unhappy. She too
stoops through the labouring year, is greyer
and grumbles. Nothing gets made any more
but money that cannot be made. Nothing
means happiness. The light comes down wires,
water through tubes. All is expensive, paid.
Silence is gone from their lives, the city
has taken that poised energy. Violence
is articulate. The deliberate motion is gone
and he moves with pain through time that is work
that is cash. He will not notice the crashed
gull fallen in the storm, the grabbing sparrows.
She cannot ease him into speech, or be content
before the broody fire. She is in fashion now.
But seasons pass them without touching.
They will not feel the winter when it comes.

Country: Keld to Reeth

Each day the earth offers itself
to the sun's heat, water.

A picture I carry, a country
all weeds, pale flowers
shaped in poor soil.
The rain drifts over it, I hear
my feet crush the winter grass,
see my father who walks in a landscape
that seems not growing but shrinkage.

Returning, he did not pause on the hill
between the still faces of horses.

We were a darker blur on the stubble,
a fragment in time gone, we left
not a mark, not a footprint;
the cold forest, the birds of the moor
do not recall us.

The hills lie on anvils of stone,
sheepcut, shaped by all weathers.
Great stones squat on the ridges
as if the ice might come back for them.
A few harebells lift to the wind.
There is a ragged field, patches of bramble.

The pity

> I cut my hands on the cords at the strangling post
> but no blood spilled from my veins;
> instead of blood I watched and saw the pity run out of me.
> MAO TSE-TUNG

She was destroyed and my child ceased in her belly.
In Kiang-si we had walked in the clear morning,
she hanging back, barefoot, childbig. Crossing
the plank bridge I saw the falling mountain
with its stream hang still. The land lay like a bowl
of pebbles, hills behind me at its rim. A hawk
splayed in the wind, dived to kill; so sparrows die.
China was patience you said: the sketched lines
of valley and the reaching twig, all still, rest in motion;
a large pale flower twitching, a flower waiting, open.
So a vast land itched for death, its people mild
and ministered.
                    But the cockroach and the grinning toad
drawn beautiful was China; the fly grown fat on flesh,
glittering in heat. I was lashed and drained
of the gentle passion. Patience was prised from me.
I picked lice from my hair. You thought me gentle still.
I ate filth, wore it, would have died in filth.

The horned and hanging bat sees a bat's world.
Fish quiver in the shallows, cold as their element,
thinking water. I wore contempt, grew hatred.
I was locked and jailed. She that was my wife
was garroted. And compassion had not anything to do
with this; she was destroyed where I could hear,
and the child ceased in her.

36

Compassion cannot go forever in the sun,
paraded, bowing, twig-like. It rests,
and somewhere takes the hawk's wing, diving.

She was destroyed and my child ceased.
I cut my hands on the cords at the strangling post,
but no blood spilled from my veins;
instead of blood I watched and saw the pity run out of me.

The Humanities, Dept of Literature

I

In April with its showers
I stood on the banks of the river, Lethe

some people were talking
in the rooms they had caused to be made

but I don't know who they are
asking is this my life also

and take from my mouth the word *love*
that falls like a water between stones

II

My child thinks her shoes get smaller
not knowing about growth

the mouths of some professors are shut
like a boot against water
not knowing growth either

Lorca

This morning a man died
he went out to the hills
with others not remembered
he was shot
he was cut out of his shadow
his grave has no marker
it opened as many graves
opened
after and before
that precise morning
Lorca was murdered

he has no sheet
no bell
the grass crops his skull
he is dead
and this sprig of words
has no grave to bear it
in Europe's long graveyard

he is the thorns on the dead thistle
the lemons' surviving acidity
a reaped wind in the olive trees

Translation

We had been caught
in an instant.
Our faces looked out
from a photograph
fluttering
down the corridors

Everything falls.
A collapsing universe.
Not a shred

of intelligence
holding
the fence-posts
that strain
in their nailed and rigid
order.
Paper and burst oranges
float from the ship's wake
plunge into
the blue mouth of the sea

on a wall
where no wall is
in ink whose blue atoms
are flying
outward
I write a message
for no one to read

Train

(after Max Ernst, 'Europe After the Rain')

In the dark
each sits alone
clutching his flag

I have more than my one death
to attend to.
There is a sickness about
and the magician has vanished

But I sit with my 26 years
spread on my palms
and I wait for the silence
when the programme is interrupted
and the actors have no script.
And I think how to carry my children
into the sewers

Roll up the cities.
Let the window explode
in a million glass flowers.
In the darkness already
the woman picking milk from the step
the ashes raked last thing at night
are postures, buried
slipping into dust, rock, ooze,
furniture of a planet
wheeling in silence
lonely as a train
waving its little handkerchiefs of steam

Between us

On this day of my life
I'd like a truce
when I would not think
what came before
what does it lead to

I have wished for a day
without thinking
who owns this field
that I'm not sure I can cross

Not to be drawn into this day
needing to possess
the food that takes me to another

There's no object
not owned
not a tree not a blade
not the white thumb of a mushroom

And there's no way out
but I wait for a day
– Thursday or Friday
it doesn't much matter –
with a great peace
between us

The hunter

On the hill three hawks
on spread feathers
fish the summer grass.

In summer on the bare hill
the light falls in sheets.

The sheep turn like ships
at their moorings.

The crows fly downwind,
their sounds fall from the sky,
downwind they are crying.

Man, dog, birds. On the hill
sheep and the wrenched grass
lie downwind. It is summer.

The birds crossing the sky
are naked, the light falls,
downwind they are falling.

It is summer,
dog and man share the hill,
sniff the air,
hunt the birds.

As we look in the tunnel
for the end
for the bleak
unblinking eye of the daylight

he is looking
for the black holes in the sky.

Water

1

a country beginning to open its spaces
a silence being broken by voices

over the first wrecked cliffs
darknesses moving in darkness

the sea keeps moving up. The sea
comes with a thin razor of water

it takes what it gives
the salt white birds fly over it

the sea wipes off the footprints of gulls
this country seems grass under the feet

its sounds are not shaken like trees
its shapes do not move like slow horses

no metal rings through this silence

in half-light the coasts lift themselves
a sea beats on them, is wild to come in

2

the cold of the wind is not from the sea
not absence of sun makes this darkness

in the dry river-bed I have seen
even the granite rippled by water

the rocks lie without ease on each other
hills scoured by rainfall wait for the sea

the sea holds a knife to the land, breaks
out the first stone shells. The sea

takes the land away, moans, lifting small
white flags in this impossible darkness

> I want to be as though newborn,
> knowing nothing, absolutely nothing, of Europe
>
> PAUL KLEE

Europe:

cathedral of the dead
to be free of you
I lay down
in speechless grass
I shut up my mind
and became
only an ear
that listens

The earth turned to its season.
Hugged to its lit side
I turned with the smallest creatures
the earth has

I could not press myself
into my shadow
nor cease knowing
of the camps in Europe

When every stone lies on a man
there is no end or beginning, the dead
are with us, we
are not children
we carry them about with us.
We cannot hush them in their silence,
each one
a sound
laid still

We inherit in this map
centuries of misery, plague, trachoma,
generations bent to the shape of a ploughshare

It is a field of listening skulls
it is a tree shaking out blood

it is a boy walking in Warsaw
nameless
European Jew, a continent
shrunk to his face
to that crying

No man envies this quiet
the dead have. The bones of the feet
do not dance
the thigh-bones do not find each other
the fine bones of the fingers lie empty

Continent of skulls
everyone tastes it
the birds carry it
the snails eat it

In the rattling grass
and the spider's quivering
I listen
to the dead
speak of my country

(i.m. Antonio Machado.
And for Europe, 1936-45)

The street

leads nowhere, cannot be entered,
down which no one is walking

into the silence, the pure sea
of boats, cryings, scuffed quays.

The grey air is empty, built into
cloud-columns. Street of childhood,
        no one is calling.
In its doorways no person is standing
nor stares from one house to another.

Things happen to us.
War boarded these windows, split walls
spilled in the held spaces.

In the growing dark only a sadness
presses the stairs to the stilled rooms

whose walls peel like maps. Here the guns
and the toys become one another. The war

has moved off. Who left can't return.
Who lived here forgot the clear lines

the far buildings had, *it has happened*
we say, the sound bobs on the water.

Who stares at the great shadows, remembers
a voice, forgets whose, who watches

the sunlight fall, there, between high houses
themselves fallen, his feet don't lead back.

      Who had a house now has a stone.

The past

      is like the sea
where we look for a light
        a blue hill

      the two waves parting
behind us
        rest at a distance

      The past is nowhere
though I look everywhere
      for it
      always expecting
to walk round the house
        into it

Perhaps I don't
see myself
        in the present
        and search
in the immense bonepit
            asking
        how silence could ever be lifted
            away from these dead

        It is sea
without rock or fish
            without bird
        crossing its face

        Only this arrow
of our world
            flies straight
        from distance to distance

        While the continents
drift through it
            the water
holds up the same look

        The past doesn't exist
where my grandfathers
            laboured
        to open the earth
            with their hands

Leaving

Putting my head to you
I said Yes
a heart
beats
gently:

a child reaching
into its fingers'
quivering,
within you
an immense
small shiver
of silence
contained like a sound
in its bell.

I, who sit over a poem
trying to see what is
pressed into light
confess being moved
more by death:
a darkness almost
not possible;

I have felt even a stone
itch to unfold itself
and the sea's crying
in the shell of my skull

We create as the husks
of the grass
bear seed,
wanting like grass surely
to obliterate
earth's darkness.
The earth we have risen from
in a blind rearing
urges us,
the earth broods under us

I ask –
tell me it is not this
a dark we go into
shut like a stone

A fragment

out of our joined
lives is grey sky
mountain and pine
grey lake, late summer
the year of our child.

For you there were faces
snarled in your coatsleeve,
you were a creature trapped
in its flesh, in its pain
the roots of your hair
the knife of my body
the night, the light
hurt you, the light
streamed out of you.

Under the wood the child
opened its mouth
to the earth of your breasts.

We became under the rain
the mountain the reeds
one cry, smaller than a minute
three mouthed
a small shrill crying.

WORK, DISTANCES / POEMS

(1972)

As he moves forward with his environment, Man takes with him all the positions that he has occupied in the past, and all those that he will occupy in the future. He is everywhere at the same time, a crowd which, in the act of moving forward, yet recapitulates at every instant every step than it has ever taken in the past. For we live in several worlds, each more true that the one within it, and each false in relation to that within which it is itself enveloped.

CLAUDE LÉVI-STRAUSS, *Tristes Tropiques* (1955)
tr. John Russell

Poems 1967–1969

Exiles

(for Marek Laczynski)

One the foreign woman

More than my life's map
of notebooks and lost gloves
I know the moon's other look.

I remember a hat rolling
and rolling. No name
no other detail swings
in that street's wind.

Counting the steps to my room
in the damp house I glimpse
the fence and the roof
of my grandfather's house.

Here I continually
open a drawer on the dust
trapped under newspaper.

I look through the glass
at an indifferent skyline.
I count the steps
in a strange house.

Two the return

Objects, clenched in their
separateness. Streetnames,
a park, the Jewish memorial.

In a place changed
out of my presence I find
known friends in strangers.

I remember I say, being
deceived, touching
the stopped door to a room
lit with child's songs.

Dead streets, dead houses,
dead people. Here I walk
with my eyes turned away
not to see absences, blind windows.

Three the photograph

Face of Kafka, the camera
flattened old shadows that moved
in the eyes and mouthcorners.

How much of our lives is filed
in deep drawers, a red form
for my birth, a black for my death.

Documents, passports, the
European darkness is trapped
in the breath of officials –
jobs to do, quotas to fill.

As we learned when the shoes
were fetched up and counted
and the long graves were dug.

Out of that darkness ashes
and letters and photographs.

Stopped in a fragment
the shutter admitted
the curious look of a man.

The smile and the angle
of sunlight survive him.

Suburb

To sleep
a million years
in the prow of the amoeba,
in the spark of the lizard's disappearance,
coming home through the long cry
from the Vistula
to wear our shoes out in this place.

The news is from elsewhere.
The postman will bring letters not yet written.
The telephone squats on its greetings.
The window shuts out the insects.
The curtains shut out the window.

I am the shoe's foot.
I am the ring's finger.

She speaks

This late evening, years
it seems, years I have been sitting,
the life in me sleeping, the chair
grown to me, drawing
round me the figure of my quiet. In which
I have sat out his silences, silences
in stone and coral, silences beyond sleep
and still water. Not him I endured
but his speechlessness –
wanting him cupped to my ear,
him shape to my sounds, years
not knowing what name rode in his skull,
what cry might break at the end of it.
Night after night, till he rises,
winding the clock, dropping his boots,
turning toward me as if he contained
other lives, as if
he were the sum of all the dead trying to get out.

Years of this. Grumbling asleep
names from a sunk continent, strange words
with salt and age in them. Or I have caught him
alone on a street saying aloud
A man lives when his name is pronounced.

Whose name? who lives? I ask
the slope of his shoulder, his shut jaw.
Or will he never speak again? I don't know
how to open him, how to enter
this difference, this mountain of quiet,
chipping it, savouring moments of speech
when he plays family man and looks up
over the offering bowls of his table
to where I have my own name ready to be spoken,
and the child's tricks, and things he must buy.
I offer tiny stones from my own house.
That he hates. He thinks he is heather
taken from the moor, continually bent
to a wind no longer pressing it, he's like a stone
shaped by water water shall not have again.

Am I to wait at the mouth of this man
the dead lunge through? I don't know what beasts
stalk me, what dancing goes on in his head.
I watch, letting him see that I watch,
catching his postures to the bathroom mirror,
talking to himself.
There'll be no steps I can't dance.
And I can't sing there'll be no song.
I'm his cynic, his lame mule,
I clatter my pans in his ear.
I shall blow his house down.
I am anti-matter, he shall be my omega.

Go teach the birds singing.
Go talk with the dead.
Go walk in the graveyard.

The child's version

Twaddle her mouth said, tired
that she knew better, given up
to the mouth's part.

In his notebook
the air takes the smell and shape
of rooms of unfinished things –
clock parts, bits to set moving,
queerly shaped pebbles.

Little use to a people hoping
one day to jump on the moon's face.
I should not put a frame to him.
Imagine him water, taking any shape
while the shape is, untrustworthy.

Everything discarded: wood and stone
he chipped to unreconciled faces,
obsessions with maps, codes, mirrors,
or wondering how it would be
to have never seen horses.

They were ashamed of their own sounds,
I know that she bore me in terror
less of pain than of pain's cry.

I am a leaf at its edge, turning
its growth back, fashioning
the image of his face in sunlight.

She is pictured turning away.
Mostly I see him staring
into a field of yellow flowers,
staring and nodding gravely
with the worldless dignity
of big flowers, curious, unyielding,
part of that tall yellow dancing.

Age

The old aches come home to be fed.
He looks through photographs of dead relatives,
the daughters nudge each other and grow quiet

Now it is the slow time
before the jaw's clench.
He accepts the idea of silence,
the street a journey across mountains.
He says goodbye to the sea, again and again

It's like being too early for a train,
nothing but to wait and grow patient.
He rages in the bathroom,
the world shrunk to a cracked fingernail
a lost stud, a button sewn tight

He contains all the planet's dust.
He's a socket where sorrow gathers
its small hard grains

They want him gone, and in each of them
two rivers, one of grief one of guilt,
flow into each other

Bitter

This is the house, good as a shoe.
One by one
the dead years count themselves.

The words are old, the mouth
just goes round them.
She sings for the wrecked moon.

For love the miracle of touch.
All the miles go underfoot.
Too many trains, too many neons.

She sings for the coloured lights.
She is singing the one word *bitter*.

Grown with water in the cracks,
bitten into the roots of stones.

It wants to make everything dust.

The boss

The stone of his life weighs on him.
My life's work My life's work he whispers
holding the stone, his hands open.

It lies on us. House-stone, stone
of his past, his years are the one stone
soothed to his shape our lives lie under.

There are other stones: his wife and her two stone breasts,
his money, his speechless look through the window,
his children, carrying their own lives.

His ambition is the great stone he carries.
We polish the stone, it is our lives are worn.

We polish the stone, his house rears in the suburbs.
We polish the stone, he dreams and fears loneliness.
We polish the stone, he grows famous.

His is the stone on us when we are still.
His is the stone announcing itself when we move.
Our lives tremble, we cry *the stone the stone*.

The son

He inhabits corners of their lives,
his cry forever raised in them.
He is running into the yard or the sea.
His voice deepens, there is mud on his clothes,
tar on his boots, it happens continuously.
He goes into the army, he comes back and marries.
He lives far away, he still eats with them.

Wherever he is now he is the same
staring at nothing or holding still
for the camera. The son who dreams
looks from all the photographs, he hides
in the cupboard with old shoes.

The son who went off one day.
The son who has wife and children.
The son who works out of town.
The son who is in another country,
where it rains the same rain.

He's in the house they made,
he uses the furniture and spoons in the drawer.
He's in with the paint, always around
with the dust, he stares through the window,
he's expected any moment, food is waiting.

Forever leaping through air, or waving,
or asleep in the shed.
His look is familiar. He is the son.
When he comes back he wonders where he is,
when they speak of him he wonders
who they are speaking of.

Everything is ready.
He wipes off his plate.
Now he wants none of it.

Gravedigger

Before him go the armies, the metals shining.
Up the green hill
go the hobbling women spitting smoke,
the processions of sadly missed wives.

So much spent muscle and bullet.
So many stopped quarrels.
The shoemaker but sleeps.
The bird sings in the high trees.
There is a silence of wheat.

Who owns the dead who are always dead –
men once trees in their own land,
women desirable as water?

He spits on his hands grey with earth.

He rules with a shovel.

His spade speaks for him.

A good fox

The fox ran, everyone ran after.
The fox's care: he drew out the pack,
he ran so we ran with him

Glimpsed red on the field, he ran
to his wood, to his own cover,
the light trembled across him. He ran
into holes, under leaves, across water,
ran in the open, everyone ran

Water never tires over the stones,
it is the stones are milled down.
The fox never tired. He worked at running.

Not for fox but for the running we went,
the fox knew it. Under the star
he lay down, he was nothing we wanted

We knew he was fox, running out
on the sly fields, we knew he was red meat
and bone and nothing but fox.
So we ran, we just ran, he with us

And the fox runs alone, peers through bracken
red against red, slinks to the house,
appears by the hedge, no one after him

We tired of that game, fox, we tired of your red slash
on the skyline. We tired of your pause and turn
and run on with a shake of the head.
We tired of nothing but fox, we learned better.
We tired of nothing but fox, but a good fox

Beyond breath

I

Beyond breath labour bread –
he feels grass shake without wind –
a twig snaps with no footstep

Fields flecked by rain and yellow –
too long he wanted more –
his hands make a dismissal

She sweeps the dust out,
the smuts of the rain forests –
she sweeps words out of her mouth –
he sits with rats in the barn –
the silence cannot endure itself

II

Tear up the map of your lands
Let the foxes out hunting

Fill the forms up with jokes
Give the schools to the children
Scrap the dead languages
Prevent nothing, prevent nothing

Behind those who pile up the bread
come the armies

You will be accused, deny nothing

Persistent narrative

The speaker opens his mouth.
The lovers lie down together.
The boy is sent to the war.

The last train leaves the city.
The sky clouds over with ruin.
The animals step back into shadow.

The speaker opens his mouth.
The fields are trampled by horses.
Children crouch in the ashes.

Survivors wait at the frontier.
Two armies meet in a forest.
The lovers take off their clothes.

The speaker opens his mouth.
An earthquake topples the belltower.
The boy lies down in a cornfield.

Soldiers patrol all the streets.
The grocer has run out of flour.
The girl dreams of a wheatfield.

The speaker opens his mouth.
Now the woman sweeps out her house.
Now there is a christening.

The ship enters the harbour.
The girl waves her red scarf.
The lovers cry out in their love.

And at last it is still.
And the speaker says *I shall begin.*
The children are all asleep.

Skull

Worms, moles, water and grasses
have brought down the mountains –
the landscape presses its messages.
The hurts come together, the eye
opening on light, a shrill of insects
flooding the ears, the paranoid skull.
Let it all go down, blue water of lakes
at prayer in the rocks, bracken, sticks,
the woods and the shivering creatures
invading the threads, the warm cells,
bone canals weepy with blood.
Pain raises its monuments, the dead
thick as porridge in Flanders go down,
the villages make do with an obelisk.
Let it all go down the voices
cry on under the helmet. The stone
image presents arms: he was there,
he was real – motion of shoulder,
too long in the sleeve, the set jaw.
He writes postcards, sneaks through wire,
he crouches again in the muck, he envies
the dead brother and the snails,
he trails home like a black sulking wing
fresh from nowhere, the dreams
ready their sights and their knives –
nothing now but this blood, this cry out

Let it all go down
till the bone hood shatters
and the roots break in

Somewhere else

Mountain upon mountain upon mountain,
assembled a long time. I am underneath
with my eye in my head, watching

I enter the sea, I fly over the winter forests,
I bring the stars back from their beginnings,
I put history under my lid,
I make everything real, the worlds reverse in me.
I go back before the stones, I examine
the first moss, I construct my amoeba

What I feel at what I see
is part of what I see
and as transient. It's all right,
we are safe from each other.
Do what you like – tie each other up,
caress, club, obliterate with love
or napalm or silence

It only hurts whom it hurts.
My job is seeing.
'I am concerned with the way we see things'

Anything else is crap. I am becoming all eye,
all jewel, panoramic or close-up
as I move. Soon I shall invent everything

Far off I am near, under the kiss,
under the cat's leap, angled
under the batons, under the tanks

Without blinking, a valved shell
following orders from the light, I sift through
the waters of everything

If you don't
like it switch
the thing off

Old mill, Newton St Cyres

Bring out number weight & measure in a year of dearth
                    BLAKE

Knowledge alone is no more than a weariness of the soul
                    ARTHUR C. CLARKE

Always this pressing for shape –
paddlewheel, gear's tooth, millstone,
wood driven on water, the force
pushing through iron to stone and the stones
grinding to quiet the shudder of wheatfields.
Centuries of grain, centuries of water,
galaxies of dust mottling the sunlight
sheened their working flesh, dust
in the eyelid, chaff in the shoes.
Somewhere are numbers and graphs
for the mountains of bread, the fat loaves
rising in ovens: knowledge of soils,
rainfall, knowledge of mills, beams, joints,
or the tensions of water – for the curious
threading their beads of fact, those magpies.
Leave that old weariness
knowing or not knowing, the earth's water
is pressing out of shape, its denial gives
in its *no* the quick of renewal, a mere
gesture of water here and not here
like a going of air. I revolve doubt
around doubt in this certainty of things –
stone, metal, wood, the running grain
beaten to meal: show me a thin cook
or a poor baker, wherever I look
I might see only wheatfields, possibles
turning about without centre,
doubt at the axlehub driving the flour
into bread and the bread into sleek girls
measuring their waists in pale slices.
Crush the doubt under words, it
raises its ear, its signal for silence;
crush out the silence, it waits at the end
of our syllables, entered this mill
like an anthem. A quiet under sound,

the doubt back of certainties, there's hunger
for bread and hunger apart from the bread.
Measureless absence, hunger is no word
it is nothing in the mouth
but struggling to say. On Famine Ridge
the bones count out loud: rib bone,
shut mouth, dead genital,
stone sounding on stone, throat whispering
eat eat in the sour fields,
charity's ashes and lemonjuice, eat,
devour the earth. To the last crumb

The Amana Colonies

Founded 1855 in Iowa by a group calling themselves Inspirationists
originated in Germany about 1714. The immigrants 'according to
His laws and His requirements in our own consciences' attempted a
community sharing work and wealth equally that persisted up to the
Depression but that exists now as tourist bait close to Interstate 80:
'one of the midwest's most historic and recent attractions.'

1

Fortitude, endurance, *amana: remain faithful.*
We survive the sea and the great silences.
Under God and the blue sky we share all we have.
Amana – we put a spade to the wilderness.
Amana – skill of our hands on the new turned land.
Amana – the word is our breath, we share,
we survive the woods that are gone
where the redmen went hearing the rain speak.
Amana, the corn roots, cattle and vines,
mortise and tenon, coins and sweat run together.
Amana, our work and our bread.
Amana. The voice within each of us speaks.

2

In the turning of wood or habit of speech
that old life may whisper, a black dress
fluttered in wind, wooden shoes in the snow,
poverty chewing its nails, winter and summer.

Will nothing of sharing survive, the cry
of what was weathered away in the guidebook.
Erosion is paint from an aerosol can, visitors
sniffing repeating *authentic authentic* –
a word in the mouth. We make and we sell,
we share our dead root, we dream of endurances

   3

What prints mark butterchurn, spinning-wheel,
what is a scythe's use, how held, what sweats
stain the handles of tools? What sleeps
in the dropped vowels or survives
in the ticking of clocks? Why these names
and *amana*, this word that remains, that endures?

Inventory/Itinerary

Illinois, Iowa
Dead grass & maize stalks
Miles, miles, $4\frac{1}{2}$ thousand
Timeshift 7 hours
2 continents, 1 ocean
Travelling, 4 days
1 good time, much being quiet
200 cigarettes, 1 bottle brandy
1 arrival in Iowa City
March 25th 1969, 6.00 pm
$3.38 in my pocket
1 cab-ride into the clapboard wilderness
1 return on foot carrying 2 bags
9 phone calls, 2 wrong numbers, 1 reply
Waiting, waiting
Hunger, loneliness, weariness, silence
1 poem written quickly holding things down
The durations of wind, cold, grainfields
Endless helpfulness, cheerfulness, on the nail
The bland faces, America America
And silence. And night
And wind blowing, right through the heart

Farmer

No tree but the one tree before the house
No house but the one house behind the tree

No earth but the land he treads on
by the barn, the plough, by the silence

No speech but the clipped yawl
he sings into the eternal wind

The corn breaks its husk, rain falls,
the house creaks and settles

He works, the grain sings on the field,
the sky covers him. Labour and bread

and a mouth to speak with, the rest
he does for himself, tree or no tree

Figures at daybreak

A woman walking alone through the outskirts
of some small town, I don't know what daybreak it is –
carrying herself and some moon of sadness slowly
toward open fields

There are landscapes that ache under birds' wings,
irreducible, not filled by a wind's length.
Magnolias soft as an eyelash, Indianapolis spills
over the plain

Fields and farms, great barns under those rooves
of a settling wing, the eye drifts on the same images,
the land cut so, stamped to familiars, each thing
shaped to our way

I imagine the water-towers growing, tiny and bulbous
out of the soil of some distant farm, row after row.
Aloud I think, Love we are shaped in our acts, in our words
for each other

The roads lie straight as a look. This way three hunters
cross tracks where trains hoot in the loneliness,
walking loose-limbed and apart into thin woods,
into grey light

Going

Going, crossing the flat lands
where the sea lay its print,
others sang of the wheat, the wheatsongs
praising the earth for its giving.
Under sun or frost the grasses pale
as if something were wrong
to grow where the land gives plenty.
Always another speaks, listen he says,
the world is dying. Far out corn
yellows on all sides, its sea
bends at the horizon where half-barn
and half-tree signify only the eye's
limits. Listen, he says to the wheat,
the sea dies, fish
turn their hulks to the sky,
in the white bear and the penguin
the threads are breaking, the whale
pressing those unlikely spaces
threshes a dead foam, its flesh
flecked by our issue. The wheat
listens and grows, through Illinois' silence
the train drives straight. DDT he says,
a dead stain inks the globe over,
feels out the horizons, grown
like a cuticle. Do the farmers
who bend to this plain know it,
their corn-haired girls who study the ways

of the lost Algonquian, do professors
of speech know? I am trying to bury
my faith in the grass. It's blown
he keeps saying. I listen for birds
by the tracks: there are none –
set out for the wrong places,
they lie in a field of premature skulls.
I hear no poems, only the stillness of light
and the feasting molecules, chromosomes
breaking the chain in a world
that is dying he says. For not singing
the fullness of wheat I make
no apology. Listen, the world it is dying

L. A.

I am alone with the shadows of my room.
The darkness gets nearer
each time I look at it, as if
it were the lid of my eyes. When I sleep
the night moves over my face

The mountains may teach their stillness.
In Orange County, in the first
orange grove, they have preserved
one tree in the asphalt

My children, far away and sleeping
in your city of looped water
where we walked in quiet places
the mind lived, how to speak to you
of this sound on the earth,
and this dark that comes close
I must speak of,
how begin to be still

Poem 1

If I am stone then I'm all stone.
If I am water I contain nothing else
of thrashed rock and salt
that is all of the sea's taste: ocean
admitting neither its boats nor its fish

How far it is it's a small place.
Mapping the journeys I outline a flower
whose colours belong to the lands it crosses
from mountain to sea, a thing of spaces
and lines that meet where confusion arrived
seeking itself in the places doubts are.
See how they swell into cathedrals,
so many police states, so many flowers

And meanwhile here come the skeleton helmets,
veterans enter the cities in triumph
saluting the monuments. Here come
the gas-mask makers, those who weave nightmares
out on the ridge and dream money, salesmen arrived
at the airports bringing the latest in death.
Here come the tool-makers, napalm chemists,
sharebrokers, altar-boys, leg-irons

I've been pulling a face so long it's stuck.
I've been sitting here watching myself
watching the sea and its motion, its move
on the shore to and from like a sweeping brush:
the sea an enormous heart beating on stones

Poem 2

So much light and there is darkness.
So much metal and stone, the nations
whirling in dustclouds, horses and horsemen

In the city glare ours
is a light that goes out. Too much alone
there are days the mind backs up

In the squared land to the west I saw
how we denied the gatherings of water,
reading the earth and the connections

The plains are forever, the sky is,
where the bombers ride on the skull,
the land's people grains of rice on a map

To be sought out, to become splashes of blood
and burnings, to be counted in numbers,
and nothing to add to this nothing

Nothing to add to the wheat
and the separate voices: power
to the lifting blades of the grass

The Stone Poems

(1971)

1

A man's work
he must bend for them,
his lifting become
stone-shut
with a stone's presence.

Stone of house, stone
of monument.
Nothing in their gift.

Stone in a man's field
or a man's shoe –
piece of the Earth's
wish to be idle, rid of us,
fraction of misery.

Not as the sea is:
weeds, birdcries, a fish
glancing the sunk light.

Sea changes totally,
stone rarely. The dead
form a new kind of stone.

It will not alter. Snap
and be nattered to dust
or the chafing of water.

Part of the sea asleep
in its own shadow. Part
of its stone.

2

Either he shifts it
or goes round it.

Dragged to the field's edge
to be grown over, useful there.

Others rise in the rain,
chiselled by frost,
tossed up by boys.

Some arrive strangely by night
or happen as comets do. In New England
frost forces them out,
stone on the move.

And some lie continually
in the field's road
finding their ways back
into bleak malevolent creatures
wanting to sit in open fields.

The man keeps pelting them
in a backward whirlpool of stones
slewed over centuries.

As if this were a battle: a man
hurling stones and the stones'
slow returns to their orbits.

As if they would lie barearse
to the sun, giving nothing growth.

3

Stonecold we say. The great music
goes on without them,
Mozart's mind forming again
in the members of the orchestra,
in the air, in the bow
touching the string, the conductor
commanding what he heard once
of rivers, of stones, birds, men.

In the blank faceless thing
nothing of our meanings
but that it outlasts us, holds up
the names that mean nothing now
in the wind wearing them away
where the scripts change
and the dialects weather
as the words shift their meanings
in the long war with silence
till what's left is a finger-traced
blur where the chisel cut
let vandals look upon this epitaph.

That it is stone, that
it is cold, that it is
chosen for sepulchres.

Nothing there: a few bones
picked clean as sticks
and the seasons drained out:

a stone flag,
a lament for dead people.

And nothing in that, nothing
can be staved off: mine
is a stoney vision they say.

Out in the strange light
grown in the world.

4

Absence of stone
assenza di pietre,
the stone
solo pietra raschiata
scraped to its usefulness.

Stone taken into speech,
stone touched in a bargain,

counting stone, stone
turning in the mill,
the ruminant, *la ruminante.*

Stone taken from the moon,
I have since touched one.

Stone ballast used again
building the shipman's house,
the miller's table.

A Roman stone I took
years ago that had lain
centuries its pavement
under the Saxon graveyard.

Stone of absence
pietra di assenze.
Stone of Beethoven's fist.

No more the miracle of gneiss,
nor graining nor quartz,
no scourings of rivers,
no granite, no dross
nor the eye of volcano
né l'occhio dei vulcani,
so little, the hot gas
of atoms blown back into space
that were Socrates, chert,
flakes of flint tool,
touch of all lovers, *di fiumi
massi, puddinghe, detriti.*

Nothing grown wild,
moving strangely, not moving
till the long ice moves them.

Not the bull's dark,
l'oscurita del toro.
Not the beasts' wonder,
*la meraviglia delle bestie
stupite della loro stessa nascita*
over their own birth.

Not lichened over
under half the stars.

Not city stone nor stone
the wind forgot.

No stone at all:
a land gleaned clean.

5

All through stone. Things
immersed in it
become stone.

Without feature or interest
to what ice or water
scrapes it to.

Anonymous,
not dreaming nor dancing.

Intending nothing –
neither the good house
nor arrowhead
nor inconvenience.

Resisting.
Not resisting.
Holding on while the planet
shudders into more stones.

Nothing to be done
but be a grey boulder
or be pebble or be sand.

No inside, no outside, no centre.
No squatting like an animal.
No nesting like a bird.

Not wanting to go back
into rock, not wanting
to enter the sea, not wanting
to be a small red flower
or a black shoe
or a lost button.

Not likeable.

Not bothered.

6

Turned in the hand, idly,
to the contempt of the busy.

What it would be
to be brought to it
forever in its place.

A man's say to be
pig figure, bird entering flight
or the tiny house of a snail,
replica of the southern wind.

A man's say. Not a thing
to do with all he says of it,
no more than birds their names.

That it may look
from the church wall
a man sharpens chisels.

From the bleak glance
of quarries came footstools,
thrones, the gargoyle's
snarling waterspout,
knights in stone armour,
the poor kneeling or stooping,
stone thumb to the stone nose
in contempt of their masters,

locked beasts, Siva's dance,
a man peering so long
till the seawind wears him away.

The man's tools seek
a stone anaconda.

Bunched in riverbeds,
abandoned, stones
lie down anywhere.

They will not answer
out of the strange mouth
of the dead.

They will never mean anything.

Their silence
applauds them.

Death Songs / Death Dances

Begin anew and put away the wisdom of your fathers. You must lay up food and forget the hungry. When your house is built and your store-room filled, then look around for a neighbour whom you can take advantage of and seize all he has.

Red Cloud's advice to his people, the Oglala Sioux,
on how to become wealthy like the whites, whom
they should otherwise avoid (1868).

(from R.K. Andrist, *The Long Death*)

Dream journeys

In the last light we made camp.
I slept with the dogs' whimpering
and dreamed of the continent, a fierce mask.
From doorways the people offered their indifference
or crept through the bush to watch us. One came,
bent and crow-faced from years listening
to the desert. I recall he was dumb
and told off the words on the palm of the woman
who spoke for him. No more of that place than we,
his way lay south as ours west by the mountain.
I knew roads to the places he spoke of.
By the fire a stranger, in the dream
I knew him far back. His was old news
of burnings and wanderings, of the people
who spread through these lands.
I half-slept, the men with us listening
for some wonder. When she described the sea
our people opened their mouths, though I had once
seen it myself, grey and endless, like our way.
I was kept silent, it was nothing.
In that woman's voice I fell into deep sleep,
all the ages of Europe elaborated,
a mathematics of blood. At the last
he walked between land and sea, a man
centuries old stepping the waterline stones
with an easy care, his eye never to one side
but to the edge of water and haze, and stepping so
a child came whom he seized and ate,
throwing aside what was half-eaten
as he came to the distance, without pause.

From the Nahua

Down from Ometeotl who is
all pairs beyond flesh &
divisions, descending
the twelve flights through
many gods, strifes, nights,
the birds & the sun,
the Milky Way that is
as a woman's skeleton we come
to the world we know at rest
on the backs of 4 crocodiles
supporting the 4 created
corners & floating on a lake
where are our stones & flesh

the soul travels down nine
more, passing a yellow dog
guarding the river, through
peaks to a mountain of pure
obsidian, met in turn
by bone cutting winds, flags,
arrows & wild beast, through
a narrow place to the final
rung: the ranks of the known
& the unknown. And all this
apart from the 3 heavens –
the sensual in Water & Mist,
the mind's Land of the Fleshless,
the Sun's House of Pure
Imagining, & last Mictlán
the inferno at Earth's core –
all this in time a calendar
worked from the stones
but precise as it matters,
and all a continuum bent
on itself where the soul
travels away through the flesh,
a circle begins as it ends
for those who cannot give up.

Consider this system, cut
into bloody cakes by the
Mexica, Dog People of Atlán.
And consider Hernán Cortés
arrived the appointed year
from the east, the way
of the people after the sun
to the seed ground, who
considered them *far from*
the knowledge of God not
possessed of reason,
dispensing glass beads
of syphilis & abrupter more
casual deaths in the real.

On the north coast, Barnstaple

Silt flourishes, easing our junk
to its colour of birds and rain,
prolongs in its pause
this wave that is breaking

The town set like a seal
shook out stiff cloth and linen.
Beads of metal
ran down the world's old map

The statues rot. In the churches
a few merchants gaze in benevolence
over the poor, elbows
propped on a skull's globe

Passing, the wave slides
over grey flats, the town
a suburb of its history,
enclosed like a plate

Where winter begins

Birds fly south, a saw
yells through the woods.
Night is coming, water
chirrs in the stream.

I want to be an animal
between one sound
and another. At evening
I come to a river, the reeds
like the dark in my own skull.
I want to sleep, to be still
away from the villages,
night is coming.

Image of bird in the sky,
image of leaf, shadow on shadow.
Darkness begins in the trees
and the tight maize-heads.

Burrowed out of the owl's look
I dream the shush of grass
in the night fields, sleeping.

Abandoned village

We had left that place, even our shadows,
and there's nothing to say of it.
A house not to be lived in again,
not to be *dwelling-place*,
our memory's house comes down
where trees hold up their heads
logging up summers, good years and bad.
That house is a lung breathing out,
its smell woodrot and leaving

Nothing of ours, not a sweat-bead,
whatever a man might have touched
or his hand rested. Odour of absences,
ants track in our rain-quickened speech.
Ours is the quiet of an animal sleeping,
the light far into woods,
the musk of the rainforests,
buried kingdoms of wood

Song for the whites

I live away from my own people among strangers
for whom words have too many shadows.
Back there my mouth turned to a taste of ashes.
I sit all night writing my songs
for no instrument that no throat sings,
and don't care if they're bad, to be tied up
with strings like a doctor's skeleton.

Most days I make small voices. Sometimes at night
sounds run through my head that I must get up;
if the world is running to death I shall take
at least my own sounds with me. I've grown used
to the strangers, their speech no longer alien
and I see they have no covering against winds.
Come under the song strangers, I shall tell you
what you don't know and don't care for –
how when we tortured it was to respect you.
Over the best fighter we put a buffalo robe,
cut a cross in the breast of the bravest dead.
We honoured those who destroyed us.
Let me tell you about the frozen grasslands
and how when we had nothing to eat
your words were *let them eat grass*.
Let me tell you about the Cheyenne who died at Sand Creek
and of White Antelope who sang *nothing lives long
only the earth and mountains*.
You may write that in books if you will.
It was his death-song, his and the buffalo's.

The Sioux cleared from Minnesota

I prefer women with flesh, the bones
have too much to say about cemeteries.
Here they're so thin I can't see them.

When I first came here I grew plants
that were dead by morning.
I went alone seeking quiet.

Then the subway burst through my sleep, inches away.
I prayed to whatever god listened,
hearing 15 million buffalo die.

Now when I close my eyes to talk
to the voices I hear Little Crow –
Hawk that Hunts Walking, speak out.

How he led without hope to the slaughter.
He's gone saying his people can't win,
he wants peace, not the life of a no one.

A year later shot down
picking berries, they threw him
in the offal pit. So much for Little Crow.

I've seen their cities.
I have nothing to put out but this hand
and this little glass.

Here

1

How they whisper the grass,
the undying. Their voices
come off the black shore
speaking their bones & losses,

possible lives.
The damned came near
passing the sea hand over hand

Mother my dreams are
a sky of spilled wings
and the stars falling limbs

The new world under the bandage
smells antiseptic, corridors,
pipes busy with plasma
for miles out of power-plants

I fear the sea's mind.
In my head I carry my people.
They have no names,
you cannot arrest them

I'm reading the books again
for a loophole, I call Ohio
and hear grainy voices
talking apart in strange rooms

All year the movies told
their disturbing journeys:
a thrashed country, laid
to the stone

The sun went down, the cities
flying below at evening –
precisely
marks on a bad lung

Driving past, their faces
white & set homeward,
soon the damned will be
where we can't reach them

   II

Goodbye deathmask, goodbye redwoods,
paper forests touched
into ash blown
catty-corner

I predict a strange dance
& yearning. Already
in the Mojave new rumours
knot themselves thickly

I shall dance, celebrations
of all we were
in that land of leaves & water

May the grass
be within me
furled & moving, a dancing

Crying woman

She is making her sounds, the ones for everyone else.
She goes *cri-cri* like a walking bird and then
sounds of a big bird alert on the rocks.
Crying woman makes the sound of a baby about to be fed.
This one is the sound of someone alone a long time,
the sound of someone cast out at sea, the sounds
of wreckers guiding a boat to their reef,
of the ship's crew who are drowning
and the indignations of those who tell this years after.
This one is from the mountains, she makes big sounds
full of cloud and rain, she begins her infinity.
This one cries *mother*, thinking of her people.
When she thinks of the south she sings
like someone asleep in the sun all day.
This one the otter. This one the gazelle
running for love of running. And this one
who is quiet a long time is a gull
pitching out from the cliff between land and sea
till she becomes the air she swings on. This one
begins shouting straight off and never stops,
a devourer that wants everything at once.
This one is creeping through grasses to ambush,
and at last she's a spilled song
finishing somewhere into the roofbeams.

Silence is hers, she makes that
when she thinks of another, when through her sleep
her children are running too near the water.
The cry of an animal kicked awake to its guard,
noises of something lost in the thicket, she croons
the names of old lovers dead in the wars.
Some sounds come from nowhere, she wants
a man who lives on the moon's back, she wants
to die if she does for eternity what she does now.
The first awake in the camp, she's about
seeking warmth, she goes out of her self's house.
She's the first creature to crawl out of the sea.
She makes all sounds, I don't know if she's one or many.
If ever she puts them together at once I shall drown
and drift with her in the sea off Northumberland
crying *forever forever*, awake to the last star.

Ghost songs

1

Only a little way the dead come with us
wanting to live in their names spoken out.

2

The wind follows its footprints.
I sleep in the owl's coveting watch.

3

This is the feel of belonging to no place:
the gods come loose from their stones.

4

No man can drink all of the water.
Think of the ice frozen a thousand years.

5

When the butcher comes give him bones.
When the clerk comes give him nothing at all.

6

When I draw you why do you pose so
unless I am taking something away?

7

All the facts are breaking apart.
The jetplanes are sowing dead grass.

8

If the dance takes an age I shall dance,
if my sleep lasts a minute.

9

Write it all down, enough for a postcard.
Pick someone at random and send it.

10

Send it away from you. Let them burn it.
Let them feed it to cattle.

Ghost dances

1

Whoever you are looking in I'm in here
looking out. Do you hear singing?

2

I want to be nothing more than the spaces
between sounds, as the air is between grass.

3

Once I was a road where everyone passed.
When I heard the dance first it was over me.

4

First I became dancer, then dance.
I shall fill all the room's crevices.

5

For music I need my hands and my feet.
Let the rest of me join and fill like a smoke.

6

Let the air be the crows', to the fish water.
My sign is an ear of good wheat.

7

The animals come and go. The sea
doesn't go down forever.

8

The automobile is a dead beast going the way
of the mammoth. Let it go.

9

I shall dance through your landscape
back to my beginnings, a thousand years.

10

We are alone here with the stones.
Dance joyfully for that woman spinning.

In this place

My hands pray to nothing.
I am the world of the little sand-grain.
I allow nothing that I am to be taken away,
I turn from the camera
against what it takes from me

The bird came, he looked maybe at the sky,
I thought he is looking at nothing
and contends with it. I contemplate
writing the history of birds – Alexanders
and Hitlers and St Jerome, strutting the branches
for the sake of this straggler

When I go back to my people I feel
like an invader. I belong no place
and live only in my speaking.
I am content with the woman I took long ago
and the children she pressed out crying.
I have what I want, I have what is not much,
a few friends, books and songs, right now
it's maybe the middle of the fifteenth century
and they've begun to fight all through winter.
If they come I shall defend these things
and ask nothing of theirs. I am the stream
that doesn't know it wears stones away,
the beaver building its dam for itself
not for the hunters and those who take pictures.
I am the leaf lying downwind and use
only a few things. I am salt in the shaker,
my hands pray to nothing

Where did I learn such quiet

Where did I learn such quiet, after the Punic wars
and the killing of those who surrendered,
where did I learn it?

Even Europe has come and gone and the star patterns
altered, Hannibal would no longer know
the way through the mountains. From where
did the silence come over the Polish Corridor
and the sleeping Xanthoi sentries?

Brothers the field longs again for its grass,
the wind travels the old passes, the snow begins.

In Pennsylvania, winter's end

A year I turned in myself
like a sail, round and around
turning to voices
caught by the light.

The dancers are turning
to look, asking who partners them,
poised as they move they see
how the light moves on itself.

I lay on the side of a hill
in summer, the hill
that is as the side of my own life.
The grasses rippled, ancient.

I became very small
and entered my body, seeing within
dancers crossing the slope far away.

Are they arriving or leaving?
Are theirs these voices calling
back or beyond them?

Under the hill an iron bell
rocked by the moon is booming,
its sound a slow tide,
wells of sweet water.

Little notes

Nick draws her brother.
In the enormous eyes
are pictures
of people and flowers.

This wood then, its grain
recorded itself growing.

And these stones of the cathedral,
what do they record?

Oh the small agonies,
men and women in time –
dancing, dancing, bread
and a short life.

The moon's a round cry.
Take a good look
before it's covered in moss.
Nick says the moon is the moon.

She draws her mother,
one breast then the other.
Draw me the sounds
of her feet, of her breathing.

After a journey

When we wake
snow will lie on the sills. There are things
happening when no one knows it.

I returned from the west finding the trees bare.
With the first cold my children came,
I don't know where they learn their songs from.

I know the dead have little to say to us,
but speak like they were the same, like clocks
scuttling into the dark with the same nothings.

Later perhaps they turn aside to a place
where they no longer need us to listen, or go out
when they are at peace like burned wicks.

What we don't know yet is no matter.
I pray not to a god but to stone,
to the grass, to the running hooves of the horses.

The Eli Poems

The marsh

Evenings the crows pass
in and out the beech trees.
Perhaps it is autumn,
she walks the lowland.

The first pinch of winter –
red docken sticks, colour
running from the pasture,
weeds leaning east.

The stripped falling
face of the willows
is part of it. The land
levels down to the marsh.

A place the river
loses itself, boggy land
of overgrown water
the foot strikes into.

October swells in the beds
of reeds and tall grass.
She blows the thistledown,
puts her feet squarely

and passes the place
horse and man went down
at a gulp: bottomless pit
of bones and lost footholds.

Oh rumours go back, soldiers
and farmers mistaking
the look of firm footing –
ghosts, river vapours.

– Or birches at twilight
above fallen leaves, there
where the stones lie
on the slope as she goes.

As she leaves that place
that after will speak of her:
face peering through water
into a face, into a dark.

The third month

Oh she is
no one's,
her belly
is big.
      She
puts her hands
to touch, she
has tried to
ignore it, she says
who will help.
      It
cannot be stopped
now it's planted
he shrugs, his hands
face outward,
he says this or that
and goes.
      Well go
she says after
and you might.

Other times
what tones he took,
what ways
and she let,
she can't recall
now there's this.

      Well
goes sometimes
a long time
between breakfast
and supper and

99

down along there
she lay down, he also,
under a bush, for
they met walking
by maybe chance
out by the water
and no they weren't
strangers, sat often
to the same table.
And not for the
last time they
lay so, and he
what was it
he said and what
matter: there's this
feeding itself
on herself, and him
walking away whose
short legs
pressing her down
whose eyes shut
and the damp grass
chilled her, he
muttered and cried
an animal sound.
      And see
where that got me
to herself
she says, as who
would she speak to
with nothing her own,
a thin
working girl,
that sort goes hungry
stopping up draughts,
goes down
with fever, galloping
consumption,
if only the poor
learn manners, and look
her skirt
can't afford to
trail the ground,

she'll work
till she's brought
to bed she yells
after him, slow
distant figure
crossing the street
to his house, *go*
and you might,
looking for brats,
here's brats,
go speak
with your wife
old man
old man
old man.

Eli's poem

I met a woman from the sea coast,
she took me aside in the bushes
and wrapped me around and said *we are alone*
as the moon up there is with just two sides.
I did what was to be done and came away with her.

Now I am with a crazy woman
who hurts herself with ashes and briars
running in the scrub. She takes blankets
and stuffs them under her skirt for a child.
She takes out the blanket and croons on it,
washes it, beats it with sticks till it cries
and tears it to pieces. Her lament
goes down the street on cut feet in the gravel.
She runs in a nightgown thinking she's the police
and charges anyone with ridiculous crimes
like wearing a hat sideways and walking wrong.
The people here know her and smile and say
yes they will come to the court to answer.
She writes everything down in her book.
In bed she's like trying to catch a hare.

She wants to sleep with me all night
till my back breaks, if I doze off
she wakes me crying for love.
I married a crazy woman for her brown hair.
At first I thought she was pregnant
but her blood runs, the doctor shakes his head at me.
I tell her your child is in the other country
and will not come here because of your frenzy.
She runs to the church crying she's evil,
the priest holds out his god's battered arms
and says *come child everyone's evil*.
I cool her with my breath, I cool her with water.
She's insatiable as the river, like winds
she has no place to go and runs
from whatever does not move. She's holding a wooden knife
and staring it down till it becomes pure menace
and I fear it myself. I sleep with her
because then I control her and know where she is,
but I don't know what runs in her.
Now she is out on the hill wailing
cutting her flesh on the stiff grass
where I go to her lamenting.

The rooming house

Dead girl what we did
was done against death,
our thrusting against
all the room's shadows.

I held your long hair
over your breasts,
under its glove of fur
your belly ran like an animal.

I put my hands to your hip-bones
that seemed like the gates
of the universe, I thought
one day to fall through forever.

And cried *do not go from me*.
I saw you walking around
in another place, in a small
picture of death.

Hearing the sounds you made
I held you against parting.
I came in to you, your dark
howled against my dark.

In the room now I breathe
for the smell of you, your thighs
wet as horses' flanks in harvest,
your heat's dumb flailing.

Dust you breathed, memory
of your throat-sound, your sweat
ingrained in my flesh,
a stained quilt, survive you.

His lament

Was it all my effort
to release you, all I knew
but to give sound to your moving,
a white to your stark face.

Words I had spoken, pulled out
and held near to myself
I released then, their twistings
ran clear as milk from a jar.

I saw as you saw, shimmer
of the rising wave mirrored
in the cornfield, a thrush bone
splayed on the air's flesh.

I had walked this way, I
had not seen the spidery roots
of the grass, leaf-vein division,
map of my own blood.

Birds combed the estuary mud,
water threading their prints.
You sang an old song, I
saw you glance through the air's web.

I touched the thin bones.
You cried out as I entered you,
a gull's yelp, breath-borne, all
the years of my life crying.

You died, so scrawny you were.
You moved out of the light though
a shape of the light still,
and you stir in my bones now.

The obsession

Months now I have lifted
your frail shell and listened.
You would not speak, you went out
the door down the street,
taking the fieldpath.

In the hood's shadow your face
is a blur I cannot remember.
I must read the slope
of your departing shoulder, it says
I have shaped you in words
that aren't true, in my dream
you move as you would not move.

You passed by, the water
looked up at you, ice-rimmed,
the marsh winter-stiffened.
On the slope where the trees begin
bird-prints had locked in hard ground
over each other. And here
you lost sight of yourself,
must come again and again
down the marshway, the dead end
of the recurring decimal.

In the wood fine snow grains
outline the pine needles.
How far it is to the hill
and the cart-rutted track.
Along there the trees thin out
where wind breaks the seedlings
and the ridge is bleakly open.
Far off the river widens to the sea,
a white mist. You must come again
to the scrubland down the side
where the brown turns to grey shale,
finding the house deserted.

Is this the place lady where pain
broke like a parting of oceans across you?
From here you have no name
but return and return to this room,
stoop over the linens, folding the sheets
and folding the sheets till there's nothing
and you but the want to be nothing
put away with them,
and the heat of you gone
as the room's warmth spends itself
on the window glass.

What was done

Push they said,
holding your limbs,
spread you apart.

So much joy they took
in the pain, the women
bore down on you.

All for men's pleasure
they said, they
looked most for a boy.

Of their own labours
they spoke, alternately
sweetened and bullied.

Turning hour after hour
the muscling wheel
rode through you.

*And he saw you now
he'd think twice.*
But they envied this.

Strangely they moved
in the old dance,
feeding up gossip.

They did what they must.
You suffered, love,
but to wag tongues.

At the last you saw
your own body's shafts
and the driving muscle

between them print out
its track, the child
leapt to their hands

and the wheel rolled
out of you, pushing
the small life from you.

The door

A few days before my father's death the last dream cried as I woke:

> *My name is Kate, I am an Irish girl*
> *My name is Kate, I am an Irish girl*

People might say the dreams were coincidences, dreams merely, indulgences perhaps, and that death's blank event drove them off at last. Over a month or two there had been about a dozen of them, almost always the same dream, or a part of it: marshland, hills one way, the tidal estuary of rising birds another. The marsh compelled attention, and the path through it that turned away up the slope and along a ridge of scrubby woods. The dream turned evening there among the briars. There was a dark quiet house, abandoned, the cold wind landward between clearings. The house lay at the track's end where the dream always ran out in a search through old drawers and cupboards of musty clothing and abandoned domesticity: but for what? Usually I saw different parts of the same landscape, entering the dream at different points on the journey she made through the marsh and up the slope along the ridge to the house, over and over. Crossing the field, walking through tall grass or wandering the marshes, she was always going away, always turned away from me. I saw only her back in a long shabby dress, her head's bulk of dark hair, a thin shoulder hunched inwards, turned towards the slope. I think she was a bit simple, a bit mad perhaps, quiet, sometimes clearly speaking a kind of song that in other times might have been taken for witchery or angelic wisdom:

> *She stood by the driven spring*
>
> *She cried my love's*
> *face down in the sea*

People didn't bother with her. I don't know who he was. Eli. Not a workman. Pompous, a bully, middle-aged, kept a lodging-house, wife an invalid, perhaps a man who called himself a master builder for once putting up an outhouse. Kate roomed in his house, huddled with others in the dark under the slates like birds, the hired girls in their sleep dreading the dawnless yells of the knocker-up. When they were let work the mill swallowed them, sent them home limping, aching in every bone.

Two lay over the clover
Sunday afternoon

Three break bones in the mill
singing another tune

The Industrial Revolution broke across England. There were still cottagers working at home, proud of their cow and their loom and their kitchen gardens. There were still mechanics who could mould and cast and file and build before your face an engine worked from a rough sketch of an idea in your skull. But more and more the independents were going under, sending their wives and then their children to the mill, coming themselves when they could get work – for women were paid less and given work first, and children barely able to speak, they too were found useful and put to long labour. The workshop became a mill, the villages grew into muddy settlements, towns, cities. Rural communities shrank, many vanished into the fields. Driven off from their holdings and commons the country poor came to be hired for day labour and entered the lives of the towns. They were told they owned half the world, their empire branded into it two centuries deep. Dour, close, with a tight-mouthed humour, they became the industrial working class, a province of the rich.

Don't ask me how I fettle
don't askit me no longer

Burdock's good for nettle
Nettle's good for hunger

Somewhere Kate lived, a thin working girl, not of that place, without family. Eli got her pregnant, she died in childbirth. He grumbled that I contain her life within mine, and stood now in his way of her: that I was once that frail girl in the time of misery. He nattered so, when I tried to release her like a bird through the poem he must step out so she went away again, nothing to say to him, he would not leave me. What I said then was to do with his presence and her absence and my impatience. I was no go-between. The dreams continued, the landscape of marsh and ridge, the clear light on the reeds, opened like an eye. Small stirrings, sometimes her face in shadow, turning away – but her face, a glimpse. And lastly the dream of her voice, in which she was speaking:

My name is Kate
I am an Irish girl

My father died and not until he was dead did I learn that his mother had died in childbirth, in Ireland. Perhaps a narrative with all its light and weariness had forced itself upon me, perhaps it was all coincidence – though I am no longer willing to believe in *coincidence* – and in any case the names do not match, the dates do not match, and I am not sure in what country this happened, and this is perhaps only a tale told by the prisoner to the jailer. Perhaps the patterns of separate events containing certain details in common as to birth and death and origin, perhaps these overlie each other, and some light gets through into these dreams with which I lived then, in some terror, through the time my father was moving towards his own death. But that place of the dreams surely exists, where this narrative happened, where a man called Eli loved a girl called Kate who died of that love in a place called Watertown in the distant year of 1790. They were alive once; they were real fictions, the mask, the face, the voice. I no longer dream of him or of her, but years later, some years ago now, wide awake, I saw her clear as I see her now in the light, in a faded dress of grey cloth with small green flowers, her coat across her shoulders, her face thin and wiry, her shoes letting wet, coming towards me down the slope's loose stones.

Half songs, 1790

1

Saw you come down the shale, love,
the stones black in the rain.
In your hand a kerchief,
in that plain bread.

Your frock's all frayed,
your face white as thistle hair.
And the wildness in your face, love,
and the cold stood there.

Come down to the mill's lamps,
a May morning.
Peewit cried on the clover.
Saw you turn and turn.

2

Rain on the running hill's back,
rain on the mill's black side.
Nowt but trouble ails you,
you're no bugger else's bride.

The lovers meet in the marshland,
the lovers meet in the sky.
There's no one comes to meet you
on the black pit's other side.

But your face so pale and sleek, love,
and your eyes like a bird's, so sharp.
There was hunger enough till now, love,
but now there's never enough.

The Wild Turkey

for John Patrick, my father, died 2nd April 1971

I should not talk so much about myself if there were anybody else whom I knew as well. Unfortunately I am confined to this theme by the narrowness of my experience. Moreover, I, on my side, require of every writer, first or last, a simple and sincere account of his own life, and not merely what he has heard of other men's lives; some such accounts as he would send to his kindred from a distant land; for if he has lived sincerely, it must have been in a distant land to me.

THOREAU

Wild Turkey One

All day walking, noticed
nothing unusual, nothing
that came to me: grey wind,
insect glitterings. Came
to the moor edge, trackless,
dull, too many years dying.
The hand released what it held,
what those imagings meant.
It was the first time, a speck
of wing came away, that merely,
the dog licked my fingers,
the robin that's bird of death
in my own country stared at me.
The event would not shape itself
as a stream's name begins
from meandering waters.

A slight wind pulls at the cloth.
On the table a dead fly,
a water-drop, claim me minutely.
I am a small x in some place
I've begun to exist in.

The rain,
fills the pasture.
I listened as one who reaches
into a dream he cannot remember,
found nothing but edges, places
that quickly forget themselves,
words that aren't true.

Wild Turkey Two

A language of afterthoughts
pursuing the moment, events
swallowed in ritual.

These obeisances, rituals,
proper marks, our prescribing
objects and forms of piety, as –
let us worship the prophet's
shoebox, his glove-shadow:
all so many farewells.

And keep moving. Otherwise
the moment is vacant and free,
evading us. Lately I found
reaches of time, open lands
to be crossed in the long step
between one and the next moment.

The forests gather themselves
never to be cut there
between eyelash and eyelash.
I grow roots in myself
that I am any place, rooted
and moving, anywhere.
Soon may I learn
a language to speak to myself.

Living in the Danelaw

Hills around. That's
one picture. Also
a sense of the sea near
beyond the next town,
behind the seawind
on the bushes by the Thirsk road
twisting home. Farms

back of trees, dutch barn,
line of poplars. Far off
on one hillside a badge –
the white horse cut in lime.
Beneath that a village,
the horse in its keeping.

Here the linked consistencies,
seeds, soil, sufficient water,
blades of common grass, thistles
lording it over the field,
bird with his message of wheatstraw,
cloud shadows moving quickly
across Northumbria.
The plain of York. In and
through which my father turns,
his forearms veined, sweat-
and dirt-grained, persistent,
the picture never quite fades.
Through it I walk from school
three miles, hot, scuffing
the road, or it rains,
the ruts fill, the airfield
groans with its war. Through
the beetfield Canadian airmen
wave, bayonets flicking the rain.
Later out of the bush
steps the German they're hunting,
a man wanting home,
asks me the way seaward. And I
showed him to walk with the white
horse to his right side
long ago, in my picture of that place,
precise as to sky and land,
red-veined leaves of the beets,
cobbles of the market,
town, fields, uniforms. My father
spat on their stripes, those armies
crossing the yard end, turned
as often he turned saying *now it is
yours this world it is yours now.*

The author, a teacher of petomania, reflects on the shortcomings of his students

I undertake what I undertook
though they flounder, asleep
in the mysteries. *Truly*
they're not swans he said,
but I'll show them the water.

A language of afterthoughts
demanding the several attentions
there is. I teach stance, posture,
composure, the importance of silence
and waiting, how to forget,
how sleep, to see and not notice
the moment the mind
takes to its channel, its
leaping and threading and listening,
the business of dreams, visions,
and distant barely perceptible sounds
– how they effect
what is brought to the world's gate.
And oh they gape, tell us
how does this far off dubious
barking of dogs involve us?
Truly they lack duende,
watching with hard eyes, confess
they cannot enter the dream,
cannot see how the bowls
offer their silences, big leaves
bounce the rain in to their roots.
Describing the buds of the sycamore
coming out boxed each 4 to unfold
is to be in the other world
listening in this one.

Is to persist; everything's
yet to be learned, even the arts
and science of farts.

The visit

I

The lady has a shrunk heart,
it is all she has, next to it
she keeps her man's life

They have reduced themselves
till their lives are two strips
of leather. Around them
the pots hold out
the disappointments,
the sighs of marriage

as if saying *see how lightly*
me take things, or, now
I'm a little depressed, cheer me

II

When I open my eyes they return,
in their eyes the hard points
diminish with each adjective.
They don't trust each other
to say anything

With such people I fell in,
felt my own name become an alias.
I was a black star
shining in another place

III

All the ranch-style houses
are gone to bed. The cars
are going where they believe
there's a place to be got to,
girls sitting close to their drivers.
The town night is swollen,
the town cop sweats in his gun-belt
and the town drunk is wading
and singing through the cat-tails.

I hear him clearly singing out loud
a farce, a comedy.
I want to go home forever

Wild Turkey Six

Wrote *walked into the field,*
the grasses waving, tall
pollen heads streaming the wind,
wind-river of seed, endless

And there was nothing again
to be said matching that flow.
It is the wind's field,
then the grasses

Walked, gathering the fall
about me, saying aloud
it is, it is. We the grass,
we shall live again

Another part of his childhood

To speak of the north
of my own life is bleak,
is to say I have
already said it.

I ran with the Swale,
clear mountain river,
around me, learned
in its stones. I was

its listener, that country
of turf and hill
falling into the cut
but oh slowly.

A hard grind, the soil
held back, the wheat
lay thin by the river,
storms raked the moor.

Abandoned farms, pit-shafts,
abbeys, monks' Latin
gravestones, the pines
reared in the drizzle.

In '47 shut in
with dead sheep the 4 month
snowfall pinned us.
Askrigg, Marske, the high

perched villages
of the Vikings
looked down on us.
My father, a small

gentle man I had seen
weep for a dead dog,
took a shotgun,
chased my uncle over the moor.

It was a life bound
to the land, to silence
of another kind, it was
the other place.

For the last time
I turn from it, I
set my face. It is
wherever I look,

shapes my life took:
the blown hill, the sun
close on the mountain,
the yellow weeds waving.

A description of the Lichway or corpse-road across Dartmoor

LICH: Old English *lic* as a suffix for -like (likely). Used as a noun,
a word for form, body, corpse: the substance of a thing. Also see
the Anglo-Saxon *hlinc* whose nearest synonym is ridge, hence a word
for a boundary, or a path cresting a ridge, and so a word for link.

From Babeny and Pizwell
west to Lydford 11 1/2 miles
as the crow flies who needs
carry only his own death.

It seems not much,
by their ways a day and a half-day's
travel got the corpse
to Lydford Church, setting

the dead down again.
Hardly a tree for shade,
none for coffinwood. In rain
the moor runs like a sieve,

the brooks flood, clay pulls
to the roll of the slope.
In what boots they went
is not said, nor their curses.

By 1260 these villages
let off that passage.
The rest, scattered farms, inns,
Merripits and Bellever

trudged on, the Forest dead
on the dead's road converged
across Longaford, the Cowsic,
under Whittor and Whittaburrow.

King's land, men struggled
away from their masters,
scratching for tin, thin
scrawny cattle, a few oats

shared with the beasts
under one roof, chaff blown
in the Atlantic wind, survived
by the rain and fern.

And gone. Their hands
lifted the stone, sifted
the streams for metal. In winter
salted the dead down.

Not long back a traveller
lifted the bench lid on a corpse
floating in brine – the innkeeper
saved for spring burial.

Cut by enclosures, mines,
artillery ranges, theirs
is the dead's print, pressing
of feet through the strange land.

A farewell to the city of Exeter in south-west England

Say goodbye love to this clock's
journey over its own face, turn
of these streets on their centre.

After four years of silence
I looked at my shoes, two shapes
of myself standing apart, ready to go.

While those others touch their lips
to their diplomas, let's leave without sound
in the living wind, saying *finis*

to the estuary reeds strange in the light
before rain, the ever arriving water.
Soon we shall learn there's no future.

The planet became infinitely small –
a turning stone mottled and veined,
a pebble alone, an eternity of shoes.

In the Americas, so the tale goes

A first grasp at land
suddenly found, in his way
he discovers a continent,
steps off to the prairie.
Fall comes, *the wild goose*
has raised its accustomed cry.

Winter approaches, the white zero
of afterwards, oh of boredom,
having seen it all, the sun
gone down on the world.
And too much yet to be said,
surprise land of river reeds

shaking in light, desert cries
strange and ancient, gaze
of the word for which all else
is afterthought, the mouth's
daft shape. And *where is*
that lawing and that song

I sang, crossing the mine waste:
pitted clay, runnels, weeds
dry and isolate, sun-split stones
of the slit hill, remember
this glazed land of the future
laid open and left by our going.

And if none may survive
we should speak our farewells
in this place. For this I turn
saying adieu to each leaf-sound,
finding the grass living again,
the red rose and the lily flower.

A journey through part of western Pennsylvania

Canvas shoes, pants,
a lone Indian walks
to New Wilmington
through Amish farmland,

green rolling, the houses
surprise each hill, white
as a smoke, blue doors
for their marriageable daughters.

We were driving some place,
two men nodded
waving their arms
from the Thirty Years' War.

The wheat waved and nodded
over the bones
of the Erie, the Shawnee,
the Delaware, the Iroquois.

We drove though there is
no place to go and
the future is shut
by our shutting it.

For we ran much, filled
all the cracks, emptied
and filled the valleys
of the complex Earth.

And it's done, oh
bearded ones, girls in-a-ring,
grief-reared face travelling
nowhere, into Ohio.

Wild Turkey Twelve

On the porch
drinking beer and
watching the cars, ah so
America

passing with
blank stares, finger signs,
advice re hair
and all

Who needs your
night spray & napalm,
what you do
the world knows

The best of you
are going away.
Some I have loved
with a grace

their open faces
the tulip-tree leaf,
their gesture
ample as landscape,

as frail, as
persistent as milkweed,
deserve more than
good luck

So love it
or leave the crow said.
We looked
at the blue lonely world

It could have been
anywhere, it turned out
this blank stare
here, here

– a gift of not much,
presence running out
like spilt milk –
was your face passing,

passing. Let's
get it over with let's
get it over let's
get it over with

Wild Turkey Thirteen

> Some circumstantial evidence is very strong,
> as when you find a trout in the milk.
>
> THOREAU

Some quit
without farewells, walked
with the knowing of woods,
husbandry, building,
making, to be gentle

Found property
what is proper men use,
men's ways and women's

Saturday nights
the millworkers' posse
drinks up
talking of rape,
each with a six-pack along

In Michigan they broke
both his hands with rifle butts,
in Taos castrated him,
took his woman, beat him
through the Sierra Nevada

*After the first blush of sin
comes its indifference*

And if there is no place
to stay then we'll go,
and if there is no place
to go then we'll stay

The dream

   1

A place you would be
familiar with, birds,
trees, men & women, world
declaring itself
moment by moment

The mountain, the distance,
the cricket's emergence,
flick of a grasshopper,
blue jay & crocus, is
or is nearly the whole

The words a country
of leaves on the field,
city of wheat to come to,
landscape glimpsed
through flashes of lightning

And moving. Their carts
creak by the fence
to where they will move
in a circle slowly,
speaking the names

Draw near the well,
the last water.
I bring my flesh
to your flesh,
a place we shall live

2

Return of the earth
to itself
like water, here
is no future

lady walling your face
to desire, gentleman
under the helmet,
the grasses take you

away from all this –
thistleburrs, pines,
morning-glories,
mashed into dollar bills

Schools full of silence,
the blue eyes, sober
grey suit, clipped head
would assure us

The day of the last
clean wind off the plain
and the lake
full of shit

The deer stand
at your whistle, come down
from the wood
to their own country

He hides down there
by the women's house.
She writes poems
full of gesture

steps on the grass
lifting her feet
as though to avoid it,
is in love or not

She has no desires
to speak of
            O friend
I would write you
you would not believe

    3

Of the mountain,
what country we came,
he said nothing

Spoke of rooms of tall grass,
Foxtail & Brome, the spread
of the Queen Anne's Lace,

a ribbon of birds dipping
& rippling, going away
wheeling its nebula –

the way we would go,
wind crying direction
yellows through maple

Described the cicada's
brief time, a few weeks
it's over: birdsounds,

shiver of aspen, briars
on stones, ripples
the summer field has

as through this she walks
step by step, her skirt
printed with corn-ears

swirling, she pivots herself
to one foot, in the glass
reflects she was young

and turns as he turns,
as the wheat moves aside
at their going, as colour
slips out, like water

4

We are among resonances,
bones of the skull

Tiny plates of the ear
move on each other

Though I speak to myself
I speak also to you

We shall burst into silence,
we shall rise from our mouths

What I have spoken of
speaks of itself:

the river over stones,
the grass repeating itself

If I'm drunk & can't see
I shall get home

Walking the street of myself
to the door, I shall go in

I will enter the dream's trick
to believe in itself

Where we are we belong,
here or another place

How the tree speaks, talks
of a fox passing through

The peewee's cry instant
by instant discovers itself

What a cry of solitudes,
sounds across water

What a small arc of a circle,
what a circle

What a small sound in which
to begin to complete myself

FROM

THE POET RECLINING
SELECTED POEMS 1962-1980
(1982)

This section includes all the poems from *The Poet Reclining: Selected Poems 1962-1980* (1982) which postdate *Work, distances / poems* (1972), mostly drawn from small press titles published in the US and UK between 1974 and 1981, beginning with *Hawk Wolf* (1974). Some poems appeared in more than one pamphlet: details of original publication are given in the bibliography. The order follows that in *The Poet Reclining*.

Wolf vision

At the abandoned farm
in the clearing shrunk
from the field it was,

woods of birch
and hickory sprung
from the forest's axeing –

American trees still awake
in their Indian names,
old field measured out

in blunt immigrant speech –
I was a man with his dog
running out

on the snowclapped
glazed winter grasses
gone into scrubland.

Some look in his eye
not dog's but wolf's
pierced me. Running

again through the edges
of clearings the late
sunlight blazed in,

pond ice, bracken,
saplings risen again
from their winters, away

on some plain
answering only ourselves
we were wolves howling.

Hawk vision

(for Tom Nickerson, vanished Indian)

At Wachusett, the lake darker
through winter straight pines,
rocks dumped in the ice sheet,
we stood for a bird's high

hovering over the inlets: red hawk
like none the books mention
circled and lazed on the air's
updrift over his watching hold

down the cone of his vision
of stone and valley tight to his eye
that fed on a wide space of small
movement he's triggered by: snake,

rabbit: liquid shutting the lens
pinpricked down to his dive –
everything in him going in one
feather spread downflight first

on the fur-stripping claws
second his bone-splitting beak.
I should shudder, remembering
victims I've known, times

I've been killer, harbour gull
snapping off crabs' legs;
other times I was running
home through the evening, then

hunched by that knived
falling out of the light.
That day we were watching, part
of his landscape, a claw's length

out from the wars of ferrets
and eagles, land grabs, horse thefts,
slavings and sack of our separate
tribes, alert for his dive

but he circled. And rose
in a spiral upward into the blue
shock of the sky diving
somehow upward and vanished.

Remembering when he was a wolf

The light on the fields
slowly vanishing,
the old dark padding back,
the old sifting of dust.

I sat by the stone, rainspots
had pitted and dried. Here the wind
carries everything off:
seeds, names, old barns.

In such light we skirted the clearing,
sunset breaking across us. And ran
through the open, we howled
so the stones must hear us.

In the scrub leaf-mould thickened,
cold to my hands. I fell there,
the pack left me, heat of my body
left me, a briar whipping my cheek.

Creatures had dug in the frost,
their small breaths melting the ice,
little wandering pumps
chewing up leaves. I was a wolf,

my work to wait
till nightfall and catch them. It could be
my boots snapping sticks
through this wood is all I want now.

It could be that sitting here
with my black gloves on a stump
keeping my hands' shape
is what I always wanted.

Another night of muttering

and shaking, cat cries,
boots kicking in the alleys
and all night I swear someone
calling from far off *please*
to come in. I dreamed
nothing, I dreamed I was asleep
with the eyes of my enemy
watching.

The sun, skimming the mist off the marshes,
trees breaking through
like junked ships. At the tips of three sticks
of the wintered elm
three crows, like three
black flames.
That describes it. On the sea
a quick slap of sunlight, the day
set loose.
       In the street
early risers with flasks
and lunchbuckets set out
for the port. There is
nothing to tell you, the city
coming awake, everyone
pulls on the ropes, from a lifted window
a man shouts down his hands
such good little citizens.

Hard to say where I've been. One place
was a thin skirling music,
its own sound, rain
gusted through rocks,
Arab music the way they hear it.
They played, each his own song
with others, a joyful lament.
A girl danced, dark, skinny-legged.
Others stood to one side listening.
In a doorway a drunk
was taking a leak
and falling. When he sat up

he was spitting his teeth out,
a gob of whiteness.

Tales of Urias the shape-shifter

First he was stone, the great sleeper,
the company of other stones
was no blessing.

Stone-still he'd talk
with the white hurrying mane of water,
no one believes it.

Glimpsed in and out woods
following the beck, by the downrush
forgot all his words for water.

Then a bird was his lifting wing-shadow
dropped down the valley.

In his skull dreamed again smoke,
mill-waste, the cotton-spinners'
dreamless sleep, Pennines
dark and satanic, so he sang *Jerusalem*.

Man again, from gutturals
making his first sentence,
singing through looms and his grudging masters
all the songs of the settlement.

A country their god had forgotten
his blessing. The birds, they sing
once there and fly off
leaving no message.

By the stream of a Sunday
would he fish, court,walk and fight.
Some time in rage a frame-breaker,
speech-maker, read the London correspondence.

And with others come in the blue
withering light at day's edge
down the mill's shadow, some but six years
picking cotton waste, always hungry.

Brooding years after he'd ask
if a man believing in silence should talk much.
Went preaching, the book of black words
in his back breeches' pocket.

Till at evening his clogs
pounding the hillsides he's famous for
he's come to the praying hole.

Behind him the gap in the rockface
is the stone's mouth speaking through him.
The birds and the beck's noise
and his people around him are one sound.

Then with the voice that learned speaking
over the groan of flywheels
he's urged his half-fed congregation
up from the stones till over the magpie's screech
and the jay's the woods
fill with their shout *Hosannah*.

My father fading out

Each time I recall him he's grown
thinner and paler, *am I*
making myself clear he shouts
from the hearthstone, already

I see almost through him
asleep at the fire, exhausted
evening by evening, his crossed feet
pink and opaque at the open oven door.

If he slams out now it will be
fainter and shake the house less,
less curl to his lip for his bosses –
Reggie Rat, Charlie Woods, Wallace Dixon.

For them he went topping and tailing
bent through the frozen turnips,
or stooking in summer pitched his fork
high in the air in blind sudden anger.

Now he fades out, the wireless
plays him to sleep, he wakes, asks news,
sees in the coals the black flag of a stranger,
dozes again, then is gone completely.

Valley

Pale grass
a long flag
striped once by the river,
the one
wandering blue star
of the heron.

In the light's early silence
the farmers crank the old box Ford
full of chickens. The cock croaks,
he has counted his wives,
some are missing,
plucked and stiffening
under the market awning. Nothing else
but a pheasant's stuttering,
a distant bell sound. I see
in the starry river
the keel mark.

Tightened into the bank's
wooded side under the steep
hill's stone shadow
a Viking boat
is still vanishing.

Childhood in the lowlands

Foweles in the frith,
Fisses in the flod.
And I mon wax wod:
Mulch sorw I walk with
For beste of bon and blod.

Hello
hello

into the mouthpiece
over and over

is anyone there?

But she would not speak
to him again ever
she tells anyone but him.

That's it she's gone.

He visits his childhood: tight,
wiry, a cable
hung in its own weight. One cheek
to the mountains,
fixed on Ben Ledi's snowtip.

One cheek to the underground weeping,
coal smell of a coal town,
image of a man
pinned beneath beams, his father
wriggling under the mountain.

Choppy water, white horses on the firth,
but no fishing in the flood.

Sunk Island, that winter

> O westron wind when wilt thou blow
> And the small rain down shall rain

O that my love O that
my love: the wind,
the reeds, the telephone wire
and I, all singing.

It's late afternoon
in a flat country,
the sea birds rise
far off and fall quietly.

But the sea goes away
leaving these fields,
this tall yellow marsh grass
and the small trees blown inland.

And last winter the gale
lifted the pigsty roof, the geese
blew out to sea, the bell
on the dull swell of the Humber

clanked through my dream
of hills in my own land.
Perhaps I am leaving,
a man stung by his woman's scolding.

Perhaps nothing. Or drunk
going home by the ditches,
singing, from a neighbour's house,
a man at the end of himself

where there's only the sea
on the sea, each thing at a distance:
dutch barn, brick letter-box,
wall of the house I will sleep in.

Old postcards of the river

View of the city with boats,
some rigged for a journey –
the canal, in watercolour, 1830.

Where the poor stew nettles and fennel,
all England affords them.

But these trees and sails
in the wide space, a woman
heaving a basket home on her shoulder
late in the daylight
seem to belong there.

If my country is slowly
lighting again,
its villages

opening their doors
and the neighbours waving –
that dream is soon over.

In the grey photograph
three who are
recently soldiers

grin from France
where they died
rifles aslant

at a slow pace, shoulder to shoulder
in perfect step, who
followed the piper

or huddled in mud
died in any case.
What for won't go

on a postcard. Fishing
down the canal
on Sundays

I find their initials
on stones
by the lockgates

standing easy together
just as they
left them.

In disbelief
at this new thing
the camera, workmen
freeze in the street,

one raising a stick
in suspicion, a boy
mocking and pointing.
Beside him a woman

dark in the face
as the sunless
underwing of a bird,
still turning away.

The swan

It happens, spring comes to the river,
grass freshens, the reeds remember the dry sound
last year's wind made amongst them.

These pollards, clubbed and splay-fingered,
are the same willows of my childhood.
These are the same birds
born over and over, rising in the estuary.

Then the swan flies, his wingbeat
through air a slow heavy applause
that ceases, sighting the weir to turn there,
takes his precise self in one motion
down to the furrow he's cut in still water.

The wholeness of him, feather by feather.
The white sail of a ship
gone long since to the horizon. Or the lance
of a returning crusader. Or
a white banner bearing perhaps good news
at last from the kingdom.

Playing field observations

In the light before rain
counting the hard little
yellows of the dayseyes I went
down the sea–opened valley –

a neat country it's said
of parkland and flood plain
squared like the blind man's garden
between the waters.

Sang goodbye to the elms,
glimpsed by the canal
blue smokey lift of a heron,
accepting my birthday.

How the shadows move in
at such news and are strange
in the light. This feather
left for his marker my brother

the crow had dropped by the goalpost
seems a dead man's finger
keeping his page
in the unfinished biography.

The Tivoli Bar

I look into the hole.
So this is where you live.

Mostly it's dark. When there's light
I look at things: the worm,
the dungbeetle hoarding his muck.

In the dark I remember him.
In the dark I have to imagine.
It's the only town left –
streets, people at tramstops,
and the eyes of young women
looking downwards.

In the dark
I roll out the words on my palms.

If I could spend them
I would spend them wisely.

I hope so. But I want
the quivering world that's in them
to pass hand to hand
between us.

Federico

They will come they will come.
They have been before.

I watched them, from my hole
under the thornbush.

The soldier's boots
were ringing in the yard.
No one's here
I told him.

Each time they come
I have to begin again.
If I don't remember, too bad.
And if they don't believe me
I'll say the truth anyway.

Wanting to shout wanting to say
go away go away.
Stop interfering with my silence.
Let me write my poem.

He takes it. Later
I see him squat by the wash house
and clean himself on it.
So take it.
Paper is scarce.
I'm glad he finds purpose there.

Take the poem. And if you
can use it
use it.

What I mean is: leave off,
I'm busy. What I want is
to close the gap
between writing the poem
and a letter to a friend.

Maria the thief

I stole the cup.

I stole the water.

So take them.

I confess everything.
On the other hand
I may deny it.

I stole the food, books, furniture,
clothing and shoes.
Though I paid cash
I stole it.
Though I worked for the money
I stole the work.

Give me what's mine,
air clean as the mountain,
the pine smell,
my allotment of rain.

Give me my portion.

Caesar Caesar

Soldiers must try hard.
They overrun one country
finding the frontier
a thousand miles further
still needs defending.

Such a profession –
soldiering.
And for the police
there's always work.

Where does it go?
All the bootleather,
sweat, curses, orders,
the lists
of those to be shut of,
those who take and are taken,
watchers and watched.

They come to the same place:
the round cry
dragging everything into itself.

Reports from the east

Days coming away from each other,
threshed out.

Stripped to the bone. Butchered.
The bones pounded to black dust
gold teeth are sieved off.
Trains, marshes, ashes. Some
request death, some walk into the wire,
one told to hang himself
took off his belt and did so.

Whether you will,
whether the clocks shedding
moment across moment record it
pain
comes to be fed, all the cries
to be uttered, misery's processions
to be numbered.

Or else
let there be singing, as at Janowska.
A fiddle, a whole orchestra
is given. We have to be thankful,
even one mercy, a raindrop for instance.

To survive

Each day the last,
each a survivor. A shaft
other days fall into.

Books, tables, lost objects
call back to us.
I remember my razor's edge,
the lift of my good bed.

Mine I said *mine*, doubting now
whether these fingers, these knees
would answer in my name.

A man assembled from nothings,
bones and tissues. He would eat,
he would swallow his name for nourishment.

At night the dark
looks out on itself, and the days pass,
a chain of black flowers.

Bowl

A bowl of soup.
A bowl of soup.

It is the hands
melded together, tip into tip.

Stains in the cracked enamel.
It is pure longing
where the soul bunches up.

Peelings and sawdust, a weak milk.
Compelled to share
she cups the heat into herself.

What the other takes
she measures in absences,
fills herself
in the warmth, in its lack.

Wants

Such effort to make ruins.

The city has emptied, footstep by footstep.

Grandfathers searching through clothes,
trousers and shoes, emptying cupboards.
The voices have left
and call in another place, anxiously.

They were neither fleeting nor wistful,
they struggled under the ban of the empire.
In my pocket on a torn piece of paper
is a word for *goodbye* in spidery writing.

I want the voices to find each other.
I want the parts of speech rising towards each other.

The veterans

Each with his president's telegram.
Each with his emblem, the grey bloody flag
he shows no one.

The medal the map the names
of his bullet-raked brothers, notes
of the book of delusions

he'll write now the war's done
and the empire diminished. *We
never gave it much thought*

is said of atrocity, cameras
noting his face, the mouth
that says it's a mouth in a face
that says it knows better now.

Now he's like everyone,
some days alone, sometimes anywhere,
with his woman who reads for him
books from the vanishing country.

Peasant

Flattening into the bank
as his lord rides by: not a man,
but a root of the elm
grown round stones.

In the field carrying straw
or straggling home beneath sticks
in failed light
two legs and a burden.

Lives in smoke, picks wheat
from the grainpit cracks,
limps through the frozen ploughland
turning an acre a day.

Dreams in flashes: rabbit
snared in the waste filched home
in his jacket, pheasant's
stuttering blur whose eggs he sucks clean.

And the boy he was with the oxgoad
tramped through the watermeads, first light
finding him still in that field
bent and ailing.

Water lifts off the land.
We are dancing.
We are not dancing.
He is a man, he is waving,

a speck in the falcon's round vision
that pins him dreaming
his master's cut throat,
the beating of ploughshares.

Duck at Haldon Ponds

At evening watches the duck
slow feeding the waterline.

Praises the duck. Such a fine
white miracle breasting the mayfly.

Green of her tail feathers,
space of her neck doubled in water
paddles off with my mind.

Ducks I have known.
Old duck mates of mine
inspecting the meeting of air and liquid.

Make no mistake, duck.
I'd like to eat you well cooked
one bell-battered Sunday in April.

And I'd wear your gorgeous feathers in my hat,
make a soup of the bones
and give your leftovers to the cat.

Fly

I woke hearing a fly
touched again to its sound
pelted into the window
trying to leave

for what was it

– something in sunlight that said
to wake now. Beyond that
pulsed and repulsed buzz
between two sheets of glass

a bird's one note

come back to the world brought me
out of long sleep. Love,
as you stir from your dream's
untrembling be still for me,

let me begin

my song for it sings moment
to moment love of you.

Lake

Freed now the lake turns
between shores distantly
heard from each other.
We walk by not on it, not

chancing the ice

drifting apart from itself
and lying like pond scum.
A month back the lake
I stood by spreading its bulk

cracked whipped and cried

and fought its bed: animals
stirring, seeds pressing out
from the milkweed's grip.
I heard the ice shifting

tight packed, it talked

I tell you. You don't
believe me perhaps.

Crocus

Leaf, green spear with white
driven through, old trackway
the fair women went, trailing
their coats. The flower

purple folded

and folding over such orange
as burns deep in coals.
New risen, beating home
ahead of forsythia's

sharp yellow fire.

Crocus glints among leaf mulch,
cornering spring, the yard's
premonition of poppy shoots,
mountain ash berry, little prints

of weeping birch,

leaf and eye. Crocus lifts.
I have news for you.

From the southern river

The proper business of ageing men is to sit on gates.
JOHN LYLE

Writing in provinces
far from each other
or any star:
greetings.

If there's news
I'll tell you
everything changes,
for you also –

the way maybe a train
stops beside yours
as you were not meant
to stop either,

hoots
and moves on.

At first we can't tell
which is moving
but the mind
comes back to the body.

Where someone is always
staring between empty sheds
at the foxgloves
and the elder bush.

Winter occasions

Years clanking in buckets, more years
snuffling in ditches, danced at shearings
and pig killings, my life in the country,
my life in the village, the owl blinks
in the thatch, the fireback blackens.

I was a girl, the sun flamed in a sky
of thistles and hemlock shaken above me,
I lay down close to the water.
Winter in, winter out
the wind nags me. Now he's back
from long absence, his boots
at the scraper, a squire
off walking the parish muttering

hoofbeats on roads I've not travelled. In his sleep
knives clatter, armies gather,
storms rake the upland, a girl
goes singing a love song over the watermeads
or he's crying

> *so then I've lost you,*
> *in the old river the moon*
> *is still glittering.*

I had been
all these years a stone to him, a hush
in his city of streetcries, or a light
he'd snuffed once and would light again,
pleading he's sorry and such, head in a sling,
dragging his deaths like a whale
round with him. He's amazed
there's life in me, blood's thumped
breath and tongue to tell him
he's mocked with his art. And he'd thank
my long waiting to greet him,
my hand at the latch, glad and a fool
when he comes home stomping his feet
with a comment I've wrinkled and thickened,
but it's years since I missed him.
                                        I was
content and will be again glimpsing
through trees the river's loop,
poppy's glare, harebell weighed
on the wind's stir.

> *Celandine bleaches,*
> *the cold field's bleating winter*
> *but in age there's fire*

he announces, surprised again
and again stares at his table
and taking his pen starts up
some tale of a woman
sixteen years a statue
because of a husband's jealousy,
and him wrong in the first place.

At the Western Beacon, the second of the songs of Urias

All this elaborate disguise.
No one's here
anywhere under Orion
and the new moon's cup of rain.

Light divided over the moor
in the fields of the bronze makers:
sheep, bracken, ponies,
stoney rainsodden furniture.

With a stone to break you.
With a stick's point
rammed through the ribs. Then came
farmers and hunters, scraping for tin,
setting stones it's a warning to cross still.

Back when the moon was the pale
banished wife of the sun
in the lost tale of the arrowmaker's vision.
All their tools, bones,
legends and gods are one wash
through the peat now.

Scoffed down a bird's share
of porridge and bilberry. Snarled
among scrawny cattle,
dogs and their stink
trailing after. Then gone to the city
whose names mean water, a people
calling themselves *people of this land*.

Among grey rocks
I took her, her eye
glimpsing a half county
stopped at the ocean: blue sheen,
two boats in the ancient distance
where she is the sea and she dances.

Moiré effect

What was always the vision
reaching for more of itself

had eluded me. How it
never included itself:

that we notice the high
turn of the bird in sunlight,

its grace
stuns me out of all thinking.

Stood amazed at the barley,
orchestra of the oat plant.

And came over me crossing the bridges
such immanence things have:

part of how the world thinks
so through us the blank
stuff of space knows itself.

Tristan Crazy

(1978)

I have leaped and thrown reeds and balanced
sharpened twigs, I have lived on roots in a wood
and I have held a queen in my arms.

La Folie Tristan (BERNE)

One for sorrow

On the ocean –
useless to say I was drunk,
couldn't help it,
useless to say any thing –
then I loved you.

Weeds on the sea, the horizon
adrift, waves' heave
hoisting the spray's flags, sea
loose & flinty, stone in its making.

I fancy I see animals,
bushes & rocks. In the motion
words I had seen
thrashed into nothing
that nothing gives back.

Only clouds, one
shaped like a raven. Sometimes
a skimmer, garbage picker,
bird's wing lifting away from the lifting.
I see everywhere the same
belled planet's edge.
And love you.

Two for nobody

How he was king
of these rocks
& gorse. Oh
he told me.

Granite country,
heather stiff
in the seawind
divided at Cornwall:

his kingdom. She
was a swallow
bringing one strand
of her swallow's hair.

His woman, part
of his stoney possessions,
ah but love
set her dancing.

And the rest: how
she sneaked off
to find me
out by the elder tree,

how again & again
in the two-backed
beast dance we went
crazy & careless,

were found, hounded,
beaten & branded.
Ah well shrug the citizens –
lies, guilt & old grief,

betrayal & such,
an old song the wanderer
sings for his bread
& each time changes

he sings it. *Love love
wherever love is
changing its sheets
come find me.*

Three: tales of the hunter

I crouched, hands & knees
beneath thornapple, mosquito
seeding its eggs in my arm.

And waited. What I caught
I killed or brought
struggling home.

When I found my enemy
I cut him to pieces & went
singing & bloody by the rowans.

But you, love. Now shadows
cast trees & I'm contrary,
rain my fine weather.

By night I'm prowling
your moonlit flesh. You're all
legs, arms, owl cry

& leaping, love, the cry
in my throat some animal,
its life in its cry.

And I swim with the fish.
I fly with the raven. I go
with the shuddering creatures
into their darkness.

Four, being a prayer to the western wind

Without you:
the moon's failed waters,
lost wheats of the Sahara.

A woman hides in these syllables.
She goes singing and dancing
through fields of tall yellow to the sea.

But the pastures are an old grit in my teeth,
the eastern forests an ash and smoke.

I pick among shrubs
for one leaf of you. On the sea
or high in the treeless upland
where I almost hear you
the wind whines to itself
be thou with me love
the corn in its chaff, or where
have I heard it?

Ships, ports, wharves, men
leaning on the cathedral stones,
I've been everywhere talking to everyone,
no one has seen you. In the snowy north,
in Germany and on the Atlantic
amongst men who are gulls' feasts
and the dreams of carrion it's your face
I fail to find in mirrors and water.

Asleep I see you
walking as once you were by the river,
but awake sleep has kept you,
I'm miles away where I barely think
how your sounds are, and must come
round the world's other side
finding again the same strangeness
opens your face in the gates of the city,
the wanderer home in his bed again.

Five, which is here by the river

Windless days reeds
tall grasses
motionless

cormorant a shoe
opens his wings
heron a stopped blue air

kestrel a moment
standing in flight come out
love from wherever

boats turned over
like the hands
of sleepers come out

from the waterbirds
of the shadowy
waterclogged marshland

come see me here
by the river but you
where are you

among these reflections
these lights do you see me
throw a stick in the water

oh then come out love
and see me a face
in the water

Six: the wife's complaint

It's for love
they told me
& brought me
across the high sea.

In his rainy country
of haunted plumbing
& traffic
not a damn thing works.

If he's king
of these fields
& wants loving
what if I'm bored

as the moon
with itself,
tired & bombarded,
a waterless ocean.

Watching the ploughman
leading a white
ribbon of birds
to the world's rim

I'm sick of it all,
or I envy
the gull's
easy lift

& long to be
lost as the larks
in larksong
over the moorland.

These my hands,
first & last
those we love touch,
that in passage

from hairline
to heels
could make you forget
till in one

gathered up fire you lose
even your name,
sight of my face,
number you thought.

So then it's true
we're meaningless
here on the earth,
tupping & dying –

soiled sheets &
nailbitten bafflement,
his feet that smell
of old wood,

cradling his head
crying love love me
till death
for through us

nowhere is somewhere,
someone is running
here in the space
otherwise empty.

For a husband maybe
I'm rope, coiled
& used, no doubt
I'll be used again.

For another I can
be woman to man:
Tristan, Isolde,
Isolde, Tristan.

Seven: when he can't sleep for thinking

Other nights of muttering,
knives scraping stones,
wanting through grunts
& half sleep to kill anyone.

Won't where he can't bear
for its loss his possessing her,
beside her thinking who else
had called through her hair

his little death's loneliness,
beached on that shore
his mind ends, and she
spent & howling.

Gossip, a thornbush. My bird,
stay with me. Her voice
a blaze in his skull.

In his mind digs a pit
& burns her, surrounds her
with razors, broods over
footprints & stains.

Love makes some sing
& shrinks some. Brings down
his fist & will own
what he can't own in women.

Or else raffle her, give her away
at the street corner,
the prize in the lepers' race

but have done anyway, take off
& damn her to hell, slam the door
forever shut after him. She sleeps,
in her pink flesh, beside him.

Eight. The singer

Nights when he is
peering through mist
at the ship breaking
coast & would be there.

A flat song: the warrior
scowling under the helmet,
a girl, her breasts
of white china clay,

nights on the wire
where his body rotted,
an example to all
in those trenches.

In spite of the knife
the club the fire
to burn him, the gun,
he would go back crazy

where she's anyway
forgotten him. He sings
show me the wind's seam
or a lovelier woman.

Continents, rivers.
A vain young man
is the singer, the
peacock, singing

oh love oh love
a mire so muddy
who'd walk there?

Nine: Shorty's advice to the players

In the flinty upland
of sheep & ravens
they dreamed
each the other's vision: birds,
these flowers bursting
a thousand years back
tramped in the battle's muck.

Forget the knights –
a fist on a field of azure,
his lady, her feet
on the chained swans, not able
to turn the stone cheek to his cheek & cry,
he would not, small
in his armour,
tender as mollusc,
stone in the cathedral.

Hitched her skirt
on his lancepoint, laid her down –
not first, last,
nor long remembered. Went,
bum, singer, a fool, the black
furious horseman, nothing worked out.

His death: full of briars,
a black sail a white sail he's glimpsed
in the magpie's jittery flying.

Little brother
she won't ever come back now.
Get used to it.

Ten: the tale unfinished

At the end there's no love
without death comes along
with the wedding dress,

in the ring on the bridegroom's
midnight finger; either way
there's death, bleak as that bird

that's king on his stonepile.
So I shrugged and loved you.
Your face sings now in my head

where without you I'm snail
dragging his tongue across stone,
I'm the bell that rings

in its own windy space, I'm out
with the ageing light
of the stars and as lonely.

And we're not love, each
as we each imagine, more lost
in each other's distance

wearing our separate flesh.
Other times with the gift
of your moving sometime with me

I am out of all mind, and recall
your running all gooseflesh
towards me. As you ran

I thought how you were
a message folded like prayer,
delivering itself.

Fun City Winter

(1977)

For Annie for whom
these were
love poems perhaps

A red carnation

Winter in Fun City. The Laughing Sailor, the dodgems and the bingo boards sheeted down, spray flung over the harbour wall. I investigate the dike, the cliffs, Oldtown and the priory church, a great East Riding farmer's barn, or a merchant's notion of what church ought to be, its vault stacked with spent prayers. After some centuries the tithes and rents and rights of pannage and verdure amount to these same stones, I think, and shut the door on it. Each day I visit my mother in the hospital, I stay in her house and order its affairs under the eyes of her lodgers, the young policeman and the French assistante, who seem almost aware of their symbolic presences hovering in the background. Everyone here is old, retired, living by the sea, even the young, you remark, visiting. One day I make a detour to visit my father's grave, and lose myself among the brick semis. I cannot ask. Everyone I pass is old. I cannot ask them the way to the cemetery. I find my way at last, and on the grave I place a single red carnation. So this is he that raged and broke crockery all through my childhood, and on the morning of my wedding, years ago, stamped on the flower – a carnation – spitting *that to your buttonhole*. So this is he.

The town, a general description

Boats, harbour swell, bone-cutting wind
off the bay, and far inland
noise of the sea beating on stones.

I sit under the nightstar writing my music.
Winter's a cry in me
that I loved you, here in a country

childhood blurs down the telephone wire,
dark with the deaths of friends, their news
coiled on the flat gull-hunted landscape.

* *

The headland in dawn light
whitens. Boats fishing the bay mouth
glitter, bird followed.

By Danes' Dike the larks
threw down song. A harebell glimpsed
in the land wind was the pale stare

my grandfather grew, years at sea
seeking this landfall, its waves
folding the first of the light

where in death his eye
pearled as the eye of the caught fish
glazes on land, the sheen off him.

* *

Centuries back they walked off the sea,
sour and Danish, wanting
the green sea-glimpsed littoral,
battle-keen and bloody at the ebb mark of the bay.

Still dour, in a tone they have
of a slighted people, short
under the easterly. And whose history
if anyone knew was to complain –

the townsmen's daughters gang-raped
under the fish quay, and him
with his head stoved in
still haunting the foggy landing.

*   *

I can believe a time my father
sulked up and down furrows
cursing his masters. Black his face was
on the white upland of the Wolds.

By Flamborough the leathery sea
gutters again in my vision. Each day
I visit and stare, calling it
grey tongue, bell clapper.

I write. I drink whisky.
I loved a woman. I write
this shell shaped like an eye is a shell,
this stone shaped like a heart is a stone.

*   *

Sea grey with fog, white
with my father's spent anger, frost
nagging its offices, lugging his grudge

home through the evening. The place
I come to bury my dead is at street's end
the old sea falling endlessly

into my childhood. And is all
that's flawed and stoney in me
by these graves and this long water.

Where that time is a bird gone
from its birdbones. Where I won't stay.
Where the sea wears out its stones.

*   *

I return. The sunlight through amber
is the bar at the Alpha Café.
The radio plays old dance records.
I visit the pinball machines in Fun City.

On the late night box it's Renoir
singing: *bullets fixed bayonets*
the single shot of a pistol
to bring down one man with a tin flute.

Ten o'clock watching the cars go by.
If we flew in each other's dreaming
in my skull I was with you
to whom these were love poems I guess.

*   *

You moved I saw covies of birds
glide through the reeds. You sang
I heard waves break. Your name
called itself at a distance.

You with the sea strength.
You from the land of green ginger.
You in the wind in your dress
a flag with its shook sound.

Now moving with ebb sounds
moving with tide change
in the 5 a.m. river on sleep's
sisterly arm you wake and break over me.

The stone gatherer

Most days you see along the leftward curve of the bay slow figures in black treading the waterline, keeping their distances from each other. They are the stone gatherers, filling their pockets with smooth chalk pebbles, some mottled by seaweed, some blue or brown veined with ancient seepage, some holed through where in the chalk's softer places sucking creatures had dug down on the one leg of their lives beneath shells, and after them sandgrains had lodged and milled through, thrashed in the seawash. The stone gatherers take a few pebbles each day, and store them for neither purpose nor profit in their houses. Often enough their habit is a source of domestic irritation as the gatherer's obsession continues; it is a lifelong and silent activity. When a stone gatherer dies his collection is dumped, stealthily, and returned to the beach. A stone gatherer must collect his own, and only as a significant gift is a stone ever passed from one collector to another. They are solitaries. They rarely meet. They have little to say. Walking into the middle distance we see one of them, ponderous and dark, coming up the beach. Occasionally he turns to the water, staring over it as if he expected some solace from it. Occasionally he stoops to examine a stone or a shell or a bit of wave-smoothed glass. Occasionally he selects a stone. Nearer, in close-up, we see him holding such a stone upright on his flattened palm against the distant headland. Old holes cut through have broken it from a larger stone, and sea-turned it is a little figurine: a head, a body, limbs folded along itself, a hole through its middle: an embryo or a relic. Closer in we see between thumb and forefinger a little earth mother, and through its middle hollow the distance of bay and cliff and rising gulls, fading out.

By the northern sea, a farewell to one woman

Your face, frame in a frame of itself
in the train window, moved off
and the northern sea fog swallowed you.

I played a pretend violin
in the train station quartet. In a Bogart movie
I walked the length of the platform.
In my mind we went
by separate roads up love's stoney mountain.

Then at the sea's grey side
I was running under the moments.

In each you were miles off
on the flat grain of the ploughland, half weary England
beaded with rain, white gulls
on the fenceposts.

In each then I wanted you
as the yawning fish on the boatmen's slab
might say of the ocean. The want
swam away into nothing,
the sea in its envelope.

I'd have lived in the hollow of your shoulder.
I'd have been an idea in your skull.
I'd have read only the book of your name
never knowing what nights you looked out from.

My life turned on its mast in that town
years ago as that moment turned towards this.
Now I no longer want.
I recall only the North Sea chill
my voice becomes mist in.

Apocrypha from the Western Kingdom

1 Six items heard in three locations in Leeds and Exeter

All I really wanted
if you really want to know
was a bigger violin.

*

So there was I
I'd painted 24 pictures
but they hadn't given me a wall.

*

And anyway it's daft my being an Irishman
not knowing how to fish.

*

I'm late because
the motorway was leaking,
so far you've shown
one grassblade of sympathy,
so I'll tell you what I will do
I won't shave.

*

I was in the hospital,
I said don't bring anything,
he brought me gin, daffodils, bananas.
I thought I'd never get out.
One day I'd die there in the rainy city
having written my epitaph
three score and ten
my heart ten cents a dance
among the small intrigues,
amongst the provincial incests.

*

On the sign in the window
at the bus station office
in some northerly town

seen in the news that night
on the TV in our front room
it said

the next mystery tour
will be to Rosedale.

2 At the collège des beaux arts Escanceaster six further items imagined

25 years dedication to the virgin
man and boy and never once
had anyone acknowledged it.

*

Can't you see I'm weary
working all day
for the last half hour
on my thesis the great work
the book of lost arrivals
the library of last resorts
a definitive history of alienations.

*

Not worried not moaning
not whingeing
not whimpering in the corner

demanding one last cigarette
one last whisky in the New Victoria
once again the fandango
under the glitter of the turning dancehall ball
till the musicians dismantle their instruments
driving off in a white VW

crying *nobody here is making me an egg sandwich*
so who am I?
where am I going?
what am I doing here?

*

Schism, rebellion, grumblings
over coffee, strange alliances,
manifestoes, knives in the dark,
religious upheavals, slander,
fanatics under arms, chance,
palace coups, gossip, non-
aggression treaties, cults,
independence movements, the wind
weaving through the wheat,
client kingdoms, petty republics,
nods to the blind man, winks,
signs under the table, flags,
beasts, bureaucrats, piles,
foreign syndicalist ideas, –
all these bother the emperor.

*

Skin of my hands the colour of cut wood.

Summer over before it began.

Whistle at the heart's finish,
bottom line at the end
of the cardiograph's calligraphy.

*

Otherwise the wind is itself,
the birds are.

       In the wide space
a woman heaving a basket
home on her shoulder.

3 Surprised again beside the river

Among obscurities, gleanings
of my life's junk and scribble: 'Boats
there'll be son, and small wading birds',

bright swans, line of poplars
fingering out the western sunlight,
windows guttering the last gold.

This is all one tale that tallies.
This is one history, all my life
same old lament for a lost country –

the same music repeating gulls,
reeds, willows, small waves
slapping in the seawind, a landscape

such as Isca the river's, the town
brisk with traffic, the treeland thriving,
streets rained on and Sunday

in the western city I called home
I abandoned. Where my heart knocked
thinking *wave, wave, high salt crests*

I'm to cross again. I'm a face
not seen any more, not waiting
between trains any more, my absence

no longer recalled on streets
falling steeply to the river crossing,
ancient trackway to the tide's head.

Merchants and shipmen, dyers' huts
now timber shards in the damp flood level
the Saxons kept the Celts to,

Frog Lane tanners, dealers in hide stink,
boats that breasted the salt plains
of the sea's pasture far from any land

gathered in the basin, sails furled,
so many birds resting on the long passage
from anywhere to anywhere.

Isca the water: *uisque*. *Pisces*
the fish: place of fish settled
by the Keltoi, the beaten Dumnonii

before Vespasian built the road
at the garrison's muddy footing,
Mithras scowling in the rock face,

chorus of Dalmatian oaths,
dog latin. More cries after,
Germanic, bleak guttural Danish

hacking out throats, breaking
the townwall and burning. The town
clung on its hill, a queen's gift

so they'll tell you, *semper fidelis*
when the Conqueror had a man's eyes,
at the West Gate peasant rebels

struggling in the open sewers,
travellers on the causeway
of the never ending landscape.

Then Dutch William. Plague,
cholera, bread riots, ecclesiasts'
vendettas, knives, women, money.

Life to life I think I return there,
cuckoo's call in spring
drags my heart out.

Nothing lasts, nothing changes,
nothing's learned from the centuries
beyond the same brotherly betrayals,

the same wifely infidelities,
same defeats, same failures, same
journey into exile, at the mind's edge

landscape carried on the long roads
remembering red clay hills
reared green and wheat again,

the townsmen's prospect, white barn
distant cresting the land's line
under the long wind off the Atlantic.

Days are soon done. Sickness or age
or the sharp edge of vengeance
have us at the end. The tale holds.

4 Some unfinished movements

Whangleather he said. Stopped halfway out of the Volvo, one foot
touching the pavement, her white face swimming his way in the
half dark: *And what's that?* she demanded to know next.

Whangleather he repeated, turning the ignition and stepping into
the evening to tell her over the car's roof: *That's something that don't
come apart in the rain the way you do.*

*

'The record office,
here or somewhere about' –
a tall brisk man in a beard

swinging the blackthorn
gives the library trees
a swift dressing down.

*

I didna sleep all night
I was throbbing
I was bad bad bad.

Long ago, a long way back,
far away from any place,
the very centre of the universe
blowing a dandelion clock
beside the river for instance.

*

Takes his supper at the bar.
Takes his wallet out to pay for it.

Opens it she thinks
like the Book of Common Prayer.

Sets his knife fork plate
down in front of him, salt and pepper,
mutters *and I hope it chokes you.*

*

The Wages of Sin is Death
saith the black spraypaint of the underpass.

The Wages of Sin are Death
it says underlined twice, underneath.

*

As for that red rainy ploughland
beyond the town wall
twenty centuries distant

that must be the other world
of the hawk's eye alert
and the grass in its moment.

5 Old business: the drowned bride

So you're back, your face
rising whitely up through the reeds
and the black bulk of you after.

Eloquent in your silence as ever.
The bell of your waterlogged body
tolls on the slow turning river.

And you won't come up from the weeds.
And this time I won't come back for you.
You would pull me in after

where you went down the rivermouth
through the cat-tails gobbling codeine.
Now you either go out in a new life

or drift on in my watery sleep.
So you nudge me awake each day
you're the light's first bitter thought.

You refer to your death
as *old business*, your laugh
laughs on in my head.

You say how the garden flourishes,
the town's found new meat for gossip,
and the children ask after me.

You say. The telephone rings,
the day begins, your voice arrives
and divides the air and I hear you.

6 A right curse on the enemy

Still around I see, still drunk,
still barely upright singing *Lily of Laguna*,
still hanging by your shirt tail.
Even though you're dead.

I don't know how you do it Jimmie.
I really don't. Shiftless. Lord Wistful.
We called you Alexander Impecunious,
forever borrowing two quid till Friday.

I've listened to your heart
that never spoke, felt no pulse
thumping in the dead wrist
where I placed lightly my finger.

I've pronounced you deceased
late kicked the bucket shuffled off
gone forgotten joined the elder brethren
with the great architect at last.

I've held a clear mirror to your face,
sent round a wreath, cancelled your subscription
to the Society of All Mates Together,
put your name in the obituaries.

And I've assigned you to the past of verbs.
You with your skin the pallor of dead water.
You will not paint. You will not fish.
You will no longer love the salmon leaping.

I've imagined you amongst the dead,
handing in your keys to the desk clerk,
handing in your name and loose change
still protesting you were innocent on Earth.

No one is. We lie to those we love,
we do not love them. Or else
we learn we cannot lie in love,
we cannot love ourselves or anyone.

So you're a man who cannot love himself.
You're a man selling salt to the sea.
You're a dead language and you its only speaker.
You're a joke in the museum of broken marriages.

And you broke mine. This is my revenge.
What else have I to do? I want
to stand beside your grave and find
some little good to say of you.

I'd like to feel compassion soon.
I want the luxury of some suspicion
I was wrong never to trust anyone since.
I can't until you're dead. So die,

old ghost, old misery,
you would have killed me anyway you could.
You betrayed me out of fear.
You tried very hard to destroy me.

So you were down, so you were beaten,
you were weeping in the bar-room,
you were skulking in the western wind
still crying for your childhood in the lowlands.

Old fox.
Got your tail in the water.
Now you die at last.
Here with this form of words. With these:

I feed you to the rain.
I sail your ashes down the wind.
I fade your name among the grass.
I think of you among the vanished.

The clearing

*

     Off in woods
a field that was tilled
isn't now: tall grass
decades deep, a caesura
birdsplit in the space
wind makes at the middle of continents.

Minnesota perhaps. Far enough,
his axe blazed the four corners,
making his own space his.

Ploughed it. At its edge
sighted his furrow on white birch
in the elm dark, the wheat
climbed his sleep
tensed as rigging.

By the stream. His face
swims there, child again
in the old speech.

As if any thing were finished,
summer gone, snow falling forever.
The magnolia stands
in pink fallen petals, a girl
shedding clothing.

Crossed the field,
sat by the water sighting
a boat come to shore –
crossed masts caught in the hawk's span
slid through his memory.

Blue jay, kestrel a rag in air,
the pheasant's yell wakens him,
rusty wheel through the bracken.

For him the wheel turned.
For him the corn the wind bowed
groaned in the millwheel,
then the bright stones lichened over.

In his ship on the pool
sails of a child's puzzle
assembling into a landscape.

He is standing again
at the seaport weeping,
the ship crowding sail
prowling over him.

*

　　　Where he ran,
bare heels through cowclap.
In the pond scrubbed himself naked.

Shy, nervous,
she'd not take her knickers off,
lay for him in the deep leaves.
It's not innocence
the fathers suffer from,
crouched in the birches, watching.

Then all his life scowling,
darker, cursing the crushed thumb,
land always resisting, forest
pushing in, pushed back
his share of winters. Years
distance lengthens down he recalls
her white thighs, peach fur
of her arms round him, pink moment
of her breasts spring wakens
year by year in the magnolia.

No use now he worked, broke
stone's weight dragging
harrow and plough. That he got sons
to farm after, fight,
curse him in snarls
they'd gotten from Vikings,
that their women toughened
and won't take his handswipe,
all means nothing. That the last
of his kin died beyond lonely

among byres and chickenshit,
the life grudged out of him
means no more. Though I can't hear
their immigrant speech, can't see
their scowl from the house
wanting me gone, there's some thickening
of air I walk through.

No use to die broken. No use
holding on to what suffering
holds us.

I am a cry among cries
in the field where I dance.

*

Hawk born from the wolf's mouth

Among sumacs, grey men
pushing their young before them
into the clearing, goldenrod, milkweed,
the space always mine now.

There is the young grass
shined by the wind, sun's broad light
as it was in the field
once when I was wolf.

Seeds passed, tumbling
their ways to wherever, the air
bringing smell of my brothers,
striking the howl in me.

I ran, the leaf shadows on me.
Bird crossed me, its shadow
swallowing the gnat's shadow,
above me the hawk's flight

formed in the updraught. I ran
through thin woods across water
the light trembled over,
wolf again, running.

*

Concerning the clearing

I carved faces in stumps. I set them to watch the clearing below the stream and pond. I set them at the corners where the man that farmed that field had stood watching his crops under the weather. That man was long dead, leaving his litter of chickenwire and bolts, a tip of tax demands and foreclosures and smashed furniture, the house as he had lived in it and died, gone to mildew, yellowed out. In the field he had cleared was one great stone he had never moved, a granite thumb. All his grown life he cursed it. He would stand on it, a man cut off by the tide, safe on his rock.

An immigrant, a Swede. A man breaking his fingers on stones he dragged off. In the dark house of stones: his woman, his sons, his daughter. A living somehow, farming the woods, turning the stream for dam and pond, lugging stones into walls. The thumbnail blackened and fell off. Cows mooned through the trees, huge and nun-like, breaking sticks, lowing before rain. Pigs, chickens, a turkey for Thanksgiving, a goose for Christmas. They were there perhaps two generations, their last efforts abandoned chicken coops, the barn fallen thick with briars, the space of a small kitchen garden, abandoned. Old iron implements shedding into rust, the soil faintly red, grainy flakes.

Up Bjorgen's Road above the city by the nuns' house. The place is secret, mine despite the little red ribbons marking off the plots that will be houses, developments on the edge of town. A place of private rituals and the continuing presences of those who called it their own, a space amongst others I can open in my mind to walk there, to return, all my days, where my mind briefly cleared of all its luggage and the hawk turned sunward.

A field of grass. A long slope the sumacs advance across. Through the elms the white glint of birches.

*

      Water's quick tongue
keeping its skin
of shaking branch, sky, reflection
waterbugs stride on, leaf floats.

I am where I am some animal
hunkering down in itself
to drink at the stream and stare
the unbreakable silence down.

Where the birds settle –
woodpecker's throb, dove's moan,
the cardinal's blood jet
as it would be without me.

To be still, a grassblade
dividing the wind, a monk hears it
steering his ship of the quiet,
his ear cupped to the stars,

in the ringing anvil of space
a bird with the birds. Three there were
at tree height driving the hawk off
his wings thrashing out sound

not part of him, not built
to fly among crow nests but hungry,
weary, wrong-muscled,
grey bird of my death

folding himself in the tree
a long moment above me hiding
demanding my silence, the watcher
watched. He stares now

in my mind catching his breath
into me, as if he were my death.
Flies again, driven out, crows
and the sunlight after him.

*

      Elm, birch, evergreen
above snow's remnants, the young firs
lost in spring, leaves
clenched through frost, folding out.

Among birches, families of five
sprung together, some lost
and some winter broken, survivors
gathered in old parchments, their skins'

weathered alphabets, pitted bark
of lost writing, lost marks,
a language left in the baggage trains,
stolen from docksides.

Tell me it's so. We remember.
Tell me someone remembering us
sitting out in the last woods
warms our old cheeks.

In water, in the greenness
under reflections I'm stolen away
waking years later among elm roots
again nodding to the ferns.

And speak again. Or nothing.
Or, children, holding the cup
drink from it, in a kingdom
to which I was travelling.

FOX RUNNING

(1980)

who could release a woman or dream there was a key

TOM PICKARD, 'Window'

Fox
running
loose in his sleek skin
loose in his slick fur

Fox
between lamp dark and daylight
loping through the suburbs
miles bridges canals rails

Through the town littorals
chicken runs long bricked over
wild places put to the plough

Streets keeping their tilt
and curve of old lanes
over Crouch Hill into Seven Sisters

Through Haringay Hornsey
Highgate Holloway the cold
wind of the subway tunnels

Out under the sky Highbury
Hampstead to Paddington
among the grey yellow bricks

Chimneys and flat house fronts
his London skyline, pencil
of the Post Office Tower
his marker for Baker Street

Along the bottom line
of Regent's Park for Camden
hiding out along the waterway

Fox
ranging the city's inner spaces
being scavenger of skips parks
and desirable period residences

Fox wanting to be alongwind
amongst bracken his own shade
the breeze at his back

One eye sleeping, shut
on some chicken dream of wire
and bloody feathers in his nostrils

One eye awake to his hunters
and the slavering jaws
of the hunting dogs, his brothers once

Being outlaw
out classed out priced out manoeuvred
hunger leashing him in to the city
in the rattling milk bottle dawn

Back of his mind brome blowing
wind sifting the oak leaves
back of a stone-littered silence

Back of his fox skull
mountain ash and the wide sky
printing his memory's tape

In at last from the wide
improbable country the townsmen
gape at uncertain such space
ever was for running: the fox

Aloof distant alert
holed up between running
in his red slash of fox body
running from the emptied distance

Crowded with townspill
of building sites' muddy footings
where will be flyover
industrial estate new bungalows

Years ago long ago late he is
skin of his name of his legend
skin of his alias son of his alibi
son of his tale told for children

Running into the tube maps
into the bus routes into the rails
learning the districts
learning connections and running

Into the city
dawn glimpsed and sometime sighted
I've seen him running
from Lancaster Gate to the Long Water

Poor winded breath shortening
and his thatch thins, wanderer

Running into his death
and his death always with him

Running into the razor
heart attack up his sleeve
shotgun pepper in his backside

Fox writes:

From a small room writing small
between the lines in the margins
on the one book left to me, *Vallejo*

in spidery lines of joined up writing
in case I shall need them
all the words for *goodbye*

Between the image and the next
instant of the image the trace
on the retina: a man bouncing a ball.

He is naked, jerky, long ago
his handsome body fed the ground.
Sunlight on him then

is the travelled light our star
sows in the thin electron milk
where will be galaxies.

Your attention please. I shall offer
a small gob of advice: *listen.*
Listen to the sounds listen
to the music listen to the fox.

And look at the pictures: our man
in the Victorian back yard
opening his fist to throw the ball

is a ripple of overlapped slides,
still frames of himself running silently
up and down in his birthday suit.

Where we see him we never would have.
In black and white.
In the space we occupy. Here.

Called *persistence of vision,*
the image on the retina a space.
Called retinal memory: the ball

through the white blur of rebound
falls to his hand closing round it
all the years since:

a fuss of white dove feathers.

Beginning again and again
beginning from what's broken.
Nights trying to slip under sleep's door
under the backwash of images:

her voice, how he turned
years through the black mill of her hair.
Came to this: nights on the stairs
not knocking on any door.

Half a morning round the phone box
before picking up the black handle.
Glad the line's busy, no one home.
Glad the number's off the hook.

All the lines through Bristol out.
From the number in his name no answer.
Outside the winter city, Maida Vale
glimpsed grainy pictures of the rain.

Wears his gasp and hunch of defeat,
his button saying *out to lunch*.
At Paddington debating trains.
In Kilburn disorderly and drunk.

Hunting alone between the city north
and the city south of the river.
In Brady's Tavern with a cashflow problem
exchanging alcohol for coin of the realm.

Twice around the Circle Line.
At Waterloo the last train north
to Camden, scattered roads of bottles,
VP and cider empties, upturned crates.

Holed up with Baudelaire and Lorca.
On Sundays picking up exotic fruit
along the market side, selling
half a dozen ties he's nicked.

Back of Dingwalls where the lads
were selling junk. His mad and
staring eyes. His mouth
repeating how she was his sparrow.

How she was his woman, faithless
as the wind turns anywhere, he'd been
better bedded with the wind
or wedded to the water.

Winter and summer all he loved
lied to him when he'd not
hurt anyone would he. Such
were the gaps in his schedule.

Such were his night thoughts.
Other nights he'd off himself,
fall into the rail, take his last
white skittering glimpse of England

down Beachy Head cliffs. Stain
the rocks. Feed the ravens.
Such was his nightly scenario,
his single movie of himself.

Happens. Crash. The fall from grace
blind drunk into the orchestra,
the bit where she sits peeling daisies
saying she loves him loves him not.

Sleepless. Nights the twenty years
of loving her are all one string
of beads on mother misery's rosary,
and how she knew to put the boot in.

And put the boot in. Lists his one last
broken wedding dish, his one last cry
in any corner, his one last cigarette,
under the glittering dancehall ball

their one last tango, one last fuck
anywhere under the stars and how
when his mouth said yes to her
there was his penis saying *no no no*.

His single ticket to the city,
a room, nights howling in the shower,
sleeping drunk inside the wardrobe,
dreamless, pissing in the sink.

And wakes to the same black anger.
Wakes to the same blank hunger.
Wakes to the same bleak search
for some fox warmth to his fox flesh.

Years, tickets, trains. Mewling
the same bleached nothings
on the salt roads anywhere, fears
he'll live lonely, die alone

in some white room in white linen
where death's angel pulls the plug
and if there's any last word of him
only she hears it: efficient, crisp,

antiseptic, laying out his body,
informing his relations, turning up
the watch at her lapel noting
time of his departure.

No way.

No way a fox goes out, no way
a man who was fox, kept ignorant
of what killed him, icy in the morgue,
ashes in the crematorium, words

entered in the black form filed away
beside the red his birth was
and between some forty years
his blood pumped out of him

the skylines that he crossed,
his memory of ferns and rivers,
distance, open country, city,
women that he loved, songs he sang.

Better die quick, if fox
at the heels of the hounds, if man
at the razor of some loonie. Better live
and if living running better run.

And keep running. Marylebone,
Lisson Grove, Edgware Road to Kew
to Wimbledon. Scattered sparks
and windblown newsprint, coming out

surprised again beside the river,
images the city has, home
the subway's groan and slide of pipes
and checking out of maps, his skull

encountering the city, his body
moving with a certain grace,
moving with particular intelligence
across the city's interstices.

And surviving through the rooms
his flesh joins other flesh
and makes some heat. Among
the endless conversations, starts, stops,

unfinished lives' biographies,
feints, gestures, cries, his life's
plain furniture, a borrowed room
in Camden to begin again from nothing.

Thoughts of a man around 40.
Notes. Maps. Things missing.
People that he loved his life ran with
all gone now, gone forever.

Just as they should be.

As they were meant to vanish
between here and the last hillside.

Between this space
and the next loneliness.

Between the image and the next
clear instance of the image
the retina remembers:
a man bouncing a ball.

Remembers how he was then
Fox
running in his long blood anywhere

early morning out
down the stairwell

sighting in the betting shop mirror
running just like him
with his same fox cunning
his brother

turning up his coat in rain
dodging in the underground

down the iron stairs at Camden
at King's Cross up and down the escalator
up the iron stairs at Goodge Street

following the lights
following the signs

running slow
running quick
in the stale winds trains shift
through the underground veins
of the city

Earl's Court to Barbican
by seven different routes

blinking briefly in the light
sniffing briefly in the air

investing in the breweries
his last Isaac Newton portraits
and never coming up all day

cashing in his cash card
ripping up his cheque stubs

waiting for his giro
arguing his earnings related

always with the wrong form
in the wrong office
on the wrong floor

of the wrong building
in the wrong part of town

and anywhere and anyway
wrong
plain wrong

we're afraid
Mister Fox
you don't qualify
for any sort of benefit

screaming back
so you sign it
you sign it Puffadder

running
running

up and down the moving staircase
in and out the tunnels

longing for the girls
saying underneath they're all lovable
being hetero and macho and lonely

his head full of underwear
his head full of skin

when he sees

in the opposite direction
running just like him
with his own fox longing
and his own fox cunning

himself

his face all surprise
his own foxy stare
carried off in the onrush
in the opposite direction

running with a wave
with a flickered recognition
beginning of a gesture
running

flying off on the train in the black
and its wind all around him
sniffing on the platform

and no one to tell
that he's seen him
Fox
his double
in the mirrors
his brother
himself
who'd anyway believe him

who'd anyway tell him
nay you're just pissed Jim

Between the image and the image
and the next motion of the image
Between the seer and the seen

Between the moment and the moment
Between the next and the next
Between denial and the fact

Between the running and the running

Comes the memory the space
Comes the man with the ball
Comes the one still space
for a brief time
in the city

Fox writes:

Tommy's space, crow nest
up the stone spiral into the wind
to the room at the house top.

Among plants and words I mellow out
watering the avocados Jascha your lady
has brought from their stones.

Avocado, *aguacate, ahuacatl,* testicle.
Above the rainy city peopled
by late quick footsteps
along the park's night edge.

Midnight. Clocks shedding
at variable distance the several sounds
of another night halving the planet
is one fancy English way to say it:

the silence, discovering itself
in what measures it at last
beyond failure, the black long ditch
welling with its dead with their mouths

still muttering their loves.
I'm alone, I have slept, I wake
from my own long wanting to die
eighteen months I can say that.

In my dream I put down the phone,
I said *that was a long time ago.*
I woke to the night's hard frost
and the dark city sleeping around me.

The planet sailed on through the nowhere.
It was the beginning of the last two decades
of the century called twenty, as reckoned
by the Europeans, I being one

of the northern hemisphere, this sector
the lights and the radio sounds

seep into space from, chatter
of our making some sense here.

By the park, where the nightjar is singing.
The voice breaking cover is mine,
the background hiss creation's
continued explosion. All the rest

being static on the tape and the airways,
late incoming plane from elsewhere,
traffic slowing to the Parkway.

Between the image and the next
sure moment
between the image and the next

Where I ease the dial station
to station, anthem by anthem.

Moscow. AFN. Stray voices
through the all night small hours

on the short wave, cop lullaby,
ship to ship interception,

quick blast of Securicor Cockney,
static crackle, long music

and two words repeated:
her hair, her hair, her hair,

some patches of silence, some
rapid reply to an unheard question,

tooth decay projects in Africa
on *Voice of America*, bulletin,

bluegrass, Chrysler, Jesus
through the late 3.00 a.m. shift

till first light shivers awake
one then two birds then the orchestra

of wide awake bells and the wolves
in the park begin howling for meat.

All night in the radio dark
the opinions arrive, urgent

hooded versions of history. From Kiev
Hangchow long grain statistics,

Sofia in impeccable Oxford
listing tractor production 1946-49.

Meat. Wheat. Sweaty feet.
Who gets what. The continent

radio sounds, neons, texts,
pools of light around tapedecks

in studios high in the rain dark
of the technicians, the announcers,

voices smooth with such facts
only the sleepless and I hear.

The image remains.

And I think: supposing it's now,
this night the voices all stop.

A flight of wild geese blips the radar
and all the technologies die.

Goodbye Newton Milton Socrates.

And so simple. One man with migraine,
loose signals in Prague,

taxi call signs in Cleveland,
some event in say Valparaiso

or one more demand and no
backout, no manoeuvre, command

begins counting to zero
and beyond into minus,

flips the alert, or a
sleepy technician goes crazy,

falls out with his girlfriend,
slips with his razor

and opens the circuits deep
in the core of the mountains.

This that they're trained for.
This that they're paid for.

This the bullnosed politicians
cadge votes for and all night

the radios sweetly reason around.
This that at age seven

I heard in the long wireless roar
of Hiroshima and prayed

and ran down the garden
sweet God let it not continue.

From Acton to Angel a fireball,
all cities gone:

'An area bounded by Hackney
and Greenwich and Fulham and Willesden,

some millions dead, houses in Bushey
burst into flame.' For weeks

we're told nothing to fret for.
Within 72 hours all programmes

switch to light entertainment,
broken by bulletins.

And the quote ends. Goodbye
radio miracle, Marconi's device.

End of message. Goodbye
to the language that failed.

Goodbye telephone nobody answered.

Goodbye Victorian nude with a ball.
Goodbye all trace on the memory.

Goodbye to everyone in Wimbledon.

Goodbye Fox, my scuttling double
gone in the hot wind of particles.

Goodbye *Areopagitica, Aeneid,*
Assyrian Winged Genius, alphabets

running from aleph to zero.
Goodbye Dürer's vision, Blake's angels,

Tolstoy's anger, Shan State,
tears of the Indians, *Malleus Maleficorum,*

search for the Unified Field Theory,
Fibonacci Series, Newton's Tables,

Occam's Razor, all gone
in the same sharp withering rain.

Goodbye republics of raw nerve,
disputed borders of meaning.

Goodbye at last, universe
thinking itself in our skulls.

Goodbye love. Woman I loved.

Writing anywhere I said once.
I had just met you. The sharp
intake of breath was mine, the long
unexpected and longed for tide

was you over me. Writing
on stones, on kerbs, on the mucky pavement,
leaving your room at first light
hearing the dawn an outrage of birds.

I write or I die: that dramatic
that simple. I die anyway
while my life is the fool that persists
and is never in his folly any wiser.

A daft occupation some say.
Swinging my lamp whether it's Thursday
or Spain. Somewhere in this
sector of infinite distance I met you,

grey lady who gave me my fox name,
dark lady who gave me my fox shape,
rose lady who gave me my fox colour,
my long fox outline, my fox tongue.

As to *goodbye* not much
to be said for it.
                         I survive
in some core of you
you through my life are the gift of.

One eye shut on the dream
one eye open

One eye hunted
one eye hunter

Aloof alert out
moving abruptly
between skylines

Afloat adrift on the city
some images on the retina

Awake

Fox writes:

once upon a long time
I was a good dog.

I ran around town
with the other good dogs.

Buried our bones.
Brought home bacon.

On paynights drank
Bell's whisky with water,

home by the moon
through the late night streets

in a bad baritone singing
what a terrible thing
is a pub with no beer

down the long hill
to the river. I was

such a good dog
such a bad dog
with the other dogs.

Now I'm Fox. I run.
I've left town.

I run & I run.

I come from a broken home
and I broke it.

Don't wait up for me
Blackbird. Your name

was on mine
like a ring. I'm Fox.

I run and run on
down the vanishing landscape.

I've not paid the mortgage,
I've not paid the bank,

stamp tax or insurance,
I'm a blur, I'm a blank

and I'm never going home.
I've cashed my ticket.

And I've thrown my keys
on the railroad tracks.

And I'm gone.

And I'm Fox, running out.

Into holes under leaves across water.

So far on the hill
and no running back to the treeline,
on in the open.

Fox: hidden in landscape,
visible on it. I run
and my sleep is a dream of running.

Between that and waking
I've glimpsed between fern
and heron's wing the old life.

North by south of Isca the river.
Days were longer there. Even I
might have lived there.

Like a dream of childhood,
willows and tall reeds.
Unlikely as the middle ages,

villages before enclosure,
before these towns I run
hunting my crust in.

Where I fade on the tape,
my shadow with the other shadows
one more missing item.

My voice on the phone
dimming out, my voice asking
are these words coming out of my mouth?

among streets and the mornings
and all these stars
is anyone

who at the end hears traffic,
the siren baying them home
on the brackish roads

on the far sides of towns, sodium
and flyway, strange blue light
that flickers on the ambulance?

Otherwise fast
anomalous
a tube train through allotments
one morning out to Heathrow

A man gone down the country
turning out his tube tickets

trailing his names
cancelling accounts
forwarding addresses

chanting underground underwear
windblown Wimbledon

Barbican
Barbie can't

send the Shah back
Shahn't

out of his skull on

learning how to vanish
hanging on the strap
thinking on his feet
covering the distance

listing strange objects
carried on and off trains

overhearing

dollar
dollar half
bunch of flowers

'Who's a big boy then?
Cooked his own supper?
Washed his socks and underpants?'

So she let you down
poor babba
my little patch of sunlight
maybe she was meant to

Clapham Common Sunday
747 hanging in the sky

split vision
caught connections
razor to the throat
bloody carnival
Easter in the city

flute sound
cutting through traffic

he dreams of elsewhere

Victoria by Belgravia
travellers' cases
scuffing the snowcem

Kentucky Fried Chicken boxes

adrift among the residences
pied à terre spacious flat
company let tourists only

down past Justin de Blanc
to the Prince of Wales

old men talking about the war

O walking in the gutter
to avoid bad luck
stepping round a ladder
he was flattened by a truck

didn't give a

Radiation
fades your genes

pagan raider

'them breeding like rabbits
with the H bomb and all'

people knowing no one else

the sixties have gone
but the moustache stays

I read the book
you saw the movie

I saw the real one
the Disney version

dick
lick
prick
tongue
NF skins
clock end
ayatollah Thatcher
kiss my willy
if you're reading this
Mildred
we're through

zipping up his fly

today I'm crow
adrift
wingbeat on wingbeat
split vision
across wet slates
lopped plane trees
hated somehow

the rainbird of Finsbury

something in me
always loving
some part of you

honestly it's my round
after all they're only people

if I'd been a woman
I'd have lost my temper

if I'd been a man
I'd have lost my erection

in Ferme Park Rd waiting for a bus
wondering where
in rain, brick, traffic

skies above Islington
blue
burdened by their beauty

blur of trees
events like birds
marking them

by Angel tube
through the crowd
through the traffic
through the flute music

two buskers, a girl
like a dark linnet singing,
her man fingering the air
to music

how she danced to him
her music
played to him
to no one else

through the tunnels
dusty light on service pipes
slid quickly
back of the brain

Urban. Efficient. Articulate. And costly.

'are you going to the circus?'

clowns lions peanuts painted ladies

Oxford Piccadilly Cambridge
split vision
pub of the same name in which

'Honestly it's my round
you've got to be good to yourself
the electric's cut off
we can't pay the rent
double malts all three Henry'

'has he for whom you
left yours now gone?'

he'll never be a buttercup
in God's shining garden

gifts I'd give my enemy:
gnawings at his brain's
thin skirting

a telephone
ringing in his sleeve
he'll never reach

facefull of fingers
decently bunched Jim

Napoleon's bad smell map of Egypt

hanging on the strap

such a vision of the street
as the street may understand

take your chance at the bar
along with everyone, squire

Fox you say your name was?

glancing on the stairs
my double
his double
Edgware Road

motion of his arm

at Paddington among the trains
grown up and riding double-decker buses
all alone

curtain in the wind
woman calling
someone home to supper

night
distant lights
moon riding clouds

glimpsed twice
his double
one who moves like him

gave chase
hot pursuit

around the Circle Line

gone again down the tubes
the black
fast city veins

to Baker Street
to Jubilee
to Neasden

where he died
easily among the skins
razor to his throat
drowning in his blood
all he ever saw was boots
and the boots going in

hunting down the trains
changing quickly

following the signs
following his shoulder

running
where he dies

running to the razor

opening the doors
awash with blood
where he dies again

spring festival
urban version
late century twenty

film events become
moment as it happens
unrecognisable

swift battering
of images
across the retina

my double
dead

my carnage

dead Fox
dead Fox
dead Fox

But I've seen him
between birdlight and Lisson Grove

between lampdark
and the Long Water

I've seen him

his file closed down the dole office
his last account cleared
his black form
filed with his red form
and his last room cleared
and his suitcase
and his girl told
and his wife told

I've seen him
between Camden and Chalk Farm

slow
easy
waiting for a bus
moving with a grace
moving with a certainty
across the city's face

One of our own they say
served his time

Gone Away on all the envelopes

'My brother thinks I'm dead
but my sisters know I'm alive'

Word

I want a word
a beginning word forming in its water bead

I want a word forming fingers of itself
in the belly of all language

I want a word fusing in the first 4 seconds of the bang

I want a word
striding in the air
all the way to the coda
growing up to be a real person
living where the grown-ups live

where each letter is a life
forming into meaning

I want a word with a gull's lift
and easy shadow
I want a word with a bat's inaudible sound
I want a word like a snail
round and round the rim of a glass

I want a word for these days these miles
these trains this distance
the wanderer covers aloof
on the star-glinting rails

Surbiton Norbiton Sanderstead
blue scatter of sparks
smokey embankment flowers
ownerless back lots of flats
Langham Court Riverdale
in Sledhurst and Streatham
and Gipsy Hill sniffing
amongst the paper plates
the Wonderloaf wrapper detritus
in Hammersmith sniffing the amyl
where I lost sight
lost my name lost my number
my ticket

To Morden to Putney to Wandsworth
to Beckenham Junction
to Stockwell to Battersea Park

Where I was anyone anywhere
on hands and knees
who would crawl to the horizon
finding someone to say *yes* to

just another face
just another walking wounded
starry in the city in a dead space
between Archway and Holloway
in the valley of abandoned bedrooms

just another bruised ego
just another fox

stepping out in the cool skinhead wind
into NF occupied country
to Lambeth evicted boarded-up

through Pakkibashers' Court
through Martin Webster Gardens
to Brick Lane to Bethnal Green

dreaming London Fields and Hackney Downs
spaces between other spaces
states or conditions of mind
a man in a yard bouncing a ball
way down Thatcherland

past the closed-down clinic
and the short-staffed school
such a vision of the street
past the road where the bureaucrats live

through Stepney and south of the river
to Camberwell wary in traffic
through which a sharp blast of dub sound
to Brixton wall-eyed beside the Little Bit Ritzy

oh lady she's long way gone now
in the hennaed rainbow of her hair
you your own man now John
step inside a minute

through the city Muggers Lane
Rape Alley
hunting situations vacant and a room

too old or overqualified
or under experienced or plain can't drive

Long ago now in the year zero
under the rule of Fatso
with my companion Alexander the Impecunious
called Knifeback
called Throatcutter
Jack Scratch
who betrayed me
in the middle of my life
back among the schisms and the alleys
of the hostile villagers
and the slow drawing of the map around Africa
slow drawing of the noose

slow sharpening of the knife
back across the foggy moors
among the stonecutters
among the bands of the black-browed
and their beaded women
there he set his watch
to the exact hour of my defeat
that is finished now

If I want to I'll weep without apology
If I want to I'll laugh
I'll sing with who will sing or sing alone
I will be honest with who will be honest with me

I want a word for a voice
trapped in the telephone
heard only by the post office police
listening for keys
dreaming of a key word listening
for drug words women words
bomb words picket words
words like *immigrant conspiracy abortion*

When all he was asking
in his hardly daring voice
was do you have a room
do you have a job
and how to get
from Balham to Clapham

where he's cowboy
grill chef
beerslinger
checker
porter
typist
punch operator
thief

standing at the cashier's window
hearing *oh we've written a book have we?*

Underneath the night sky.
Star. Star. Star.
I would pray were there any God to pray to

I want the word
for the many lives he might have lived
if he'd gotten off anywhere, Moorgate
for instance or Tooting
in a single room or Dagenham
at the end of a lousy marriage
to a woman hissing in her sleep
alongside him. When he cries
in the onrush at Victoria
and his cry comes out of him
into the world I want
what his cry is: sharp

Always on the wrong train anywhere
with the outdated ticket
in the wrong skin with his
long forgotten biography

Rolling up his last tobacco
and it's midday and it's Monday
and time to feel bad
and it signifies nothing
just another person on the line
when he tips down his hat
and sleeps and wakes knowing
he is called *only the protagonist*

Arrived by the wrong train
to the wrong town hears

no she don't live here no more
your kids grown up and gone
heard she married again
your mother died asking for you
where you been and where you now

At the last there were phone calls
from people who didn't exist

Word I want his word
of the dotty professor
of the salesman hating the product
of the sleepy technician
of the jobless
of the fat man in first I want
word uttered in defeat by the captain
of a wandering band of chartered accountants
word of the bad architects
the government of tax lawyers
all the little stockholders
voting protection in a free economy
turning back the clock
deciding what the country needs
is a damned good war

I want word of the tramp on Kingston bridge
dreaming only a warm mug of tea

I want word of the bloke
who leans over with a razor
and slits the protagonist's throat
and walks off scot free

Just another of my feints
Just another invention
Just another of my lies
Just another skin coming off

Switching trains in the train game
playing games with my name game
middle-aged and seedy in rooms
living with a woman it was said
in Eastbourne by the winter sea

Men I knew years back
when I was young and daft
delivering the *News of the World*
round Pearson Park. Faces
mentioning defeat saying
bankruptcy desertion failure redundancy
lost bottle. Their light
that had gone or never lit
or they burned now on the lamp oil
of necessity the pure oil
of ageing euphoria the door
held half-shut on privacy
sheet smells dusty odour
out of second-hand couches
rent due smell of woman
glimpsed in the kitchen dark
some other dark pursued
room to room through suburbs
in a slow terminal frenzy
their last dance anywhere
under any glittering ball but they
when they talked had not much to say

Such was Fox

In the technologies of terror
On his road to the terminal ward
On his way to the knife
In a taxi to the hospice
In the corner of the interrogation room
Reaching for his last drink in any bar anywhere
Saying *to hell with everything*
Sleeping it off in some room
his night full of idetic images

Fox drawn to the life to the bone
 to the yellowing teeth the bristles
at chin and cheek singing barearse
clap hands here comes Charlie

With his word that was word
of the unmasked betrayer
a beaten man knowing better
and had he his time around
but it's too late now Valparaiso

no such thing as a free lunch
sings the radio
where's this highway go to?

him and his egg sandwich

his suffering was only good for when he had to

like a wheel
like a wheel
that stops turning

smiles in death's little sad face

he speaks
from the lengthening floor
of his blood his conviction
not me not me Jack

he speaks
with his word
from the night's narrow places

with his moment
a man bides his breath for
at the end forbears boastmaking

a wise man holds out
his enemies destroy themselves
he defeats them with words

brother shadow
I greet you, goodbye
go well on your road
leave the way open

he is anyone
naked under his clothes
alone his moment

anyone at all wandering back
from the laundromat late Saturday noon
clearing his throat
speaking again
in the white room
sweeping his hat off and asking
who all belongs to this blood then?

The Poet Reclining

Spartan communiqué

Over in this sector
in the limitless nowhere
setting the mirrors
facing each other

the face shrunk
to its eyeball
its one act
of looking and looking

we find coming between us
ourselves and our vision
that would otherwise be
to infinity

merely our eyes
only our looking.

From the Vale of White Horse: some news

At some cost
I achieved some detachment.

Finding this distance
here in myself
I first had to cross.

Say I got out of the traffic.
I was no longer even curious.
I said bravely *no more bullshit*.

If I lost sight of myself
on the landscape smokey with towns
that barely matters now.

Nor do the years I marched
in my bright brass buttons
behind the wrong flag.

We're each one of us
separate countries I think,
tricky and wary as states.

And the language fools us,
each in the yammering skull
with our messages fading at the border.

I've no complaint in the silence.
I'm alone at last with the stars.

I'm connected by voices and footprints.
I've one eye on the distant foothills.

My news is as ever:
it will not be the last of me.

Being the third song of Urias

Lives ago, years past generations
perhaps nowhere I dreamed it:
the foggy ploughland of wind
and hoofprints, my father
off in the mist topping beats.

Where I was eight, I knew nothing,
the world a cold winter light
on half a dozen fields, then
all the winking blether of stars.

Before like a fool I began
explaining the key in its lost locked box
adding words to the words to the sum
that never works out.

                    Where I was
distracted again by the lapwing,
the damp morning air of my father's
gregarious plainchant cursing
all that his masters deserved
and had paid for.
                    Sure I was
then for the world's mere being
in the white rime on weeds
among the wet hawthorn berries
at the field's edge darkened by frost,
and none of these damned words to say it.

I began trailing out there in voices,
friends, women, my children,
my father's tetherless anger, some
like him who are dead who are
part of the rain now.

In transit

(from Mari for Mick)

Some place a horse
shines on the field. Some place the ants
trek the foothills of the grass.

Maybe love comes and goes
and maybe comes back, scrap of news
from places we lived.

Or it's too late for everything,
childhood and sunglaze
gone from the river. And this
is a grim little song, sister.

As we fly away from each other,
unrepeatable, ordinary,
years away, miles later
chewing love's bit of bread.

Or we're free. That's
what I wanted, always: to be.

Among the white horses.
Among the fields of yellow kale.

Hunéus the shoemaker

He was content all those years
carving his children from wood.

Two nails banged in for eyes
and you're done he told them.

Twice wed he was, his first
lost in childbed, six
that survived out of infancy.

One son he named *Walk in the Lord*,
another *Go Forth*. Taught them his trade
that they make provision.

Working late, kept by his lamp
to prayer and close study.
Frowning under the lintel.

All his life the same music,
patching and stopping up draughts
through sixty some winters.

So much to ask out loud for.
The dark space in his mind
he called God told him so:

mend, shiver, make do when hungry,
suffer when must but make good.

He was content anyway, at nightfall
hunting the wild birds of the river,
a man in his own space.

Or so we believe. That he died
blameless and lonely I'm sure of.

Operations undertaken at or near the surface

Mornings of long silence. I wake late
to the wind and the grey light
of winter coming. The milk
stands cold and alone on the step.

In my dream you shook your dark hair
and turned from me at last.
I bring in the milk.
Yes you loved me for certain.

I think of you. How at times
the world stopped in your hair
where I cried my cry uselessly.
I pour out the milk in the jug.

You betrayed me, having no choice
apparently. Did what you must.
For love of you I scattered my cries
across England. I make tea.

I make it like everything slower these days,
and consider my lack of compassion
back when the world melted in you.
I pour out the milk.

Now your letters no longer arrive.
Your regrets don't whiten the morning.
Winter does that. And my fury.
I pour it all out. I pour it away.

Shallow dreaming

it scrambles time and seasons
if it gets through to you
JONI MITCHELL

Sitting in the bus station
where else mister? tuning the transistor
thinking that lady waiting a good lay.

Wearing his snow white bandage
digital timepiece pentacle and earring
a silver razor blade to the throat.

Later with the wires to his head
coasting the big bird from Seattle
beyond the Aleutians and the Circle

or takes the long shift to Bear Island
waving to the Mig *only kidding man*
dropping down the Murmansk approaches

seeing the sky's edge turning south
fuelwards to the Turkish bases
over patchwork Europe and rest up.

That's one duty man over beer and smoke
later the same day *boy that was close*
shooting pool all the world one rush

through the skull one wing of geese
on the snowy wind of the prairie.
Between us and the stars only stars.

Six miles down only clouds more miles
over their shadows. The plane
in the bare knuckle light of the sun

makes at times a rainbow under itself
and the bright ring of colour goes with you
in the radio silence. *It's a pain chief*

that I can tell you. Nothing for hours
over the Baltic probing the Polish margin
testing the Reds. Times out of mind

I've watched them trying it out –
Ilyushin or Bear or flock of wild birds
homing over such landscapes

that show in my scope still –
the long shores of cold where the ocean
batters its freezing continents

and if grass grows there it is chill
rasping and stiff in the sea-brought winds
at the tops of the world.

There the caribou come in spring.
Their hooves still thrash in the sea's ebb
through the tales of the grandfathers.

All blips now. Data printout
as to latitude and the old ice geometry.
I'd quit but what else? I see

white sky on a white world, cities
stubbed out, ash blown catty corner.
I tell you I'd go on an acid tab singing

glimpsing at last a pattern in the grids
kissing goodbye all the ladies
on the planet's side flying in

sliding under the radar yelling
this is a good day to die brothers
nothing lasts only earth and the mountains.

Old movies

It is long ago in an old
old movie, the print bleached,
the soundtrack scratchy and flat.

The actors wear suits and speak
upper-class British, the workmen
are always cheerful and loyal.

They smoke a lot, poised at windows,
their knuckles folded to their faces.
They are all dead now. Overhead

in the high auditorium since demolished
a moth flits in and out the projector beam.
Lint catches in the corners of the shutter.

A film I saw years away in childhood,
in rainy Ripon in the north of my life
before the world showed me its backside.

At the station he waits 40 minutes.
She never arrives among the steam trains.
They never meet again this side

of the last frame of the last reel
before the movie runs off the sprockets.
They won't drink, sit to table, bear children

or share one grain of wheat
of all the world's wheatfields. Before stars
blink out and all the silence starts

her eyes won't be the last he looks into,
her hands the last he falls through,
his voice won't be the last she hears.

In the grey blur of film the protagonist
smokes one last cigarette, loops the butt
off the platform, claps hat on head

and pitches his bag into the next train out,
a nomad pulling up his tent pegs,
his wanderer's reflection in a whisky glass.

And he has no ticket. In the buffet car
the barman counts his change, he says
they come and go they never say their names.

It is another night of trains, blue light
that fades across the fields, a last crow
on a telephone wire and the movie's over.

Transcription of the crying woman

I was making my sounds
I was making them for everyone
I was walking bird alert in pasture
I was wingbeat labouring the easy air

Did he expect no change in me
who was not one but many?
It took the two of us I told him
the drowning and the drowned

I put on silk I put on lace
I oiled my olive skin
I was the mirror's glance
as I was dressing for my lover

All through these woods I was
beating in the bird hunt
too long I was alone
and he where was he where?

While I was hennaing my hair
while I was in my mirror's silver
while he was numbering the roads
while he was calling up from Maida

I took one lover then another
I was buckling on my purple dress
I was straightening out my seam
I was still dreaming of the south

I was the seal I was gazelle
I went running by the strath
I was tucking in my children
I was sweetening their milk

And I was running for the running
I was the otter's skin
across my lover's skin
I was infinity of cries

I took him in my hands like prayer
I took him in my mouth
I took the wafer of him to my tongue
I sucked the sweetness from him

I took the salt I took the wine
I was his nun I was his whore
I was the gull pitched into wind
I was a song spilled in the beams

My name was being called
my name was *bird on water*
my name was *spent and howling*
my name was *he is butchered*

I was undressing for my lover
I was pronouncing all my words for him
my shoe my clasp o my sweet moth
I was unravelling my tongue

When I was fiddling with my button
when I was picking out my comb
when I was lacquering my nails
his death came beating on my air

I was whirling in the thicket
I was thrashing in the sea foam
I was running in the scrubland
I was falling down the mountain

I was calling for my mother
I was dressing for my lovers
I was calling to my children
I was crackling in my satin

I was staring at his death's head
I was remembering his hands
I was encountering his blood
I was alone forever then

I was all Ivan's seven wives
I was Sobakina meaning *canine*
I was Nogaya meaning *naked*
I was the fury in the light across my flesh

Planting aloes
(for Judi)

Days of random events,
waking with no plan,
all the city mine to play in.

And whatever else I do
I'll be no damned richer
by the evening. *Can't dance*

too wet to plough.
Cut myself shaving.
Unsnarled the white kitchen.

Emptied out the trash.
Filled little red pots
with dark London soil,

planting the aloes
my mother gave me hours ago
yesterday in Yorkshire.

So come live with us
little green-sleeves.
Like the throats of birds.

A slow careful work
that's repetitive,
my mind drifting off

hanging in the moment
I'm tucking roots
among muck's spaces.

Sounds of far traffic,
blackbird, woman's nextdoor voice
and rattle of a bowl.

Dog's yap. April light
warm across my shoulder.
I am awake again, my life

suddenly its centre.
You I love
who taught me aloes heal.

Red blossom through the suburbs.
Yellow blaze forsythia makes.
Skies forever changing.

Words forming into meaning.
Take the aloes. Take from me
of all my pages this love.

Mouth

Mouth of a soft shell
I put my ear to hear the sea in you

Sighting eye of the sextant
I put my own eye to read the constellations
where are no stars no starcharts

Mercury
mirror without glass
scoop
sickle
shoe of the first step in Pavlova's dance
telephone to the sea's deep
I put my mouth to hear the word in you
I touch you with my tongue it is a prayer

Sibilant
first mark first ideogram
first aleph for all alphabets
first futhark of the script of pagan raiders
first winter count of zero zero zero
a language made of vowels only
words spoken into water

Like a day of leaves in rainy wind
like the tongues of shoes
like the first plants come ashore
like a cabinet of drawers and secrets
like the flickered pages of a book
like the spaniel's ears
like the flaps of aviators' helmets
like the lips of horses
like the petals of magnolia flickering pink, white
like the blue of burning anis
and the strange translucent brown
beneath the rose skin
where your blood is hunting for the surfaces of light

Like the fish mouth risen into air
like the moon's reflection stretched on water

A chanterelle
a cedar chest
a cupboard stocked against a coming war
a cave of smuggled liquor
ogival arch where no madonna is
a box of soft cutlery
the flower's throat going back in you
far into the centre of all liquids

Where was my terror
where my joy is
where my anger is
where my fear of the dark we come from
and the dark we go into is

Like a bird through a byre of the Saxons
like the swan's road on water
like the first stages on the long journey into Russia
like the tracks of fish
like the keel's shuck into waves' trough

The long afternote of a bell
the anemone
sifting all the sea through its marrying ring

Tongue

My tongue is a flute
filling all the tunnels of the subway
with its flute sound

My tongue goes before me
My tongue says my tongue
in the chatter of my quiet

No more a singer than the reeds
my tongue's a bird sound
a throstle
singing in the tree of memory

My tongue's a busker
much interested in loose change
but my tongue plays anyway

My tongue has no stops
My tongue has no reed
as a flute has none

My tongue goes rolling into words
My tongue goes running into language
My tongue goes rifling the alphabets
hunting through vocabularies
saying *honey ant   palanquin   labial*

My tongue unlocks my word hoard
My tongue says I'm a fool to let it speak

My tongue is all the fortune that I have
for any of my children

My tongue's a daft errand boy
running on ahead
My tongue's an old messenger
forgetting what he came for

Telling women that I love them
Saying that I'll stay
Promising *I'll pay I'll pay I'll pay*

And when my tongue gets me shot
my tongue will ask for one last cigarette
compliment the squaddies on their turnout
order *ready aim fire*
and quote Lorca
to the gunfire
I'll never hear

The Ubi Sunt variations

1

I shall account some lost things:
twelve songs for a missing flute.
I have lost even their titles:

> *He returns from the frontier*
> *He finds his house deserted*
> *She writes from far away*
> *He despairs beside the river*

2

In some lost book I recall
in a photograph taken Brighton Beach,
Lee Miller, Paul Éluard, Eileen Agar, 1936.

The seawind blows in their faces.
They sit in deckchairs in the sunlight
of the moment that contains them,
gone the road of all moments.

3

Bones no bigger than a child's
that were the warrior's, the fierce
man-killing frame of him

mineral again, climbing the bog-cotton,
rounding the sheep's horn,
singing down the flute singing
in the love of you I lost myself.

4

In the long lost weekend of my life
we gathered herbs she and I
with the full white moon in Orion.

And all night crushed and blended,
mortared, pestled, pinched
finger to thumb and scattered.
But who knows what that meant now?

5

They lied about the heart:
that it's a soft pink cushion
sitting in the left wall of the chest.

A lie I outlived. Time passed
in the study of linoleum in basement rooms,
an old slow war that fought itself
over the long slope of my life.

6

In trunks packed in haste,
randomly, my lost books, notes,
photographs, lost again as they must be.

The wanderer resumes his journey.
Makes do with what's to hand.
The air fills with banal words:
how I love you, we'll meet again.

7

And each night in the dream's house
the hand was a hand waving *help.*
Say I ran, say I was hunted

ditch after ditch, life after life,
a creature that slept by water
and woke among cities, strangered
and half way human. Say that.

8

Traveller on the old road
of the wind between towns,
say I endured.

Singing *short of nowt we've got.*
Singing *not much but we eat it all.*
Singing *clap hands for Charlie.*
Singing *love this is my country.*

9

In the capital as in the provinces:
disaffection and less work, scattered riots,
the imperial currency worth less and less.

Rebellion seethes in the suburbs.
The governors strengthen the police.
Dark clouds, no rain yet from the west.
The ugly prince marries the virgin.

10

Set the fire up. Let there be drink
for these travellers. There was a time
once my brothers I was young

and what lay till now ahead
was mist along a river, the kestrel
in sunlight hung his moment
over the tall reed beds running south.

11

Dear mother father aunt Jessie
it is no picnic, it's France I think
there's no white tablecloths.

We're all that thinks in all the stars,
inventing telephones and missiles.
Then silence from the planet.
Nothing more. The hiss of radiation.

12

Hills blued with distance.
No goodbye. A little further
we begin to see the mountains.

And the river's small beginnings.
And the sea turning its only syllable.
And the nights where no one sleeps.
And the song that is the last.

The poet reclining

(after Chagall)

What still holds me,
where I stretch in my skin
at the day's edge:

a particular landscape,
the fence at the field's side,
what my hat keeps the rain from.

The moment, once and once only,
sufficient, taken on trust
in the wheels of the watch.

The wind stirs the foxgrass.
The lapwing enters the thicket.

Where had the world gone?

Did I invent it,
making a fiction to keep off sleep
for fear I'd dream worse?

So I devised the grass
and the raggety birch bark,
the spider's morning extrusions
beaded white with the mist.

So it was. When I snapped my fingers,
when I turned, when I opened my eyes,
when I clapped my hands and called out,
my voice came back empty.

The morning, the evening.
Everything vanishes, generations
fading into the grass.

I lay down. I counted
the words she had written
in barbed High Gothic script:

behind wire I can't live.
The wind took her words off.
I lay down without sleeping.

Mine always the want
to make more of what is,
the world from its nothings:

the assemblies of grass,
fallen leaf ticking pavestone,
water drop forming and falling.

Out of sight were old gates
swinging in wind, far hiss
of a highway of traffic.

Further off smokey towns
with their townsmen's scandals.
City glitter of gossip and money.

In the streets coffee smells
and newly baked bread.
I met train after train

but her train never arrived.
I wrote *kleine Mutti*
so far you can't walk
to the wire you can see it.

I should forget such a place ever was.
I should concern myself with the city,
living there and surviving.

That's enough. I should forget my thought
the best's gone and the rest gets darker.

But for my belief
in the grass, that it is once
and once it is
it is forever.

I hear it all still: sheep's bleat on the moor
and the peewee's thin calls in the weeds.

The geese: I hear their cry in traffic,
the gate's squeal in brakes,
in the high thunder of the planes overhead
the wind gunning through the pines.

Long ago. A psychiatrist
told me not to listen to the wind
but the wind tells me not to listen to him.

I'll be the one holding the forged winning ticket.
I'll be the one with the devalued currency.
I'll be at the airport with no flight anywhere.
I'll be on the quayside in the bombed-out harbour
deciding once again to abandon my luggage.
I'll be in the right and I'll be dead wrong again.

Let this be the scald of remembered country.
Here the river turns east.
Here the geese fly over my grandfather's house.

Soldiers march off between trees
into the dark elbow of the road's curve.

The gate's lost its sneck.
Tiles rain from the barn roof.
Trees break in the gale, lightning divides some.

There will be sleet, then long winter.

There is a dotted line dividing the house from itself.
In the general's office this district is maps.
In the war college the cowshed an objective.
There is a red pin where the pig's snout roots.
Tank radios chatter in the fir trees.
There is a bullet-hole where the horse crops.
Here the rockets fall and the fallout
obliterates the grass and the old field divisions.

He lies in the paddock.
It is mid summer.
Not a leaf has yet fallen
but the sky changes towards day's end.

He dreams the dark evergreen,
the resins in the calendars of wood.

Waking, the byre and the brown horse
will again surprise him.

The night music

Long notes of a late instrument
drawn out across the balconies.

The stairwells newly painted.
The windows open for the night air.

By day small cage birds
hung over steep streets
dropping thin weepy notes.

The sadness of the bars.
Their air that's thickened with hashish.

By night there is the distance
like a blanket and the heavy air,
a man's breath pared along a reed
played late and to no purpose.

Across the streets in moonlight
the music fading off into a nowhere
made of dark and dog yelps
battling for the suburbs. It is
another night, another country
in another lost city where I scribbled
if I die leave the way open.

All my years one bullet
travelled from the mined-out minerals
through assembly lines until it found me.
At the end I never saw it.
So goodbye my heart, my name.

That was long ago,
a life that was or would be.
It finished somewhere halfway.

Moment by moment it sheds
more of itself. I move away
in a new name with a new biography.

This is the next world already.

Everything shines much as before.

Nothing has changed, even I.

Fox in October

He forgave the grass its persistence.
He forgave the sky its blue indifference,
no longer angry with the high wintry cirrus.

Horizon to horizon across prairies,
oceans, towns and villages the planet
spun day in day out through sunlight
into dark again, century by century
of rainy violence what was the sky
but a great yawn
wherever he was on the Earth
in any of its histories,
small in all his armour.

He forgave it. Were there a god
among the rafts of stars
he must be bored by now or had to be joking.

His eye to Herschel's telescope,
his ear to the radio noise
out at the last edge of the little we know,
in the dark of the planetarium
or in the pavilion at Kew
staring up into the points of light
he saw himself.

He was merely a protagonist,
his bag of words across his shoulder.
He forgave that.

He forgave the brown leaves.
He forgave the pigeons their dullness.
He forgave childhood its passing.
He forgave the left side of his brain.

He forgave his enemies.
He forgave his friends.
He forgave himself.
He forgave his betrayals.
He survived his own foolishness.
Some he'd damaged he hoped survived him.

Wind clattered the dropped leaves
across the afternoon park,
the long sunlight guttered,
blackbird with traffic.

He forgave his mother her growing older,
wiser, braver. He forgave
his father his death after decades of meaningless fury,
a flint pitched at the sheer injustice
of his bosses. And everyone else.

It was hard on the Earth.
He forgave everyone that.
Some that had almost broken him
he supposed he'd forgive. He did not forgive
in the name of anyone else nor the years
spent wasted and gone asking
were some evil or just daft,
either way meaning the same word *trouble*.

He forgave his children
miles years stars falling away
since his abandoning them.
He forgave their forgiving him, loving him.
He forgave even her.

He forgave love its almost ruining him.
He forgave its illusion.
He forgave himself that.

In a mood to forgive all,
make his peace, live his life now
with the woman he loved who loved him
without need of forgiveness.

Those we properly love travel with us
some way down time in the distance
the stars scatter their light
particle by particle forming new dust,
new tides in new galaxies,
perhaps for no reason.

They don't give up.
However many tries it takes.
However many lives it takes.

He concluded, one day in October,
at the beginning of an early winter,
sunlight sheer between the plane trees
at Crouch End, in his cold northern country.

FROM

BURNED BOOKS

(1981)

AND

ABEL BAKER
CHARLIE DELTA

(1981)

Burned books

Recitation at the burned books:

taking a handful
of rainy ashes
crimped half burned
paper into his fist
what was some tale
of fair women or
tinker song how
Queen Miracle was
with the stable lads

he's caught sight
of hawthorn hedge
drizzle & honeysuckle
asking what chance
of nirvana for this
wet rubbishy fistful

and longs to be
merely a grassblade
the singular stare
of the speedwell
maybe a reed flecked
by the reeds
his brothers

San Quixote of the cinders:

what was salvaged
& all but survived
ruin. Was sent
to the binder expert
in calfskin & vellum,
restorer of margins –
good man with a pastebrush
clicking his teeth
at the occasional
lacuna, gap,
hiatus.

A beam
fallen lengthwise smouldering
its fire's black terrain
of collapsing
lynchstrips & plate armour
maps of some western states
has inwardly marred
a good chapter or two, the
last uncountable pages
will always be missing.

We have then
some tale all unfinished
of the knight gone crazy
in barber's basin
helmet & paper shield
dragging his boots
from one rock to another.

A pity. And yet
watching the sea slide
in on the beachstones
under the sky's plump
indifference, how
with each swell it returns
to itself, now
I'm not sure
I'd ever have read it.

Some notes on Perdu:

Poet.
President of the Republic.

Made use of his first term
to prolong the second.
Founded the library
of gutted works.

His memorial.

Self-styled *Jacko, King
of All The Birds.*

Alchemist turning gold
into lead. Maker of
scarecrows. His mark
a black circle giving off
darkness. He recalls
the people hissed *Crowjack*
Crowjack, his name
on the itchy boulevards
of the city as they burned
his effigy and with him
all the books by him
collected from the ancient
kingdom, each one
in one place stamped
with his spidery logo.

Proclaimed *God is an ant*
but which one. Patented
wheel & fire since
no one had. Was
'a gentle fool' & spent
years writing the longest
sentence in Christendom.

Forced from office
some held him as others
burned down the library.
Or was it he in pique
fired it with petrol bombs?

A question for history,
and who writes it.

Either way it burned.
He picks up the pieces.

Lost letter to Didot:

so they have
done in what you
for years carefully
brought in my love
& nourished:
books, waifs.

How you dusted
& catalogued while I
tried to catch you
up ladders & once
on the open spread
of the *American*
Heritage Dictionary
with *nighthawk*
night heron &
night blooming cereus
under your backside
had you at last.

You found the floor
gritty & fearful
of visitors smoothed
out the pleated skirt
& must go
for some other thing
swinging your hips
to the tune of that
Spanish song (end shelf
top row big greying
volume with pictures
of mountains & Arabs)
light years ago.

A survivor:

So the one book
that was all Leofric's
Donation survives,
chopped at by drunks
slopping boozy cupmarks

to be opened, spread
to the fingers'
handsbreadth following
script into mouth speech
where some monk had

marked up the page sighting
his pen as the ploughman
sights on the hawthorn
& mutters his song to himself.

The exile puts out,
storms break on the stone hillside
seabirds broad out their feathers
through these vowels
that reach us thinking
how come it's so late so early?

Fragment: memo to Milto:

how it was for us
newly recruited
subalterns young
in the President's service,
far away, days & nights
on the sea, in the Americas,
so the tale goes.

Who sang *où où*
est Perdu in another
of his damned toasts.

Long ago before both
earned promotion upriver
to fresh woods, never again
to crumple together
our dixiecups over some joke
on the hierarchy
of Albert the Fat. Now
I think how is it
for you in wherever,
hung ill sustained
above slippery rock
as the long poet has it.

Do you still keep
such perfect balance sheets
and turning in sweetly
drunk from your labours
is there perhaps
at twilight a blackbird
exploding the same pulsed
riveting cry I hear
now off in the hedgeback
and is that sufficient?

Nicholson's advice:

35 years
drinking Guinness
man & boy & never once
told a lie.

Learned the hard way, son,
in Korea
where embellishing beggared description,
anyway a man
got shot for it. Before that
with Stalin I couldn't lie
& Siberia froze up the brag
in a man's teeth.

In the two years I spent
in Yenan with Mao
often he said to me, son,
don't lie to those people
within you, they'll
find out.

So I don't.

Hunter's piece:

on the doorstep dancing
with mouth harp
& bourbon bottle

to welcome us
chugging home late
stoned & weary

all through, bones,
stumbling in
caught the screen door

saying *sh* to the cat
when quiet & naked
ready for sleep

the wife opens her one
owl of an eye
in the next day's dark

says *You're late.*
You're drunk.
You're in the wrong house.

The discovery of metal:

Little tears
leaking from stones
of the stoney earth
our mother

keeping the hard shape
of crevice & stamped
burnt white firebed
they settle

am I
tired of this long
panting for meat
& cries of my brothers

picking these different
pebbles the heat
runs off
grainy & knuckled

the first or the last
to see how cunningly
run this stonemelt
makes tool or weapon

& not see how again
for dawdling here with my
daft notions I may
be kicked seneseless?

From Belmont, a ghetto song:

you hear the silence now
over the tumbled pits?
That's what was promised.

On the wall a child's scrawl:
I hate me.

No light on the stairs,
cabbage stew. For this I came home
wondering why.
The roaches feed well:
dust, wallpaper, plaster.

They never complain
to whom nothing is promised.

From the plain:

And if one day I open my mouth
finding nothing
not vacancy even

looking out of my head
there's no tree no fields
easy in sunlight flatness
the glacier's scouring
stones and these rocks.

thrown behind winds what became
of the mountains
as this numberless grass
fattens?

From the book of changes:

Could have gone
fishing or some other way
to waste time
& grow wiser perhaps.

All day
throwing the tall
coppery yarrow stalks
asking the book

whose reedy voices
surface & drift sometimes
swamped by the river's
onrush: battles

without names any more
plots cries old wounds
picked clean & at nightfall
the scavenger people

snatching off keepsakes
& coins no longer in use
now the empire
picked up from dust

in the mares' hooves
has closed for the last time
its book of changes.
In pleasure the people

forget how hard is
pulling on ropes,
forget risk & dance
drunk through the cherry trees.

I shall encourage
the conversation of friends
& though restless
& staring across

this country of wars
& old poverty you
may be sure
I'm still listening.

A note to his landlady:

what was the
germ of The Work lost
in the rushing
of fields, poles, stars.

In your racket
lady clattering
the steamy lids in your
smothering basement
floor grey with fagash
cat moult & you
yelling *rent rent*
in a crimped brown
cardigan clutching
a letter perhaps from
the abandoned husband.

I was trying
to tell you despite
my dislike of explaining

how what I do
that pays so slowly
concerns
the difficult matter
of silence & how
to prolong it.

Towards a coda:

now they had
sacked the great library,
never another
collected works of AZ
or the measuring flood
of the Canto Triste,
no one may ever again
curl up with a book.

I am in the ashy silence
hearing again the groan
of timber & burst
of waxed leather bindings
of pages & glimpse
at the burn's edge
crowding & hooded
the foxgloves.
                And think
as I think I see them
how might they
ever be lonely?

Perdu: his last appearance in history:

so much nuts then
to the zeitgeist & minutes
of kitchen conferences
all down the ages.

I consign my books
to the fires of the people
& will speak & will speak
if no one listens

or whether or not
if they heard all
they might hear is
how lonely it is.

Burned out in Washington,
bombed out in Shankhill.
It all burns o my brothers
all but a few words

we've sent off the planet
in our famous address
to the nowhere.
I would be content

to get one word through
as I hone & seal them
to open their boxes
& live in some other place

starting bank accounts
passports, party cards,
going down to the postbox,
getting sick, screaming.

But just one thing
before I go back
to the ribbed ancient life
of the ferns let me

hear you sometimes
as often your journey
permits it
laughing.

Abel Baker Charlie Delta

the pussy willow song

course it were different
when I was a dog

bristol to china
twice every weekday

no weather at all then

fish chips ten woods
pictures bus fare
change from a monkey

and little lambs wore underpants

where that seagull stands
stood the sailor's return

I used to frequent
many a moonlight
with the old ukulele

met my missus in the bar
slim as a whisper
16 years ago

where all the money that I spent
I spent on friends of yours

& all of this was pussy willow
as far as you could fly

without lime that is

me here
her in the lounge
he comes in exits left

crippled with the dandruff
resting the lung
weak in the whinge
fits of forgetfulness

permanent ridge
approaching high pressure
heart attack up his sleeve
that again

only here colouring my breath
once around the town
white lion malt shovel

ring o'bells artillery
eagle prospect of whitby
welcome the case is altered

end up always the valiant soldier
bloody all plastic

belting out the white cliffs of dover
piano man's song
last one's on me

abel baker ashore

dom polski captive nation society
taxi to listerhills social
train bus home to the queen's arms

leeds & bradford up for sale I see
north sea crated & packed
says jolly jack the sailor

mixed my fanta with cocacola
muy valparaiso
near blew me apart

if I'm going I'm gone
all I can do I said
all I can do make a splash

supposing it's friday

I'm dancing with beer on my flies
now you're gone it grows dark

little miss nemesis
of the six peacock feathers
o the malady lingers

you've left me
my bird my brown lady
other roads other strangers

his appearance in the white hart

nice place
when you don't have to be here

takes a window seat
pot of coffee for three

here among the rich invisibles
copyholders of budleigh salterton

so how are the chintzy-schmalzies
middle management mummy
cheltenham the doberman-pinschers

not in front of the cod roe cyril
remember we're english
hundreds of ways to complain

we repeat ourselves
we repeat ourselves
suffering is so good for one

try the lemon sole darling
off he goes in his porsche

remember young squire

college we called him
everyone dipped to
even the hatless

bit of bully nose in air
no time anyone soonest
women strangers seen off

remember gardener white hair
cocked *yes sir yes sir*
back step into cold frame

laugh

should be dry for town show
last saturday august
remember he say *now lads*

best trust tories
agricultural interest
all gaujos together

o you remember he came
that day it was raining
make it a double jeff

we were camped in quarry
kicked off shithouse roof
one there yourself charlie

next day joined up
killed operations off crete

now there's a subject

thursday they fetched her
in the wee wooden box
put her in front there

don't think much of mr death
joe that just went
like your last cigarette

turned his face to the wall
fell at his post
same stool in the abbotsford

in harness as they say
shuffled off
to join the elder brethren

happens in the head
all him her & me
this cold wifeless world

lay my hands to her breasts
she minded no more
than ever she minded

so once again round the floor
with the glittering ball
one more round there guvnor
we won't go home at all

and as for you lot

trick or two I could tell
tale or two you should know

young buggers like you
I was out in the marshes

rifle & sidepack sten
mortar small arms emergency ration

56 isle of dogs
russian airborne division

you wouldn't know
I'd like to forget

lucky for you the bolsheviks
were only after me

ambush landmine tanktrap
ackack double line trenches
improvised nuclear device

soon had them cornered
on my own all alone
solo mio all on my tod

some thanks I get for it
not a drink young bastards

take a look at this headwound
that's amnesia son

charlie delta adrift

right then lads
back from winter sleep

next question

who bashed the bishop?
how many trees in italy?
does the pope live in a big house?

some of us were wondering
about some of you

midlander irish shiksa
gentile scouse of barbados
welsh geordie bangladeshi
brummie pakistani cockney
fish & chipper cantonese
gaujo jew jock wasichi

o screw the national front

the little brain cells
winking out all over europe

or have I lost it again
my old invisible thread

knocking out the epic sonnets
this is the joined-up writing

an it's a union job jimmie
30 quid an Ah'll speke clerely

otherwise I'll mumble mumble mumble

sight of the enemy

not from you mister
ah'll hew ma ane

great big wee malignancy
mr bouncing cheque

mate of mine once
screwed my missus

causing me to roam

he'll never be a buttercup
in god's big shining garden

my only ambition was
piss on his grave

now he's dead
can't be bothered

then there's my publications

surgical blades & handles
young wives praying
tripping for cripples

all written in haste
for money & fame

no I've no real ambition

nice one

knock at the door
can I come in?
bloke four feet high
I'm your paranoia
I thought heyup
got a licence chummy
you're joking he said
examine the fitments
counting the forks
routine visit
countrywide survey
government programme
national importance
double glazing inspection
stand aside chief
his brothers & sisters
uncles & cousins
up in & all over
hadn't expected
no drink in the house
if only I'd known
could have dusted
papered the dog
unplugged the piano
curried the biscuits
forgotten amnesia
vacuumed the fridge
hidden my large supply

best jamaican euphoria
but that's it pal
I'm botany bound
on the good ship blue
and it's too late now
california

where francis drake did drink

'next to mine owne shippe
I doe most love that shippe
in st martin's lane exon'

he do say
had to put he out didn Oi

customers upset
all the half-pint bandits
of the half-timbered interiors

young accountants grockles
decent clientele

and he's language
spittin on the floor he was

six month on the water
fish stink & tar

wore a dirty great sticker
two three knives

couldn be havin that
brewery at my back

call a jam sandwich
put he on the plymouth train

gropin all the spanish au pairs
and completely upsettin nigel

the one you got three days for in achiltibue

goes into the pub with his elephant
evening reginald

drink for these travellers
coin of the realm to invest

so the barman gives him a glass
in walks little pierre with his duck

agin says the highlander
agin or Ah sleece yer heed off

and the little old lady recited
dedah dedah dedah dedah

a pound each to look at the swans
the kerry man did say

so the colonel takes his bet
the curate opens the window
the postman does it again

and the actress says to the gardener
and the salesman says to the farmer

two aspirin and a wire brush at 6
three bananas and a mars bar

dollar dollar half bunch o' flowers
but he never found out the greensleeves method

she gives him his shirt & says
this time you hold the pigeon

the milky bars are on you kid

charlie growing old

manwalked in to a bar
itwasan   ironbar

i say any   vac an cies
ex per ienc ed drink er
years faith ful ser vice

ref eren ces sup p lied
all lead ing   landlords
ownwords   made up

small glass sau ter nes
five pounds till friday

thus the way of exile
egg and sandwich rd

empty stom ach blues
squeeze a half in tom

seven bells aqua pura
one of old ex hibition

a wooden leg woman
one lady with a lamp

one iron duke & one
discoverer of gravity

silly songs of spring
where beth they now

fifty   shilling   tailor
ubiubiubiubiubiubi   sunt

no reply to that

aye an there is
another world
mister rimbaud
an it's this yin jimma

saith the barman
ye don't have to gan
someplace else
still ye canna stay here

and finally

old mates of mine
broom reid & harris
timothy white & taylor
freeman hardy & willis

put a few away together
stopped a few going bad

monkhouse & glasscock
where are they now?

sluggett & pow butcher
just an ordinary person
who'd have thought three legs

not a man of them
for the brilliantine
oil & vinegar two of chips

every one a gold watch
four acres & a cow

all gone for a burton
bristol & further west
in the weaver to wearer raincoats
& the marks & spencers vests

TERRA

(1986)

Hawkwood

SIR JOHN HAWKWOOD, *miles anglicus*, 1320-1394: Born near Colchester in Essex, the younger son of a rich tanner who owned the manor of Sible Hedingham, Sir John Hawkwood died a citizen and freeman of Florence, where Uccello's equestrian fresco portrays him in the Duomo. He was, said Froissart, *a poor knight owning nothing but his spurs*, though he came to possess estates in the Romagna and Tuscany. A classic example of the younger son without inheritance who goes for a soldier, Hawkwood fought at Crécy and Poitiers, where he was knighted, early in the long English depredations in France of what was not yet called the Hundred Years' War.

Under the Black Prince, Hawkwood learned the tactics he was later to employ in Italy: mobility, forward intelligence and knowledge of the terrain, the devastating use of the longbow (a good bowman fired six shafts a minute, the sixth in the air before the first found its target), and the dismounting of the lance, transforming the cavalry weapon of the mounted knight and squire into a two-man infantry weapon, a third man holding the horses for swift pursuit or withdrawal.

In 1360 the Treaty of Bretigny suspended hostilities between England and France, the armies were paid off in the field, and the free companies turned to plunder. Sixty thousand of these *routiers* went down the Rhône to Avignon *to visit the Pope and have some of his money*. They were known as *skinners*. Gascons, Bretons, Burgundians, Germans, Scots, Irish, Dutch, Flemings, Welsh, Cornish, French and English, they were *those villains commonly called English, who wasted all the country without cause, and robbed without sparing all that ever they could get, and violated and defiled women, old and young, and slew men, women and children without mercy*. After their passing, it was said, *the forests came back*.

Hawkwood was amongst them, and appears in Italy in 1364 as the elected captain of the White Company, so called for the brightness of their armour, fighting for Pisa against Florence. Like most campaigns it was short: the Florentines bought off most of the Pisan mercenaries, including the bulk of Hawkwood's men, and the White Company disintegrated. Hawkwood himself would not be bribed to ignore his contract. He was, by all accounts, very particular on this principle.

Over the next 30 years Hawkwood was a mercenary and fought variously as a condottiere, a contractor providing his own forces for one side or another amongst the Pisans, the Milanese, the Papal States, Padua, Naples, and Florence. For the latter half of this period he was on contract to Florence, while free to undertake other commissions.

Many of his victories were gained by stealth and deception; he was as adept at avoiding conflict as at entering it, as efficient in the timely withdrawal as in advance or ambush. His reputation in an age of cruel men was said to be brave, fair, merciful and honest in his dealings, and little of the wealth that came his way stayed with him. His reputation rested on his military skill and on his principle that a contract was a contract.

In 1376 while in the employ of the Papal States and under the orders of Robert of Geneva, Papal Legate in Rome and later Clement VII, first of the Anti-Popes, Hawkwood was instructed to *administer justice* on the city of Cesena. Asked for clarification, the representative of Christ's representative on Earth replied he wanted *sangue et sangue: blood and more blood.* Whether in fulfilment of his contract ('obeying orders'), or whether as a means of paying his men in loot what his paymaster stood in arrears of, or whether had he refused his men would merely have elected a new commander, Hawkwood obeyed. The citizens having first been persuaded to surrender their arms, for three days the people of Cesena were systematically slaughtered, the town looted, and what could not be carried off destroyed.

In our terms, Hawkwood was a war criminal, responsible for an atrocity. Shortly thereafter he left papal service and began his long association with Florence.

He was twice married, the second time to Donnina, one of the many offspring of Bernabo Visconti. For some years he lived the life of a country squire such as he might have lived in Essex, though at the age of 70 he was still campaigning.

In 1387, fighting for Padua against Verona, he scored a decisive victory at Castagnaro, and in 1389 he undertook a forced march from Naples when summoned back to Florence. When he died in 1394 he was buried not in the tomb prepared for him in Florence and subsequently memorialised by Uccello, but at the request of Richard II in Sible Hedingham, the village where he was born, in a grave that has now been lost.

*

Seated, a man with the tools of his trade,
solitary in the company of weapons,
always the warrior, apart,
etched into metal in a moment of brooding.

Mostly he sleeps sound till first light,
by day lives the life of his time:
fighting to live he will fight
for cash money or credit. Or not fight.

At his ease when he may be,
who can never go home now,
his landscape the blunt northerly speech
glimpsed through the window to his left

where the hills are already going to sleep,
the road hatched away into more shadow
always closing round him. In the foreground
a single candle he has lit against the night.

*

Messer Giovanni condottiere
I thinke this worlde a boke
and wolde rede it

turning back the pages
chapter by century
into the distant background

where all that's certain now
has already happened –
an argument for lawyers,

each day's skin
stitched to another day's drum,
another season of wheat,

another year of tramped corpses,
some words falling away
for instance *brother, victim.*

*

Who knows what any of it was now?
I move between the dead and the dead,
always erudite and fractious,

in their different speech the same:
the same dangerous commonwealth, men
totting up loot, stacked heads,

the harvest of scrap metal
at the engagement's end, some thrush
puncturing the heavy noon air.

Thereafter come the keening women,
gulls to pick out eyes,
the broken citizenry in halters.

A long tale the same again sir
repeating itself *o misere misere*,
burning what we could not steal.

                                        *

In truth sirs
I merely disable myself
in this condotta with words,

so many flags
under conflicting allegiance,
meanings that dodge

across factions and borders,
lights over the marshland,
smoke or the shiftings of water.

Men's speech is all cunning,
bragging and grief.
We must make some agreement.

And honour it,
clause by condition,
down to the letter.

                                        *

At the eye of all shadow
if I sleep by the tallow's grace
I sleep wretchedly. My heart
flies out of my mouth and away.

She is perched singing all alone
in the plane trees by the river,
all thought of this quick planet
sweet even in war snuffed out.

One wall of fire sweeps the vineyards.
All men are with women instantly angels
vapoured in swift rising air,
their bodies shriven in sharp metal.

This is my skull's dream. Meanwhile
my heart stretches wings over woods
singing out of our childhood once
in the abrupt speech of my own land.

                                        *

And this I do is my dreamwork
late and unwilling, the watch
posted alert, rattle of irons,
long death cry of some creature

caught in the hedgeback alone, stars
and the moon's pale face over all.
My heart goes away, flying north
to the snowy passes she will die in.

Night by night she is fainter,
further and colder, her voice
in the star maze at the far range
of my hearing.
                    Where I

working late and close to the page
draw up the sketch for a medallion:
my heart between a falcon's claws,
my name *Acuto* and the versant writ

What am I but a vicious labourer,
the iron grub that kills for pay?
What I am now so you will be.
What you are now so I once was.

*

Awake and sweating in my flesh,
my heart gone off without my leave
perhaps for better pay elsewhere.

Or she must beg her way
through warring neighbourhoods alone,
and like me sell her only skin.

Or limp a penitent to Rome
whose bishop is one of two great lechers
and I but one of his butchers.

Between the birthstool and the planks.
Between the slippery dialects:
Auti, Auguto, Giovanni Awkward

sharpen your good blade, shine
in your beaten armour, get horse
and a good ship ready and go home.

*

I am a blank slate on which is set
menace and *oblivion*. I sit
witness to the witch's wick
studied in the candle's hiss.

I make war because there is no work in England
and profit from necessity.
I who have privatised war,
I have made of my life great industry.

These cities made of fluencies
and money, rich hinterlands
stood into wheat, the ripe grapes
bell and split their juices:

all mine now. I who reap stones
from a seedcorn of ashes,
I who grind out the future
between millstone and millstone address you.

*

You who live between knife and cut
and hone the blade, dragging wood
across a muddy evening home,
another day with nowt to show.

You will come to the harvest of swords
the same. You who nurse the heart
in its ladle of blood and sing
lullabies to the love you lost, you also

to the pit's rim, tar hissing and the devils
delighting in your misery, all fire
suddenly upon you, the preliminary routine
of rape and mutilation done, they will kill you.

Your moment in the sunlight will be over,
the sparrow fleeting at the yard end,
some field you walked beside the river
between the willows and the ripened wheat.

*

I mark the changes: *none* and *none*.
Some day between some years of peace
we hear fighting break out in the valley
and the unending warfare comes home.

A river known by many names: *The War*
or *The Rocking Horse Expedition*,
The Campaign of the Seven Brown Loaves,
it is the same miserable waterway

we dream the river that will drown us.
They say dreaming is to forget,
in which case I have forgot much.
My dreams show clear them I killed –

301

in a three-day butchery at Cesena
a nun I halved from neck to waist
from worse between squabbling soldiers.
I, Giovanni Haukkuode, did this.

*

Who might have been anyone,
a tanner yellow with the lifelong stink
of burning dog muck, a pilgrim
limping to Jerusalem and back.

I might have lived my days
in some slope of the hills,
a man reckoning fleece,
hides for the Lowlands, wineskins.

I am a man becoming an emblem,
inscribing the book of his name
who must shift across ploughlands
because no one will have him at home.

I chart the cries of other sleepers:
one a fat drunk cherub must have *sangue sangue*,
another has designed an engine
to flatten cities and will use it.

Another weeps he is the King of France
and mad and made of clear glass
and will break. His cry
a wounded man's, a pierced bird's.

*

Some nights the blood rush at my temple
hammers *you will die you will die.*
I see white images of the ditch
at Castagnaro heaving maggots.

Pink and fleshly, they are cribs
of black flies everywhere in Europe,
the arrow shower, the lance thicket,
nails of the cross everyone walks with.

My enemy sends a caged fox for taunt.
I let him go. I take hawk and horse
and ride to inspect the fortifications.
Later I will rally all with my cry

Carne Carne, given to the meatwork.
And where's my heart? Friend,
I dream she is in a far country,
her message fading as it finds me.

*

Persistent as the rust in unused iron,
from The Serene Republic of Slaughtered Innocents
and The Most Royal Kingdom of Branded Thieves
my heart sends greetings.

My heart sends coin to pay for all,
meat and the red sleepy wine of Genoa,
bed and a fresh horse at sunrise:
Signor sithee take cash

in fair dealing or have none.
I have made a proposal to my heart
that if she will come back to me
I will declare war over and go home.

It will be a long night's parley.
In short she writes I cease delight
in fighting, end my part first, withdraw
into the country but I can't see how.

How may a man lay down his weapons
before others who envy him?
Merely for living I have enemies.
Useless to say I made them so.

And there it ends: in failure.
My heart won't come back now.
I draw the long wine from its leather.
I see the long night to its close.

*

Because of my kind nothing.
Issuant of me the long war
centuried and worse weaponed
than any wedge of longbow.

And finis. These cities
kindling to one furnace,
one tangle of astronomies,
one burn across the campagna.

Goodbye my heart. We fade
in different directions.
There will be less and less
we ever shared: the woods,

the distant terrafirma,
the cypress and the silver olive,
blue sky, white cattle,
measured out in fire,

all counted out in one
and time since Adam ashes
in the time it takes to read
and in the time it takes to tell.

*

It has already happened, the flash
winked out its message to the other stars,
the ink burned in the engraving, such record
as survived now in dispute.

Already pain has eaten through the page,
so many words gone into air
and we no longer here who dream
over and over the whistle at the finish.

Such is my bookwork: a contagion
of shadows, maps of warring neighbours,
border posts shifting in the candle flare,
white fire and the nothing I foresee:

the centuries of hate bloom there,
the paper in your hands is ash.
So goodbye to the voices in the alley.
So goodbye to the spiders in the wall.

*

So now I must step smartly
yet with long circumspection
through the last of the landscape
before the century collapses:

a tangle of cut limbs
burning on some bloody hill
where all ends in carnage
and pray God I've an advantage.

Pray I've taken the measure right
of the land's lie in my favour
and last in my skull as I die there
some mapwork of hedge and ditches.

I cheat none but a worse death
in some ratslicked dungeon
or dropped in the pesthole,
death's shilling in my armpit.

*

I shut the devils in their book,
I set the hellfire back into its star.
I plan to cross the littoral in good order,
swiftly and without my enemy knowing.

Between daybreak and candle sput,
a first blue light around the poplars,
between nightingale and cockcrow
dreaming I'm awake I dream my heart's dream.

And there we fly, in air sharp after rain
to evening water, two birds anywhere
across fields, the landscape pieced away
like the dropped jackets of soldiers.

And the wars over, the harvests
taken in order, history a meaculpa
not much happens, the images
of troops and weapons fading in the stone.

*

Thereafter little to report:
the business of good women,
tradesmen sleeping on their takings,
flags fading in cathedrals,

farmers and journeymen along the road
of the never ending landscape,
the continent at peace their country,
its government a distant rumour.

In the text known as *Where I failed*,
in the addendum *But we tried*,
directions to this place are fanciful,
the maps white terra incognita, or lost.

Etcetera etcetera. The ways of men
are combative, each locked in his defence,
his territory forever in himself
he carries in dispute, less space

than this the candle lit, a thing
no larger than his name he calls
his own true sovereign republic –
on the move, sharp, tough, and hungry.

*

My heart's caught in a thicket.
She has forgot to fly
and plays the lapwing's game.

I see her falling far away
in thorny quickset, bleeding
at the hands of strangers,

like me fading in the other lives.
Soon little will be known of us,
she with her dream of peace,

I hearing *blood more blood* in my ears,
still hunting for what bird
she's taken for her shape now.

There will be two seasons –
war then long winter.
There the tale ends.

I shall leave this place,
for choice without wailing
or fuss in the Italian manner.

                                                *

Say of me if you can: a man
that kept his word at any cost,
trusted nothing less.

Goodbye England, *that nest of singing birds*,
tall ladders of the hearth smoke
climbing on the valley air.

Somewhere's an end to it,
the landscape leaning skyward,
the slow oncoming to the sea's edge.

And then the last page turned,
the candle finger thumbed into a smut,
the book shut and I tell no more.

Colden Valley

North I'm convinced of it: childhood's over,
in the narrow valley in the mist the frost
is silver in the veins and edge of leaves,
and last year's briar's coppered into stone.

Then more stone dragged to quarter fields
in which the miserable lives of beasts in winter
whiten into breath. The valley pulls –
poor pasture, poorer footage, water falling.

And all its children gone through millyards
into stone they chiselled *Billy*, *Emma*, *Jack*,
and gave their dates and shut the ground
in work and prayer. Or they are almost here,

their short days closing in an owl's hoot,
crows labouring over woods, along the road
a footstep always just about to fall
and all their voices just about to start.

Roads in the north between two seas

As ever, the straight track between trees
receding out of the eye of the painting
into brown distance, water, a haze
already forming on the vague hills, sky.

I am again in my own true country
that surely existed, a map in a drawer,
a postcard, a print in a seafront café,
a place it has always just stopped raining.

The macadam shines, two bands of emerald
are kerbside grass, trees in the wind
and the afternoon sunlight's arrival
down the prim brickwork of the avenue.

So much childhood: the sun's raw eye,
the northern sea grey and unlovable,
the swift constellations of birds
over the bayline, like silk's shine.

Like salt scattered across tables.
Like the Pleiades, some place we'll not go
past the flightpath of the terns,
the cold salt aching down the easterly.

Salt. Stiffens locks, the keys
jam in the doors, doors in their jambs,
the windows in the windworked shutters,
the widows stiffening in easy chairs.

Clear again is one moment, as to detail
precise in my imprecise memory, it begins
this long tale I am telling myself
as to why and who am I on this road.

I am six, I am getting in wood,
it is evening in winter, the ice
plates the horsetrough, in my hands
the sticks in the woodpile are frozen.

On the third step of the mounting block
there's a white milk can, waiting,
the air round and the winter stone
wear off the milk's heat: *the moment*.

We will die, all: my father, mother,
such kin and such friends as all love
and the world lends, and I
no exception fall out of knowing.

It was death looked at me then
in the white shadow in kindling,
a dark brief face in the ice,
the cold closing my fingers.

I broke sticks. The sun lay
over field frost. The farm clanked,
humming milk, moaning complaint,
long ago, its moment comes back now.

I am again under Orion, the moon again,
by the sea that returns everything lost
in the tide's rope tangled up, the birds
at the watery limits of the English.

I'm the sea gone sour, going radioactive,
betimes touchy as anti-matter, untouchable
in the north, I go down hissing
leukaemia between the lovers' sheets, *the blood*

will wither in its artery, the sperm
shudder in the egg, the marrowbone,
the molecule unwind within the heart, the brain
stare into nothing and be dumb.

This is not a melody nor a tale told for children.
This is not a telegram to the poets in Minneapolis.
This is not an answer nor a question.
This is not a message. This is not a song.

Now we are travelling into Cumbria, the road
running out to water down the lost peninsula.
Now I am far away recalling winter and the fog
across another country, continent, biography.

When what I think to say is that we're done,
where everywhere is in the crosshairs,
everywhere is targeted, we are the printout,
we are the coded blips, we are the software.

'Filled with longing, capable of grief.'
Tough luck Susie Rainbow fare thee well.
She got the hero not the message, hostage
of a government that failed, my friends

this may be all too long a night along the road,
and I begin again. Again. I who left
everything behind I have forgotten nothing,
so it appears. With our desire we continue.

Grabbing any end of rope, we might be anywhere
or anyone under the blue star of evening
spreading out our maps, we might be
you and I my love and love each other.

A white sheet perhaps, the glance of shirts
across the winds of March, a glimpse
of washing in the gale in next door's yard,
the kitchen window staring into nothing –

soil, these fingers and these tongues
the crocus and the snowdrop put through frost,
a cat's dance through the cold we hoped
would grow to summer, last the flash

across the wind-whipped shrubbery,
the shed in fire, the glare that wastes us
with its glance, the crack of sheets
in wind, their sudden whiteness.

Commercial break: RSK Porsche

This is the dream: such distance
the oncoming wind is brother to,
long silk of the highway spun off
between the shoulders of the roadside.

All day the singing in tall weeds,
the grasshopper's confession, the birds
remembering their plainchant, reciting
little bread no cheese and the nine times table.

Some dawn the mist blows free, some
afternoon of dusty sunlight, the soundtrack
a far falling of a river over stones
Mozart's ear might have listened to.

West through willow country, villages
of woodsmoke sleeping in the valley,
or on the causeway through the lowlands
beneath the high white music of the larks.

Or anywhere. Across the upland,
sunset shimmering the treeline, gone
across the cobbles of the market,
the tall road only halfway to forever.

Communiqué from desk 19

One we've dissolved our office,
scrambled the files, regrouped,
our propaganda no longer exists

in which to deny *Two* the war's lost,
the phone book the new roll of honour,
it's not true we were beaten nor

Three we're dead meat now
in the deep stale air of the bunker,
our voices taping instructions:

What to do when the current runs out,
What to do with the blood, the world
taken down like a line of washing,

full stop. We're not here,
we're all moving on, some at work
on the new speech, the others

planning the deployments,
counting the syringes, the blankets,
the new ways to be nothing at all.

Lilith

Some far country she speaks from,
she was born there, can never go back
nor will where she lost.

Everything. The earth rippled
waves of the sea she tells.
Then soldiers, beat her and used her,
burned her house, broke everything.

Her man broken, her children, how
to get out then, *the airport broken,
the ships.* Suddenly again

the interrupted carpentry, the wheat,
the young trees and the apple
stopped in the blossom. Her complaint.

Het achterhuis

A glimpse: at the high window her face
a moment at a corner of the blind,
the frost forming its flower, in the garden
all the winter leaves so much leather,
so many tongues, scraps of old gossip.

For so little you can die: the price
on a second-hand coat, a finger ring,
the brown shoes in the cupboard, the mirror
where your mother powders her face.
For these you will be taken.

Mice on the stairs, grey packets of dust.
The ice making its maps out of water.
On the square stones of the Prinsensgracht
soldiers' boots tapping *links rechts links.*
In its season the chestnut's sudden blossom.

Letters from a lost uncle

Postcard of Chicago streets,
one blurred brown figure ringed in ink,
then written on the back *it's me now.*

Wherever he was then. He drifted west
along the railroad ties, went north
to work the dams, south to the rigs,

through Germany and the lowlands, spoke of Alaska
and the deserts of Arabia, he'd seen
more gold than all God's grains of sand.

But no one's heard in years, he may be dead
or changed, all memory of a life
he sometime lived blinked out like stars.

And all his laughter stopped, the voice
that rounded out in bitter beer
broke forth in *Crimond.* Where

does it go, that presence in the air,
brightness of a man that sang,
a breath that answered in his name.

Bogart in the dumb waiter
(after Dashiell Hammett)

This is genuine coin of the realm.
A dollar of this buys ten of talk.
The cheaper the crook the gaudier the patter.
I'll see you at the inquest maybe.

I'm a reasonable man. I don't mind
a reasonable amount of trouble.
All I've got to do is stand still
and they'll be swarming all over me.

More than idle curiosity prompts my question:
how'd you like to turn my chops over?
Yes. I'm tired of lying, tired of lies,
of not knowing what the truth is.

So listen carefully here's the plot:
the grieving widow walks on, grieves,
walks off again still grieving.
You want to hang around you'll be polite.

You get loose teeth talking like that.
You're taking the fall, precious.
If you're a good girl they'll give you life.
If they hang you I'll always remember you.

The shortest farewell's best: adieu.
Here's to plain speaking and clear understanding.
I distrust a close-mouthed man. I'm a man
who likes talking to a man who likes to talk.

Three from the freak house

1 *The Tattooed Woman*

On each arm a blue snake wrist to shoulder,
jaws apart, the long flicker of tongues
forked to each nipple, one lettered *mild*,
the other *bitter*. She's my snake lady,

the anaconda circling her waist, the cobra
rippling her belly, her neck a rattler,
each thigh a garter snake, her crotch a pit,
a snakey river many men have failed and fallen in.

On one rear cheek the anchor of the wandering sailor,
the other wears the lucky horseshoe of the landsman.
Above a skull a scroll spells out *forever love*
below a name scratched out she can't recall now.

2 *Tiger Lill*

You won't remember me. I'm the one that tupped
in the wall in the brass bed in the next room
of your father's dream the night he sired you.
Not that your mother knew. No wonder you're stunted.

In my time I've fucked under flags of all nations
and all for the love of it, banging the bedsprings
from Cairo to Cardiff. I'm the same good whore
in every man's port, in a window in Amsterdam

where I sit behind glass in my credit card fur,
in my black suspenders and tigerskin chair.
And I show them my tongue. I show them my eyes
and my lilypad skin. And I purr.

3 *Tom Peeper*

My name's Tom Peeper, I live in Gropecunte Lane
among the other animals. Under this woolly cap
I'm entirely made up of the private parts of lovers
busy at each others' bodies in the ferns.

I'm a mixed bag of tits mouths cocks cunts
and little boy bums, I'm a sandwich of meat in meat
and I dream every night of the gold skins of women
naked among leaves with nipples like diamonds.

As for you. You never see me under the briars
in my charity shop cast-off hush puppy shoes.
You're too busy. You come with a bird's fierce cry
in woods where the lovers are both one beast now.

Hatred of barbers

Imagine being anyone, a barber
for instance honing his razors,
shaking the tall white sheet
from its corners and sweeping.

All clippings and small talk,
a deft stroke from Saturday's game,
how weather is, how money,
the punchlines of six jokes.

His contempt, his power
to make any man ridiculous
in a glitter of scissors and mirrors,
one arm a brush then a hand:

You want anything Guv –
blades, rubbers, a change
(wink nudge) *is a rest.*
And then:
            When he gets there

When he kneels in the Sistine Chapel
with his missus for the blessing
on 20 years wedded bliss God's bailiff
the Pope says
            So who cuts your hair John?

The ballad of Eddie Linden at Earl's Court

When last I saw ye brother
you were falling on your face
as one copper then another
held you fast in his embrace.

We were halfway down the road,
we were halfway going home,
we were strangers in a crowd,
some of them in uniform.

Though none of us were virgins
and few of us were straight,
the constable and sergeant
had your number from the start.

And before the bust was through
and the punchup yet to come,
two gentlemen in blue
declared they'd have your bum.

Send in backup cried the jack
in his jacket radio.
*A hostile crowd is at my back
and they bid me let him go.*

And all in just a second,
in the space it takes to tell,
they came as they were beckoned
with the funny squad as well.

We were rapidly outnumbered,
oh the shame it is to think,
if we lingered we'd be lumbered
and we'd all be in the clink.

There was filth upon the street
and it took you for a ride.
You were just their kind of meat,
they were never on your side.

You were buggered from the off,
you were always on their books.
They never liked your stuff
nor cared much for your looks.

So they beat you black and blue
when the brown stuff hit the fan.
You were falling off the waggon
when they threw you in the van.

The London Poems

After Mr Mayhew's visit

So now the Victorians are all in heaven,
Miss Routledge and the young conservatives
chatting with the vicar, visiting again
the home for incurables who never die.

The old damp soaks through the wallpaper,
there's servant trouble, the cook
fighting drunk at the sherry, and Edith
coughing and consumptive, fainting away.

Only this time it never ends: the master
continually remarking how the weather bites cold,
the brandy flask stands empty, and the poor
are pushing to the windows like the fog.

Encounter at St Martin's

I tell a wanderer's tale, the same
I began long ago, a boy in a barn,
I am always lost in it. The place
is always strange to me. In my pocket

the wrong money or none, the wrong paper,
maps of another town, the phrase book
for yesterday's language, just a ticket
to the next station, and my instructions.

In the lobby of the Banco Bilbao
a dark woman will slip me a key, a package,
the name of a hotel, a numbered account,
the first letters of an unknown alphabet.

The meridian at Greenwich

We find the river again, the ferry
south over the great water, on the shore
you read *Take Courage* and you're not joking.
In my fear the city, the blue misty planet

vanishes, a curtain ripped away
and nothing in back but fire, the river
and the busy roadway rolled aside
in our bad dreams from nights we don't sleep.

And no one to remember. No messages
passed late at night across borders, by hand,
by word of mouth, we who are lost together
telling tales the prisoner spins the jailer.

Movies after midnight

From Canning Town to Woolwich
the tall cranes rust. The pub's shut
and the lift's out in the towerblock,
everything you see is up for sale.

But there's a night movie: the well fed
soldiery with fancy weapons come
to stutter out the liberators'
brief philosophy: *up yours Commie.*

Even the prime numbers are giving up,
all the best words have moved to Surrey
and we have just a few at discount now
to make farewells that vanish with us.

In Silvertown, chasing the dragon

The police are called *Syncromesh*
wailing desolations on the flyover
playing the two tone music. Greetings
and goodnight from the kingdom.

Whose government is known as *sh*,
they own the miles of wire, the acids
that devour forests and white words out,
and they are listening in the telephone.

But we are all going away now
into some other dimension, we speak
a mirror speech there and count differently
and no one stands for the Queen any more.

Beyond hope and the Lea River

'She's five foot four and falling.
Either you come get her right now
or let her sleep it off in here
and we charge her in the morning.'

My friend Napoleon visits Farina's Café.
There is no message. He meets no one.
It is mysterious because there is no mystery
but Napoleon is now in the house of numbers.

We are entering the capital of a lesser empire
where the plans of our masters surface betimes –
pins on a map at the Ministry of Natural Calamities,
and the statistics like crisp new folding money.

Clipper service

In black and white the Isle of Dogs,
slow workless docklands going cheap,
the great outworks of power stations.
I'm living on two eggs and no bacon

here beside the river, smokey as ever,
among strangers. Ships there were son,
and lascars, then as now the afternoon
brought sulphur on the wind and no comfort.

Now the natives are proud and scattered
and lonely in the high rises, living
as they always lived: thieving or work
when there's work. There's none now.

Message on the machine

Your protagonist is not at home just now.
He's out, a one-way window in his head
with everything coming in fast across the city
and always an alarm bell ringing in the buildings,

a jammed horn streets away, the town winds
lifting documents along the Broadway,
along Commercial Road a signboard
banging in the night reads *Smack*

Disposal Systems, he fears skinheads
in the drains and angels in the elevator
and the number 5 bus will never come now.
After the tone leave a brief message.

Unfinished portrait

Today I'm Red Rover, late the Queen's
Own Leicester Square Irregulars, DSO
and several bars, ageing in my trades.
Today I'm doing double glazing duty,

I'm on the weather watch, especially
for the Greek girls in Minnie Mouse shoes,
I'm with the CIA, I need a fix, say friend
how came we through the middle ages without whisky?

Henceforth I shall speak basic and fortran.
I'll say *excuse me sir I don't have a dog to walk.*
I'm primed, armed, fused, and now I'll tick
till I go off. Think of me as a deterrent.

Out West

Here is the moment holding its belly:
water swills from a main an iridescence
of spilled oil, the broken street
and scattered *this is raw human meat.*

Your man now is the frightened rabbit
fixed in the oncoming traffic, headlights
swirling the wet, the bleared music
of the squad cars and ambulance.

Caught in the shutter, run off
in the final editions: *you bastards you,*
and last in his last glimpse the rope
made of the hot blood spilling from his head.

Leaving the Angel

This far the trains are still running,
the night still awake. Then you're gone,
angry with me, late and lost in the city.
Love, our two furies will wreck us

blazing in the black space between.
I meet the man with seven omens there,
the one who sharpens knives and sings
in neon light *I put an edge to an edge.*

And I've encountered some river
of grieving in myself and drown in it,
living some days a half life on the stairs
defining *lonely* by not being there.

At the Barbican

Oh men she says, and means
their rigmarole, half truths
muttered half drunk on the home stretch.
There's always one man boasting in a bar

recalling how we slew the enemy
at Agincourt or in the far Malvinas
or spoke with Homer – still a boy
with others in the woods inventing stories –

changed, misremembered, *lies most of it,*
still bawling on the doorstep for his shilling,
bragging all the lives his conker has,
ridiculous, in short pants.

The talk at the big house

By nightfall when they hope no one's looking
the paramilitaries are out shifting fences
dressed in each others' uniforms. As intended
the signal from the government in exile

is opened by the wrong hands, so much lost
in the foreign tongue, so much of meaning
is a border always shifting in dispute.
No one gives an inch. No one affords it.

Then war, then peace, then normalisation.
The other side sends fraternal greetings.
The dissidents are hosed down hour on hour,
the guitar player's fingers smashed by rifle butts.

Dosser

I am says he *an exploited human being*,
half brother to these men at Charing Cross
sleeping in their cardboard apartments,
fighting in a line at dawn for work

if there's work scrubbing in the entrails
of the Ritz, and every man jack of them
upholds the free flow of market forces,
weary with his tale of dull misfortune.

I own two wrong shoes and a tartan blanket,
a spoon, a pencil, and my famous collection
miscellaneous plastic bags, my bequest
in lieu of taxes to the nation that bore me.

Slow dancer's epitaph

He was the black boy skating in the cars,
some city music on the headphones,
or at the video game, there being no other work.
He went to sea. He didn't want to die.

And on the radio that day a song of Souvla –
so long ago the bright lads sailed,
good men and ships blown in the water.
But he would go. I didn't father sons for this.

Soon he was hunting down the radar,
targeting the bloodbeat. By then
there was no other work for him,
no dance but shitting when the missile hit.

The house of the androgynes

We are invited. We're offered
tea or whisky, cushions, incense.
Their room is hung with damasks, shawls,
tall bowls of flowers, peacock feathers.

In love they have the music of each other,
their topics and a place they go in Portugal.
Later they promise indoor games: *the parcel,
kiss the postman, chop your candle off.*

All's softness and ambivalence, the air
breathy as recent sex. We say how like one
the other is as if two mirrors but which wife,
which husband, that we never figure out.

Of things past

I know they're never coming back now –
Malice Aforethought and Gay Abandon,
Sister Alabama of the Amateur Latin Americans
shedding her shoes for the compulsory dancing.

It's Sunday and World War Two on four channels.
It's the fifth day of Christmas at a sick friend's.
I'm out giving my credentials an airing
and my provincial's contempt for the provinces –

little towns where there's no dancing.
I remember the 60s. In another life
we would be lovers living in the suburbs
making fickyfick and many bambinos.

Tube talk

She tells him her dream, she arrives
with a suitcase full of her poems
she's not written yet, her initials
in cursive tooled in the leather.

It's a wide-angle lens. If you had
two chops you'd end up with two bones.
And the young barrister's speech *Sir
I address myself last to the window.*

When the open society closed I was drunk
your majesty. Now what I hear is random,
names back in use like *The Titanic,*
the heavy rhythm of the snatch squads.

Nobody's apartment

In the next place of the dream a voice
is beginning to whisper loud in the late
flicker of a TV nobody's watching:
razors available on request.

Nobody lives here. No one at all
remembers the next war. The buildings
whine in their own way their own adventures:
such a good building such a nice space.

And the pipes sing and the telephone rings
and the fridge tunes in its only song
about rented spaces and borrowed tuxedos,
but nobody's here that will fix me a drink.

Your friend the drifter

Too many years up and down the world
chasing some light that goes out.
She's always moved, the job turns out
to be some people talking in a train.

Some work up cures for new diseases,
some we never see decode our traffic.
Others are mapping the new dictatorships,
others the movies they will make of them.

But all night long I have been underwater
mining the harbours off Nicaragua,
I need a place to dress up in my uniform.
I have a deal for you. I'm your imaginary friend.

Talking with God

First the productivity agreement,
the vote of confidence, the loyalty oath,
then the standing ovation to mediocrity,
and still the powers that be are peevish.

What lies in the muddy bottom of the well:
curses rolled up in lead, fixed in a nail,
petty grudges and greedy prayers to be rich
or richer, the clenched fists of revenge.

And the words *How I rejoice in my enemies.*
You who gave out my secret, beware,
addressed to Minerva the owl
and for her eyes only, as if she were looking.

The window of vulnerability

Sure today it could come in a fast plane
named perhaps for the pilot's mother,
the city ends in a smear in the road
and that in a child's shoe. No one

will say aboard the Missouri *all these*
proceedings are now closed, by nightfall
hours beyond zero no one remarks
it was grey, it had no beauty at all.

Now what to do with these postal districts
drifting downwind? It would be
routine enough on the autopilot,
flying home till there's no home to fly to.

A bad day at HQ

Today's not good. We are enduring
une abaissement du niveau mental. Next door
banging on the wall all night and now
everyone is looking, sliding in and out

the flat mercury of mirrors. We are perhaps
the last citizens of an imaginary country
hired to destabilise the client kingdoms,
write the royal speech at Christmas,

broadcast to the disabled nations
and vanish on a cruise to oblivion. Friend
we need a space, we need a stretch of air,
most urgently we need another walk in the woods.

Drinking at Dirty Dick's

Truth is I'm a prince among princes
with my own bit of a dukedom hereabouts
but my betters keep saying I'm a lizard,
a common reptile that understands nothing.

And I love the young princess, the way
she steps from the helicopter to bless
with her smile the disabled children
and cut the ribbon on the new hypermarket.

Otherwise my life is bad Dante, brown rice
or acupuncture, or waiting in the takeaway
for an order of dropped duck and noodles,
playing *Defend Cities* till it kills me.

The soldier's tale

What hit him was the pain, his hip
blown clean way they said, his bearers
argued in two foreign tongues which army
owned the blanket he lay bloody in.

Then he was going home. Someone
had put five Woodbines to his chest
and that was all his medal. The wife
was blitzed and took off with a fancy man.

He writes, *she was another beach*
where all my efforts were in vain.
The inscription on the back reads
the dead piled on the sea stones.

A case of medals

You find me sir, eleven of the a.m.
of a weekday drinking by myself good malt
with indifferent barley. I love a woman
but she's gone into another time zone.

I own a case of medals like a spicerack,
my days so many stars and wars there
with my dicky soldier's heart. I was a runner,
a disaster looking for a place to happen.

I've quit that. Somewhere the running
and the putting on of masks must end,
the tale turned dull and cloudy April
in the city, or will spring never come?

Absolutely no selling

I don't work she says on the top deck
in machine talk in a little girl voice,
a tape announcing the fault in itself
they say there's no cure for, over and over.

I could pack shelves in the supermarket.
I could calibrate the ages of the rain.
I could say again again *I can I know*
I know I can like the little red engine.

It comes to this: we will be happy,
we will laugh, we will be loved
some place we never come to, what we want
we will not have, and so goodnight prince.

The Botanic Garden Oath

Each of us, each with a tale to tell,
each one starring in the scenario called *me*,
sad for all the little of our lives
and all the short days of our loving.

But today I leave that out and take a train.
I've joined the Rupert Bear School of Poetry
and I'll not say anything controversial.
Here there's peace, the traffic tuned to a blur

and only the flightpath of the great planes
to disturb this fuchsia magellanica.
Especially I love the tropical conservatories,
their great ferns and the hot air full as sex.

Not talking on the Circle Line

Let's take a slow dance on a fast train,
thee and I love, since all the news
is bad news, and now the radio
is yelling *gas gas*, and still the heart

delivers its message: *get on with it*.
Maybe I can work on the nuclear facility
or maybe I'll just wander off like Lao-tse
and disappear beyond the western frontier.

Or you and I could slip out anywhere,
take a walk around the park, a cup of coffee,
start the peace talks up again
and take the next train out of this place.

Person to person transatlantic

You're away, gone over the heavy sea
and *I miss you* is everything I say.
I say it *oh I love you* down the telephone,
the electronic chatter in the deep

sea cables at the bottom of the heart,
I bounce *I love you* off the satellite
and let the listeners in the circuits
make what they can of it, a code we know

for *I would take the world's end with you,*
we may have to, we know the state
conspires to kill us. Give us peace and to eat.
We hear it in the wires, the radio, the music.

The John poems

I

And so: the cannons, the fountains, the fireworks,
the oratorio and the aerial display by the Red Arrows –
so educational, so good for the children – and last
the dawn chorus of the orchestra and the curtains:
here I am centre stage with a name like John
and hardly a damn thing to say for myself: merely
I am the man that can never spell straight,
the envoy of a country that won't negotiate.

II

I wake, I make my first tea in all the world,
surprised the downstairs and the kettle, three
green bottles on the windowsill are present
and correct, not vaporised in sleep,
the sirens weeping through the short night's
many possibilities: a line crossed, a wire
singing in the radar triggering the rockets.
I am awake, the blackbird's song against the sky.

III

I have been walking my domains, where everything
and nothing much has changed. I have been here before.
I have a photograph of who I was then, standing
ill at ease in a borrowed suit of clothes
in the room of bleached light, one workman's hand
across the chairback, the other halfway to his waistcoat,
the silver Albert and medallion on whose clasp
there is no timepiece, but only I know that.

IV

Most of us with little, a christening spoon
or on the wall a souvenir of some daft war
our grandfathers had died in, before the sperm
homing on the egg on a 48-hour pass from Boulogne
burst all their passion through us to our children,
here in the rainy kingdom, in the long peace
fought for in another country. For my inheritance
I had a pair of copper cufflinks, now my son's.

334

V

I have examined the leader's brain with my nightprobe
finding not much but fear of God and strong language,
random events I have no vision or power to read.
We are got ready for war again it seems, the hiss
of air released again from the dead, and the band
going down with the ship playing *Abide with Me*.
I'm jumpy when the allies practise mass graves,
or when a truck goes by that says *the real thing*.

VI

Listen. Everything is still as a Dutch painting,
forever Sunday. I'm a man clearing space round himself,
one hand signalling the gods, the other a gardener
of balm and sweet savoury, living my secret biography,
my name and a self-addressed, stamped envelope
by return of post: John with his book of anyone,
his bell and light, his exit left, his tall tale
as to our masters' thinking and where grow weeds.

VII

This moment now someone is mining the waterway,
closing a frontier, someone is arming the missile,
someone makes love, makes a profit, an objective analysis,
someone is torturing someone with telephone wire,
someone is listening, *this is routine* someone says.
The women join hands at the chainlink fencing,
the convoys the colour of gangrene sneak out at night,
the microwaves weeping out messages we can't read.

VIII

The president is in his rose garden, I in mine.
All afternoon discussing Armageddon with the evangelist,
he's thinking *dammit time to open the good book*
and strike first, the work of a moment meanwhile
to admire the fuchsia coxinia, the lawn, the tea rose
opening itself, the white blaze of the magnolia.
Here in the same moment it's dusk, my love and I
plant marigolds, alyssum and night scented stock.

IX

We talk of another rose garden, by the long shore
you call home. Your mother, call her the rose lady,
grows blue flowers there, the shade her eyes
and the seas possess. *I have the truth* you say
but where the hell's my purse? Tonight we drink,
we may weep over the floor if we want to. Always
the low itch in the skull to give up, to forget,
go crazy and keep running till the heart bursts.

X

Always on the shore of great events, almost a witness,
or are we merely a reserve set well apart
in some cupboard in the suburbs working out
our dangerous purposes, here at the finish.
Caught in the playback I'm the man with *Time Out*
walking the square the moment the other world's
ambassador opens up with a machine gun: that man.
I'm the missing witness. And they never ask.

XI

The nights end in cat fights and backyard wars,
bad dreams and between a little night music perhaps,
a little work experience. East of the city
the missions are still preaching boxing for boys
and the evils of drink. West at Kew the mandrakes
in their glass mausoleums form my last exhibit,
last offspring of the city's hanged men, last blip
across the cardiogram across the city's narrative.

XII

That's it then officer I'm John with my invisible.
I keep changing my name to fox the government.
I'm John with my music plain speech down at heel
making a muzak of everything, the ice cream bell
and the roar of the crowd risen up, and the sea
on the beach stones that are all wearing white
for the evening. Officer, I'm one among others,
every day we are more and we're all called John.

Ignore previous telegram

The Olympic Year

She was a dancer and I loved her once,
perhaps again. I was loyal as the London plane tree.
I simply thought of her to save a phone call.

He was another runner in the relay sprint,
the wind behind him twice the legal limit,
a new breed with an edge running from the front.

How many broken records and a medal, secret letters
from the unknown Tasmanian in the shot-put?
Let's say a normal sort of life, *o solo mio*
on the ice cream vans when all the war breaks out.

Aggie's advice

You don't have to insist on being yourself.

Never make decisions on the road.

Never put your papers on the table.

And never count your money in the wind.

The actor

I'll close the window he said over the telephone.
Someone may hear us. Ignore my previous telegram.
I've played Lear in Hamlet and the fool in the Royal George,
I've played Departure, Rumour, Exit, Jack the Lad
and the buffet car from Paddington to Penzance,
the lodgings always filthy and the trains late,
stuffy and over full from Clacton to far Wigan's shore,

the whisky in the taproom always watered down.
I never had an encore, never saw a proper script.
From the tyranny of everyone sweet Mother defend us.

Eva's story

The other woman with the other man.
The kind of man that bites the bullet that feeds him.
The kind of woman keeps her orgasms under her breath.
Him saying *I can be a behaviourist if I want to.*
Hers the kind of cake he can't eat all of anyway.
Him with a wife and a wedding ring and a pussycat.
She in a portrait of wind in a white straw hat.
He with nowhere to go, no one to go there with.
She with no one to show it to, nothing to sing.
He was an actor she said, asked to stay a while.
Just a couple of boxes, a trunk. Six years ago.

Autumn with full summer

He's from the department of offers she can't refuse.
The plot is the same as ever: need of privacy,
love of solitude, fear of loneliness. The locale
contemporary London or Truth or Consequences New Mexico.

She knows he's gone beyond his shelf life.
Way past his due-by date. Mother knows it.

Old Westerns

So tell me what use is a stagecoach to an Indian?
My money's on the pony express getting to Laredo.
Does it have a zipper, does it have enough pockets?
Can you take it home and make a lamp out of it?

He's stuck with the myth of wandering herdsmen,
moving by stars between pastures and women.
Summer in another country. In the mountains.
I guess it killed him. How would he know?

How to get a job

Be prepared to work hard the first million years or so
banging about by the buildings asking *what's this for?*
Expect little pay and overcrowded conditions.

You should have been born clever.
You should have been born rich.
You should have been born in Saffron Walden.
You should have worked in school and considered
the example of the future Sir Robert Maxwell.

If you get an interview don't sniff any glue.
You will be offered less than the whole ten pence.
And wear a tie.

Two parts haiku

This was my first love:
the numerous wind through grass.

The Russians

Ignore all previous. We are totally surrounded
by dark shaggy bears, mad drunk on honey and vodka.

The program

Ignore previous couplet. Recode. Reprogram.
Reenter at line 69. Enter: *I'll be myself.*
I get in trouble being anyone else.

At the rostrum

If you speak up what to say but everything?
You will have a medal stitched to your chest.
You will be called a hero of the silent republic.
You'll be its spokesman brought home in a glass coffin,
given a state funeral and a very fancy motorcade.

Better sit close to the wall o mi amigo,
dealing the cards tight to the chest as they say,
hanging on to the hat and the pistols well oiled,
a silver .45 bullet clenched between my teeth,
what passes for a smile the bitten leather of my lips.

The 1984 Tour of Britain

Miners hunted down the corn by the mounted division.
Sad poverty's lament around the garden festival.
There's work in nuclear construction and security.
And yet much bitterness in the land of the butter mountain.
Sad junketing around the wine lakes. And here
the missiles we can't see move in their circles
on a page deleted in the interest of national security
while we were standing round in groups of one or less.
But we shall build Jerusalem. Well worth a visit.

Visiting Americans

So the other side dropped out of the guessing games.
Our runners compete best in non-anabolic steroid events.
Just the athletic urine samples are a security headache.

I'm aware none of this means anything or just more guns.
I guess I'm a cynic. What use is this program?
That of itself proves nothing like smoking and cancer.
I was born in California but left no forwarding address.

If she marries him he'll be a non resident alien spouse.
She just loves London, spent the whole two weeks in Harrods.
Surely money's not the problem. Doesn't everyone?

Think I'll make me some money John, a whole piece of it.
Go live in New Mexico in maybe Truth or Consequences,
eat peyote and breed me some ponies.
Did you ever fuck a horse, John?

The previous telegram

She's gone at last leaving her honey musk
in the white room of their athletics, and no
forward address, no final note, no valediction.

I find her white straw hat with no ribbon,
some stray hair of her head, one blue shoe.
On my breath the mint of adultery, on my mind
the total recall of her skills on me. I send
c/o the wind two red roses and a telegram:

If you vanish I'll appear. If you go away
I'll materialise one sunrise on your doorstep,
I'll find you in your sleep. Across a square
my face will be familiar in some city, country
in whichever life, a voice a mouth you will recall.
There will be partings but no end to this.

Message from the Basque country

Give yourself the benefit of the doubt: nuclear power
is killing you. We have no crock to brew it in,
no bucket to contain the power of the sun.
What we get's more wire and chainlink fence,
another 32 varieties of police, more secrets,
more prisons and more central government –

and less and less the wild country to go to,
less and less the seas and rivers.
And there is nowhere for the waste.

Daft as a brush, Mother says.

The black report

Ignore previous telegrammed emotional outburst.
That of itself proves nothing like leukaemia.
Years of copious enquiry will vindicate my words.
I'm the Minister for St Elmo's Fire and I repeat
ignore previous unsupported bias. The government says
it's OK the rain isn't eating the forest. We think
some topsoil may remain and some of us survive
occasional nuclear holocaust. These matters sub judice
national security subject of course to a D notice
and the usual 30-year rule, the files deep in the mountains,
the long tapes whispering in the nightwebs, all safe
in the hands of our allies the white male Anglo-Saxon
protestants of North America, some already born again.
End of announcement. Perhaps later in the day
there will be a recital of *o solo mio* on the bicycle bell,
to be followed by the Didcot Sinfonietta of massed sirens
playing *Bye-bye blackbird* for barbed wire and geiger counter.
There will be scattered outbursts of caesium and strontium,
showers of alpha gamma beta followed by a very bad smell,
scattered backgrounds where loving anyone may be difficult.
It's OK the language isn't really a disease like Windscale.
In any case the place is called Cellophane or Sellafield.

They make only spare parts there and routine replacements
for several of the bad dreams you've been having.

Bonnie over the ocean

En route from elsewhere with some rare diseases.
She's a very sick puppy and ought to be in quarantine
but nothing stops the peace train or the pony express.

Oh they know what it is she says.
Except they never heard of it and gave the Latin name.
There is no cure, no treatment and no charge.

On exotica you get no better price per pound, Bonnie.
I say you're not guilty of anything but love.
You don't have to take the medicine.

Conditions in the west

It is the first condemned building in North America,
a bar on Third Avenue, lunch. Ignore stage direction.
If you got an imagination it's the ham and barley soup
you want we don't have. This guy came in I said Mother
he's either a very good customer or an asshole.
So maybe he did coach the San Diego Graverobbers,
Quasimodo for quarterback, Quetzalcoatl running back.
Anyway I was right. He is an asshole. *To the bank*
to the bank to the bank the tall man with the stetson
is singing his winnings on the pony expressway.
You think those Indians wanted that stagecoach?
Check the zipper on this whisky, check the pockets,
check can you take the bottle home, make love to it,
will it sing, will it write a sonnet, will it fly,
will it stack the storm windows in the basement,
cut the lawn, clear the bitter snow in winter,
will it keep you warm in age and will it last?
There's a thing to own a sweater outlasts the girl
that knitted it oh years ago and do you know her name?
Every Tuesday I get even. Today is Tuesday.

For a living I design meats. This ham & barley soup
Mother makes. She knits it underwater, naked,
singing *Oh Susanna* weeping for the world we inhabit.
The Russians are right: stay drunk. I've come to think
the tall guy lives a sheltered life under the hat
but then I never saw the movie. Next thing I know
his wife's calling on the phone from New Hope Pennsylvania
shitface come cut my grass or I'll disable you.
There's no reply but I keep knocking on the third drink.
What can you say to *Mein Vater war in der SS*?
So what it's the Olympics with only half a medal?
When does the stagecoach event happen? With Mother
you could have your cake and eat it but you can't.
And then this crazy killer with a car, the creep
shoots out McDonald's and wanders off the porch
with a cool can of beer in his fist. And this:
this is Mother's soup the 23rd today and you know what
it's like the 23rd psalm it just ain't hot enough,
it ain't like Mother.
                      She checks her waitress pad,
takes down the order, stares beyond the window
past the bar strip's neon signature of city skyline,
Manhattan deep in elevator shafts, the haze
of traffic-darkened air, the splutter in the airwaves,
peripheries of speech turned advertising copy,
the wordy trains a babylon of territories and codes
that make the fast train anyplace, the women
on the sidewalk minding their own sweet business –
and speaking of the valley of the shadow Mother says
and gets the soup. West of her is heartbreak country.
Fifty states of paranoia. *And that* the barman says
is a sign of good health round here. I'd say the map's
unreadable but I'm a stranger in these parts, a man
under his hat moving his shoulders in embarrassment
and looking tough among the towers of speech. I'd say
the trains and scribble in the subway. I'd say
between the whisky sours and ham and barley soup
the language is on fire, shot, taken out, erased
with extreme prejudice, irradiated, burned away.
I'd say the stagecoach. I'd say the previous telegram.
I'd say the elevators or the wailing chasm of the city.
I'd say the sirens. I'd say I'm out of signs
and running from the front when all communication cuts.

Nielsen's visit

Meanwhile in London Nielsen comes to call.
On the river bank a boot a bottle a wine bucket.
Old brown sails in the seawind by the Prospect of Whitby.

In another life Nielsen we were mates thumped drunk here,
and woke together in the Queen's Navee.

You want to know what Ezra Pound said to me?
He said *Thankyou* and walked off in the railway dark
of another black Italian night in his cape and cane.

Pound. Proud. From Wabash College. Weary.

Living with the boss

Don't tell me objects don't have feelings.
They resent our intelligence and fall down.
Telephones and police never when you need them.

How did it get way past midnight without my noticing?
It's enough having to remember all day who I am,
how important, my number, my callsign, my cues,
where I keep the suicide pills and the silver bullet.

Am I or am I not the President of the United Shirts?
Did I accept this part? I have to call my agent.
I have to remember all this only to forget it
night after night with Nancy, and no let-up.

The space salesman

He's wearing a grey suit and not at all like Richard,
and he wants to talk to you dear. In confidence.
He says he's from the New Church of the Holy Loft Insulations

conducting a survey for the University of Double Glazing,
and this joke's wearing thin. He dines out
on his famous namesake and he's famous for it. I hear
her say oh years from now I was depressed my time there.
I guess I loved him. But there was never anyone at home.

Snobby Roberts' message

You're wrong she says. You'll do it my way.
I'm the head girl and all this democratic stuff
is for the firing squad and a short sharp shock
at the back of the gym with a rubber truncheon.

No cure. No treatment. No natural justice.
We have a business to run here. Sell everything.
Give the miners a stiff course in how to sink.
The prefects will know what to do with their hockeysticks.

I think she's never been lived in, Mother says.

Remembering the Fifties

So there I was with an open heart and a closed mind,
in love with the dancer. So where are you now,
the brown Armenian from the house of women?

I barely knew what language to tremble in.
I was in love suddenly with Italy, with Venice,
her many masks and silks and lace, her musks
and all her yellow birds singing in the water city.

A city against nature Chateaubriand called her.
I too danced and sang, a silver weathercock
strutting the Riva where I spoke with Benveniste's doppel
and went about sniffing the insides of tombs.

A normal sort of day, a typical existence
eating mayonnaise and pickles, the sweet red wine
uncocked an hour before dinner, and a fine view
across water to Our Lady of the Perpetual Erection.

I heard women calling from windows *Droppa your breeches*,
the sign across the waterway translating *Two Men Pissed here*,
and on the gramophone the voice of Signor Primatur Seniliti
when war broke out and ended all at once.

Graffiti in the hall of athletes

'Rajid Patel is a puff.' That gets everyone.

Good boys, all educated. All good clean girls
in clean white sheets. But no reward for being good
and I was never any good at being bad.

I fuck and sign her, cross the *t* and dot the *i*,
and dream the fat rain singing in the applemint.

Long distances

Her man's away beyond the mountains,
always moving with the herd. But he visits,
sends money, word of himself in other travellers.
Some of whom love her also. And she them.

The relay runner

Delete *rain*. Delete *applemint*. Delete *f∗ck*.
I have to get in touch with my controller.
I have to plug myself back into the electricity.
I have to check in with my Earth Station.

He is running, he is running, the faces of the crowd
like water scattered in the sun, all eloquence
a blur across the wind in the distant city of the angels,
the fiefdoms of the Barreras and the White Fence Gang.

He's pumped with cortisone and anti-inflammatory.
This boy needs rest and more rest sing the airwaves.
He hands the baton on. Dark lady of the sonnet,
by now you will have guessed: all we ever do is gesture.

Disco dancing in Streatham

Ah sweet land of green money. Such a life
put together of posters and signs, gestures,
images in the TV flicker of another continent,
another decade, stars of stage and screen,
characters in movies, all good consumers,
loyal citizens in borrowed dialogue
and borrowed clothes bearing urgent news
as to what's on and who's wearing it
in languages that don't compute.

Reasons why they met, reasons why they parted,
never reasons why they were together.

To exorcise a blackbird

You say OK blackbird that's far enough.
You say OK I'll give you the plot but the treaty's off.
You say you missed the point lady. The butler did it,
or the barman with the ham and barley soup.
You missed the joke about the stagecoach.
You remember the retired schoolmistress?
You remember the deserted cottage on the estate?
You remember the laird back wounded and blind from the war?
He fathered her a child and called her *princess*
once in his terrible dark, perhaps again. That child
became the priest in the black cummerbund and dog collar,

clicking his lilywhite fingers whistling sanfairyann
at the end of the performance but you never got it.
I've had it with your Olympics. You wore the medal out.
Ignore previous marriage. Ignore telegram.
There will be no midnight release from the tower
where the virgin sleeps unkissed. These days
she's working a funfair sideshow on a block of ice
always melting. Stay off my territory blackbird.

Gone for gold

Faithless. Alone and fatherless, a long starry highway.
Here's John again with his chat in and out of uniform
serving with the blood and guts brigade, cocky,
fly and unreliable. Don't depend on him, Sunshine.

He'll do a runner, change his name, reappear
in Stratford Langthorne living with another woman
as McGinty, Bartollini, Juan Day Sam the noodlevendor
selling 32 kinds of ice cream and home improvements.

Suburb city

Men tidying Sundays in their backyard sheds,
the nails and screws assorted in their boxes,
the hooks and fishing flies laid up for winter,
all the windfalls picked, the soil turned over.

The things women put up with from men and stay sane,
enthusiastic even. She imagines his private parts
and walks into the nettles. She keeps going back
to the source of the inflammation.

Maybe she can get a discount on her next life.
He frames her photograph and all his thought of her
twisted into loops of picture wire with pliers,
hung in any of the last rooms he will rent.

Words like rain in the applemint. In my trade
I'm a journeyman living the life of waste nothing,
odds picked in skips, scraps my dead father kept,
all the words I can steal so look out for yourself,
my sisters, my brothers. I'm Thief, Joker, Twister,
Departure the weathergrained theatrical beached
at the Colony more often than not weeping in whisky
muttering *stagecoach*, *vulva*, *rain in the applemint*,
anarchist-in-waiting to the republic of survival.
For instance I might say *dry white Chablis pray*
and the barmaid reply *we've only dry roasted*.
They were led out in groups of five by the interpreter
across St James' Square. An ordinary sort of weather,
the usual sort of planet. Sir Officer Your Honour
I worked hard and drank only in *The Onlie Running Footman*,
he that cries the road clear before Their Lordships,
and takes the brickbats, sods, clods, sundry turds.
Now it seems I'm in trouble and nothing makes sense.
I've a severe condition of the gyratory system,
my inner ring road's clogged, I have flyover,
underpass, roundabout and Blackwall Tunnel.
I've been hammered in Hammersmith and Battersea,
I'm Tooting and Barking and Ealing and Southend,
I've Epping and Ongar head to foot, White City
and Parsons Green and probably terminal Shoeburyness.
I'm a sick puppy going home on the 12.15 to sleep.
For 30 pence you get at least one sort of cheese.
I'm a stone too light for its weight and full of holes.
I'm on the blink and fading fast. In the French
I thought I saw Chicago but I think he's dead now.
I closed the window on the telephone just in case.
I am become the destroyer of worlds Vishnu himself said.
For the loss of one day one thousand years regret.
By the omission of a letter, the variation of a constant.
In a sense we're all dead already Milton Keynes says.
And in another we begin every one by crawling.
Thank Christ I've recovered my deadly composure,
found my thread again, forgotten my euphoria.
I'm just a normal sort of crackpot. Do ignore me.
Throw me out if I snore, if I bore or offend

or raise two fingers to the photograph of T.S. Eliot.
I've been all over England, to Scotland and Penzance,
I died in the Winter Gardens when I saw the ladies dance
(– and pray to think they will dance for me again).
I made a mistake the first time around and settled
for a pair of tits. Her body. Designed I thought
to make men mad, but she's actually her own business
taking the late air along the Broadway. *Pig.*
What use is a stagecoat to an Indian in any case?
Who played the Bartender, and who took Mother's part?
So now you're all here ignore all previous telegrams.
Delete *applemint*. Delete *cruise missile,*
delete *Brook Street Girl,* delete *one blue shoe,*
delete *and oh the runny honey of her labia.*
And cut the sexy stuff. Pretty soon now
I shall deliver my treatise *Language as the Management
of Sexuality,* bored as ever with my Ph.D notes.
Truth is I'm a Wally with a Walkman listening to tapes
of his own voice in the subway, metro, underground,
tube. Once upon a time this was a live performance.
Once I was a puppy, a young poetrie apprentice
in the school of Whingeing Willy's blighted adolescence.
Now I get snotty letters from the likes of Anthony Thwaite,
my line is overextended. Is there no end to this?
Will no one switch me off, unplug me at the wall,
disconnect the supply or seal me in a vacuum flask?
Will no one tow me out to sea and sink me at night,
shoot me into space or the pony out from under?
I'm probably the ideal consumer. A million dollars
and a piano don't speak to each other at all
Quincy Jones says. I'm caught in the rain's graph.
I'm riddled with statistics, toxic, overtaxed,
overloaded, I've barely enough bytes for the program.
I'm contaminated and there's no discount, no treatment,
no Latin for it and no charge. Will the planet
recover from our wounds? Will the pony rider
make it to Las Cruces? Will Ronnie Armageddon
swat the planet flat and go to heaven in a sheet
and all the believers meet in the rapture?
Send now for catalogue. It's in the standard.
See it in the mirror in the news in the times
that's fit to print. Tune this channel next week
to the same exacting performance. In the privacy

and comfort of your own home blow your own head off.
Telegram your representative urgent soonest express.
If not the world save Venice, mother of poets.
For sure there's trouble in my mill. Surely
the government can do something. I'm lost
in all this complex electronic weaponry to defend me.
What if anything at all goes off, the wrong goose
in the wrong radar in whatever management of error?
May I enquire the name of this place, strange,
dangerous, the centre we suppose of what is known
of spacetime, on every side the anxious citizens
each with his and her different map of the district.
Till now I was content, my voice singing me to sleep.
We need peace Mr President, and quiet conversations.
And for vegetables a patch of good land Mr Chairman,
if the soil be workable, the ground cover sufficient,
the radiation in retreat, the sniper fire fading,
the depredations of the mercenary bands less and less
till year by year we reinvent the wheat, the spinning jenny,
the working of the differential gear and the sonnet.
I fear the program ends abruptly, one day the stereo
playing *o solo mio* in the city where the other woman
with the other man is waiting for the right bus
at the wrong stop when farewell all the rain:
the rider never makes it with the message, the words
roll off the page's edge like lemmings to the sea,
the marathon goes on forever with these jogging men
somehow puffing through the long nuclear winter.
How shall I find you in your sleep to whisper
there would otherwise be partings but no end?
Your eyes are soon enough, love. Ask what song
Mother sang us all to sleep with. Speak again
as Lear spoke and the dead in Homer, called again
beyond the ditch's lip to be an upright bag of blood.

WORMWOOD

For Nicki in December

I walked by the sea,
for the last time by this sea.
Give up your dead I said.

No dead came ashore on the white
lines of water, by the white stones.

Not the knife that cuts
but the hand holding the knife.
Not the sea but its element
– hostile, bearing no ill will –
drowns us, she said.

I walked a long time.
No dead came ashore.

Mine are the cleanest dead
she said
she said.

Airport silences

On the eighth day whiteout, the 747s
ghost vague and mist drenched
and like us grounded. *Fog* they say.
Announcements will be announced.

So much promise in departure.
So little comfort in promise.

A drink, friend, let's talk
in the last of this currency
minted from courage and silence,
let's talk about weather.

From my American period

Point is friend, you & I
we don't go much further together.

Either the whisky dislikes us
or we smoke different brands.

And the landscape's brutal, repetitious,
with no deposit on the empties.

Or maybe just my horse
don't like your horse.

Fun City encore

On the headland wind and the wide sea,
as above: boat distant, gulls, sky,
beaded spray on the leaves of the grass,
at my feet its wild stitchery.

And these old graves, stones
wind has scribbled the names from:
Messrs Grimgrind and Whingeon
still bleating their unpaid accounts.

Thereafter the relatives.
They moan like the North Sea wind,
generations that shoulder complaint
on and on in the grey sea weather.

But the battery's flat at last
in the plastic parrot by the amusements,
and the bingo caller's throat's been cut
at the pier's end. At long last.

The rope

Away in some northerly distance
remote province a far interior
my heart's royal ancient republic

hunched across thin upland wind
chilly fields rainy sky that darkens
inking the rolling table of moorland

drum tight to such effort
a man folding a fist of himself
drags his rope through rain-heavy bracken

in case he may need it:
cable he coils out of himself
into more distance he's crossed.

Such a length of hawser that man I was
stoney pasture his cold country
over the treeline of linnet sound

windy holdings nailed to the ridges
hard bitter soils black as a raven
stones set to keep track of stars

he considers *for no particular purpose*
him with his rope he drags after
in case he finds use for it

when he can't even hang himself
not with the braid of his blood
not with the skin he was born in

nor the long skin he will die in
nor the blue coil of the umbilical
connecting him to anyone who ever loved him.

*

Whoever I was once
a boy that began tangling string
I was never innocent from the start
everyone my toy everyone my tuppence.

This phase lasted far too long.
Fists knives a black metalleta
the ink green eyes of the Guardia Civil
in the iron city of Bilbao convinced me.

We are real as the rain and die
we are as brief we are what hungers
wondering at the stars each one
the nail sharp eye of the universe.

Where is one great tatter of string
all my days have become unravelling
or more ravelling. I take one thread
it runs back in the same labyrinth.

Back into the museum of marriages
along the clogged thread of weddings
she and I each other's business
each the other's final telegram.

Each other's audience each other's movie
who might have been anyone at all
wanderers in the city with everyone
a separate event more often lonely.

Now if it ever comes out this string
it is the bare light shedding back
off stars spreading into separate distance
and the long rope ends in a noose.

A seawrack of ropes snagged up
lines grafted with other lines
the last a drowned sailor held
as the wave shocked breath out of him.

Nothing now but faulty connections
the deep ocean cable burned out
the continents no more in touch
than she I was wifed with and I were.

*

I am awake who was asleep and dreaming
the dark water he will drown in,
the rope that will hang him at last.

In a 3 a.m. city of clocks, the traffic's
horizon note or the first sleepy bird cries
or a scream woke me that might be my own.

I had dreamed ships rigged on the winds,
the last ropes slipped from the quays
down the long stones of my imagining.

And I falling with them, the light
the good star makes thinned underwater,
the coiled sea tightened till it woke me.

At the rope's end there's no rope.
I'm falling away with my hands burning
into a world at the world's end.

Where the black nib dribbles its ink
down the casualty lists, the transistor
whispering news from all the warfronts.

I am where I feared where the ocean
has washed us all ashore, I am
with others at the end of things, goodbye.

And mine is a black song brothers,
a book of the many bladed rain
but the long rope comes out here.

Where I open the buttons of my shirt,
where I keep the black rainbow
tattooed over the space of my heart.

Serbian letters

I

I'm back from wherever: highways
twisted through mountains, the road
of the armies, the caravan trail
down to Istanbul dumping flotsam
and camel dung. There the river
sent me one dark caress, one glimpse
of a woman's white face and her hands
through leaves and the rain. Again,
we're surprised each time by autumn,
the trees shedding their ribbons,
rainy flags of the corn fodder,
upright fist of some fortress
raised in the mist. *In the mountains
a small dark people*, I read now
in my notes, in my mind the rain
still falling, the patriarch saying
look what our fathers have done.

II

So then I got lost explaining
how I got lost, I would be all day
writing my message to myself,
I with a thirst no drink slakes
in the dark city. *Nema problema.*
We were having literary evenings,
discussions followed by general
fuckings, speakings in tongues,
moments of silence, brain damage.
So how are you my brother,
we meet in a dangerous season,
my sister? I recall how we peered
through the bars of cyrillic
to find water, finding you
peering back: through the bars
of the alphabets, through the bars
of Belgrade singing *Jerusalem.*

III

On the seventh day of singing,
on the sixth day of laughing,
a man fell from the fifth floor
dead at my feet in a sheet
but his last breath blew through me
with all the bad air of the city.
This was the last day. He jumped
down the air with our voices
last to next door in his skull,
now I bear him a little way on.
The rest was parts put together,
drinking toasts, declaring *stop
hunger stop war stop bomb stop*
to the actors without shadows,
the smooth-suited, the well-fed.
Miodrag or Pedrag, he jumped
down the world's well. Share him.

IV

Bear with me brother once more
the long ride to Novi Pazar,
the white sheets of the mists,
the rough landscapes of grief:
wild Illyria, scree black, scrub
red with autumn, heaped windfalls,
black fruit, black flowers
of the mountain. We remember:
the halftrucks fallen in,
troops, bullets, those taken
to be lettered in stones,
names that never give in: *Adam,
Jordan, Stepan*. We'll pull wild
mountain thyme, we'll be half goat
half singing in the tall air,
your words through our mouths,
our mouth's through your words.

V

There was the error: the telephone
singing in a locked room. There
where I was standing on my hands,
words squealing under my bootsoles.
There was the world in a mirror,
the words upside down, the lettering
bars of light in the darkness. We
have no proper study of failure,
we merely grow used to it. There
in the dark town of minarets
where the lists were reversed,
the dead counted living, the missing
listed as dead with the quick.
And worse nightmare: the glass
said *cut*, the window said *jump*.
I'm alive to deny it. There, sister,
my last encounter with darkness.

VI

Maybe somebody lost the key,
maybe it's world war three.
These were our *Balkan Nights*,
Balkan Time. We were having
Romania said *A Scotch Affair*,
drunk again, where we'll all
go together. The Poles smoked,
the Russians were circumspect,
the Czechs quietly intelligent.
We spoke of the neurosurgeon,
an open-minded man, we think
that's a beginning, him sitting
on the bus with a knife in him.
Tell the president I'm gun-shy,
tell the Greeks I surrender.
And turn off the camera, whose
movie is this we're appearing in?

VII

This for the Greeks and my sisters:
why should you ever forgive us –
my countrymen, cousins, uncles,
my brothers the conscripts firing
into the square, so many we left
smashed on the stones in the red
red ropes of an autumn of blood.
So soon all we recall in the blur
of roadsides is so many trees
that were squabbles of starlings,
windy leaves at the year's last.
So long in the moon's shadow,
now it's too late. In my own
chilly northern country the gates
slither shut in the prison house.
So let's dance. So let's sing.
Let's be one tribe made of many.

VIII

Home again in the enterprise zone.
Am I looking down a telescope
or is it the barrel of a gun
or a rolled sheet of paper this
letter is written on? Innocence
I've some remembrance of, some yarn
the slow wind tells itself
among birches. I light a candle
for Miodrag or Pedrag, you also.
Now there's small lights burning
east west, in distant cities
where the desklamps hood the paper,
the words come, letter by letter:
peace and to eat. So who cares
what the birds call themselves
or what the grass sings? I'm well,
friend, trusting this finds you so.

362

A theme of razors

1

One cut and the blood rings:
Roland's horn running in the mountains,
the dark Vascos inching rocks to ambush
manoeuvre through the deadfalls.

Some nights the clock's hand will not sleep,
night rides her cargo out at anchor
on the tide's approaches, and the blood
is thumping out its message to the pillow:

you will die, your heart
imploding like a busted TV.

You hear the static in the phone.
The drum of waves ashore.
The ticking out of every grain of sand.
The itch inside the instrument.

There's wanting to be done, to cut
the singer from his song.
And there's desire. Along an edge
we are to act the moment as the last,

reporting from the frontier of the self
all present and correct a tale to tell –
the rambling message of ourselves,
the target of our swift arithmetic.

Where at the line's end will be death,
the swiftest answer to the shortest prayer
with a daft sense of humour and bad grammar
repeating himself *death death.*

And all the bloody mess to think about,
the insurance and the weeping,
the fact the sentence came to nothing,
even those we loved were strangers.

2

Therefore I shall befriend the razor
stolen from the rare book room in Ohio,
sharp as intelligence that never learns,
keen and as I am quick to the thiefwork.

Observe his grace that fits the hand,
the curve of finger grip and shaft,
the steel arc of a wing to nowhere,
and all his speech a single syllable.

I fear the blood. I fear the moon
bruised in all the sea for his ego.
I fear the man I meet at morning
in the mirror's frame, as he fears me.

His eyes that meet me in the glass,
what do they know? I glimpse him
in the blade's glance, so carefully
his other hand shaves his Adam's apple.

His eyes catch mine but nothing's said.
Some days we hold the razor well apart
and stare each other eye to eye a time
but what we know we know and cannot say.

We shrug. That moment's all we share
along the sharp edge of reflection,
a pair of borrowed blades who meet
to carve our separate faces from the air.

The final blessing on the suicides.
The sickle at his ancient labour
cutting through the blood the air's
immediately filled with and the light gone.

I clean the cut. I stop the blood
and wipe my blue-eyed double's face.
I fold the blade back in the shaft. I put
the shaft back in the box still priced $2.00.

The wanderer Yakob

Three things always threaten a man's peace
and one before the end overthrows his mind:
illness or age or the edge of vengeance.
THE SEAFARER

Yakob she sings, *Yakob*: his name
in her mouth in the new tongue
she knows now she knows him:
the dreamer, the wanderer, Yakob.

All this life he complains
searching for wells. He's away
shepherding across the mountains
into Andalusia, all summer long.

Driven by necessity, happenstance
one way, heartsease another,
always at adversity's far edge,
gone into everything he's scared of.

*

Torn apart, as were the valleys
to be the way they are. Thereafter
everywhere he looks it is her face,
her hands that meet across his flesh.

What's given them before the ground?
He finds the prickly pear's legacy
months after, its spines invisible
in his skin. She is a photograph.

They are as always: scarred, flawless,
stained by each other, a sketch
one moment makes in the next
in other zones the heart has.

*

Either he bad mouth misfortune
or whinge or sing supper, laugh
or clap hands for Charlie, dancing
to the flute's quick currency.

Let him begin with nothing much.
Relatively harmless he will end
relatively legless, his piss
a glitter dancing on a stone.

So far away he's vanishing, drunk
knocking at her dream's door,
his echo smothered in the canyon,
on its rim his speck of shadow.

                                        *

He will be back he writes her,
over the border, stepping
the Earth's meridians, gypsy,
horseman turned trader.

Master of tarmac, his shotgun
under his shoulder. Thief.
With a skin or two to sell,
Navajo rings, combs, watches.

And a coat worn but the once.
In men's nature he writes her
*hunting with dogs or herding
lowland to upland, moving.*

                                        *

A gambling man, dice and a fancy
Italian deck in his waistcoat.
A salesman with his patents,
survivor on his silver tongue.

Comic. Piano player. Drifter
with the railroads, poacher
of other men's work and women,
on the moon's tack, a migrant.

Or takes to the sea's roads,
a carpenter, bright tools
in a box made him shipman
twice round the world's rim.

*

Busker to the subway come winter,
wild geese or Cape May. Mechanic,
mercenary, preacher, poet
or magician, all come sweet April

attend the spring wind's message
warm on cheeks: *Thanne longen
folk to goon*, the pale forsythia
yellowing the landscape.

Moiré of railings again. Water
willowed, still, aloof in motion,
townspeople shimmer on a bridge,
the high jets cutting X on all.

*

War's ruckus took off many.
Some a bird bore, born again
to a season of Jesus, in fear
as he is for the night coming.

Others mad or went wasted,
some glimpsed in the mirrors
in the cold country of cocaine,
one he knew flew from a window.

Death's usual doings. *The dead
knowing nothing but through us
always inviting us in. I
who am crazy sing in their faces.*

*

Yakob in the desert: the sun
striking its single note, all day
the Panzers crisscross tracks.
Thereafter rheum and the prickly heat.

Thereafter a new name and a gammy leg.
No man endures distance unchanged.
In his sleep grey columns of smoke
advance along the night wing.

Fighting thunder and cactus.
He recalls: a following wind
and fair weather. Writes her name
in the tall sand's side: *Rachel*.

                                        *

Yakob wakes in the city, Chicago
traffic or Moon Township, counts
bird, *water*, *metal*, his trades
always taking him town after town.

In the neon her name blinks,
in the glimpsed passing of graves,
among trucksides and storefronts,
a chain round the vagabond's wrist.

Beauty a feather, the lark's life
indecipherable. The road to Wide Ruin
wet without rain, dark without night,
and all the AM stations fading out.

                                        *

So each day his gob's given
grievance's assonance, chant
to complaint's counterpoint:
tribulations of marriage and money.

Years blunt and brief, beyond
worse uncertainty, his mind
in its narrowing margin remarks
in his time stars haven't moved.

Yet makes him some song of it.
Shapes it for telling. The blues
and the dark colours his cries
among towns he is travelling.

*

Whiteness scribbles his scalp,
winters enter his face, a map
to the freeways, the bone
in his breast burns homeward.

The continents clutter, fenced
from the border to Santa Fé,
and all the Spanish coasts
hazy with condos and hi-rise.

If home there be and his name
still known there. If his eyes
long staring at bulkhead
and sea bile be not star blind.

*

Yakob on the home stretch,
dreaming warm grey bread, his name
along the wind in women's songs
imagines places of arrival, home.

Tales there'd be told there
by lamplight and the dark rioja,
a wineglass franking the table,
the wind's twist to the chimney.

Wishes, horses, stables, bolts.
There's no home but the roads,
smokey longings for the distance,
stones that curve along the canyon.

As it happens

This Prison is a House of Care
A Grave for Man Alive
A Touch Stone to Thee Friend
No Place for Man to Thrive

INSCRIPTION, YORK COUNTY JAIL, DATED 1820

On the swings

to the far fall of my own weight
that carries me there, east, west,
over the city between the prison
and the place I come from, go to:

either's a moment pausing itself
on a rope's end, all of me there for it.
Then home watching TV: *don't make
damn all of a difference* the boy says

to the camera *in nick or not.*
All this here as the lens eye pans
bleak cements of the buildings,
the units opened once by a princess –

All this is prison. Myself I want
to be me and be useful and not be
where I'm somebody's social problem
and time's the whole sentence.

> All other wormwoods, the nearer they approach in taste to
> pleasant and palatable, they are so much the worse, for they
> are weaker, their use requires so much longer time, larger
> doses, and yet less success follows.
>
> NICHOLAS CULPEPER

Down and more down. Down the ladders and down the snakes
and never passing *Go*, never winning the state lottery nor so much
as the Christmas raffle, never throwing double six, never dreaming
of the winner in the 2.30 at Cheltenham, never finding sixpence
in the plum pudding. There was never any luck that was good.
And so down the steps in chains and down the stairs in cuffs, and
backwards down the up escalator shackled to the jailer, and at last
in a bodybag down the well under the cellar under the basement
under the crypt under the undercroft and still some down to go.

So here I am, drinking the green absinthe of my wounds, weary
from descent, from falling, drinking to get drunk. Enough of it and
I'll be crazy and forget everything, I'll be wide open and talking
aloud to myself or anyone or no one about the yellow dust, the
ragged leaves, the palest green, the serotonin.

I dreamed you were not who I thought. You were at the airport
opening your passport to another identity, a name I was not familiar
with: *Jessica. Jessica Snow*. You were who you were before I knew
you; you were who you are without me; you were who you are
anyway. Your look said *But I am always Jessica. Always have been.
Always will be.* You were leaving, going home to your own country
one way without thought of return to answer old letters and the
questions of old lovers, to look through shoes and coats still hanging
in the closets, mementos in drawers. You were a stranger in my
life, I in yours: someone I never knew on a long vacation under
another name, the one I knew you by. You were a country only
visiting mine in another country I only visited with you.

Artemesia absinthum: yard high and wildly divided. Green ginger.
Curer of worms and quinsy and the bites of rats and mice, vile and
bitter, beauty's name for solace. Opaque, iced, sweetened through
silver, I drink to her, to Artemis, *destitute of delight*.

For the lost boys, sleepless:

The usual sniggering on the stairs,
and from the night park the shrill
peacock scream might be rape or mankilling,
pierced rat or some tortured innocent.

No one calls the cops. I don't.
The night somehow goes on, whatever riddle
the owl alone in wet rainy leaves
knows the answer to. I don't,

don't sleep or awake each night dream
the same black, the same trains
made up in the yards, last word
of a late argument, the door slammed

in the house of green ginger

where I'm banged up inside as if dreaming
the dream shut tight and I never get out.
So wide was my journey.

In the dark yellow hive I'm in with the bees
where the last man out was a spy for Russia
dreaming of wings on the fourth iron walkway
of D Wing: cell by cell in its socket,
the bolts home early, the smug keys
sleeping it off, the late shift at the spyhole
counts each man alone, and there's no honey.

In my room as it happens I've a view
east over wire and the wind and the wall
to the nurse's home and the city beyond –

the remembered city

Camberwell Clerkenwell Muswell a haze,
glassy steel etched on tile was the city,
its traffic clear over to Canning Town
where I don't want to go as it happens
by wheel or by water. Wind blows there
through the towers, the spraycan sneers
this is white man's land and the shadow
on scrapyards is soon rain, it's forever
the mean meridian of Greenwich, coming in
off the flyover to Rathbone and Silvertown:
all the lost boys hunched on their knives –
the Posse, the Firm, the Little Silver Snipers

in the flats, flat voices

betwixt traffic and trains, boats on the tide,
dog grunts and the midnight rain between blocks –
upright streets as it happens, the lift shrieks
at the 17th floor in the airshaft
the wind hunts ruins to howl through,
the doors open on blue video voices.

You hear glass split, long clatter of heels
on the stairwell, a man's shout and a slam
all the way to the street where a car
coughs like a baby.
                            Later you hear
through the breezeblock *it's not her
car as it happens, it's not his baby*.

Elsewhere, the same night:

'You in there. Beast on the wing.
You're not my brother.

Not since you buggered my sister
chopped up my mother and stole
all my father's blessing,
dressed in another animal's skin.

You bastard. Go sleep in the desert
with a stone for your pillow
and dream if you will your dream
of a shining ladder of angels.

Jacob. Given a blade and a half oz,
I'll kill you.'

As it happens

the lost boys are playing their music,
one with a flute one a knife one a pistol,
keeping rhythm in the dark flexing muscles,
some like the dead in their stone jackets,
all serving time in the orchestra's beat
to the unfinished murderous music of men
so far below salt. Time is what it is.

As for me I was making the myth of myself
I'd come to prefer in the authorised version
fair copy and carbons security cleared
with the censor's approval, years ago
with my mates on the Bendy Rd when the world said

do this for me daddy

I love you

you owe me

as it happens it happens I forgot myself,
what I knew of distance receding away
into more of itself to Cyprus and Woolwich.
Some feeling is too much already I think,

so much we can feel belongs to the gods
who are sulking, thin water our prayers
through their hands, what with the river's tale
and my shadow there small by my father's.

So much for childhood: grey boulders
the dale's length, the rainbow's high arc
and the river's fast speech that runs
through my life now. That was no dream

it happens

nor am I awake nor am I asleep now
in the walled city, the boy in me still
bawling for love, and in me the animal
prowling, and the shadow of my shadow,
and the man I am sometimes a glimpse of
almost half human again, so where am I?

Where on the road was I distracted again
no doubt by love when whatever was hunting
through her eyes met in mine what I hunted
then down the landscape, the small firs
thinning off to the valley, the flaw
in the rocky distance far snow on Mt Taylor?

Talking with the censor

In me someone believes the tale I tell
to distract from the night's terror:
diversions, dreams I don't wake from.
'I want some place to be I'm not a problem.'

Love forgive me I speak of dark things,
men's shabby concerns as to women,
through the sad nights of the masturbators,
the fist always closed on the self.

Some days I meet monsters, men I encounter
in the house of green ginger, in myself
as it happens, drawn up or caught short
with my father's lost knife in my hand.

My father with two knives

One he found shining in a furrow,
red amber, bright German steel
fallen from the sky, a blade grooved
to thread air in a man's blood.

In a cold white room I recall him
staring that knife down all Sunday,
his one thought to be done, and I,
eight, at the curtain's lace edge.

His pocket knife I keep: bone black,
brass head, bird's eye for a rivet
sighting the lifted beak of the blade –
useful and home made as he was.

Like him plain and of little speech,
given to blunt surgery on sheep
or whittling sticks any weather
out on the hill's side, long ago now.

Towards daylight:

all this and the rain's endurance
Lady I've aged, maybe you've aged me.
What I wanted: to roost in the nest
in the dark tree of your body.

I'd live alone but who would I tell,
alone as it happens. From this place
months go looking for years and hands
for each other and night after night

your voice on the tape in my skull
pauses for breath, breathes, speaks
your name with my own, as it happens,
as I grow old thinking of you.

The bee dance

Let the grey dust thicken on the landings,
let the spiders tick in the wall,
let the locks rust and the keys be lost.

This is the yellow hive of my skull
where the bees dance on the honeycomb
their tales of direction and distance.

They tell how high the sun is, how far
to sweet marjoram, borage and thyme,
and the tall green masts of the sunflowers.

Cain's songs

If there's a tune no one remembers.
The words fall away and the voice
remembers in bits, trailing out –

> *O when you loved me*
> *When the wind in a garden*
> *When the carousel*

In our songs innocence comes back,
our childhood some moment a throstle
sang in the orchard at day's end,
you sat among blossoms and moths.

> *O when you loved me.*
> *Till with love's fury I came*
> *to murderer's home.*

Don't I know you? Did we meet
when last time you were victim,
I the persecutor? Maybe.

> *For the prosecution:*

I arrested him.
His reply was
I've got nothing to say.

He then said *Answer me truthfully officer*
how many pubs in Weymouth
am I not banned from?

I said *None sir.*
It was 9.10 p.m.

Here's a man with a hammer
banging the sound under his fist.
The sound grows as it travels,
dies down its wavelength.

Maybe that's his wife he's beating,
beating with a hammer. Maybe
with the nails between his teeth
and the hand and the hammer raised up.

Maybe her. Maybe him. Maybe me.

Where love stays. Where
there are no prisons, no police.
That world you speak of, friend,
lives in another song in a tune
I can't recall, another tale
told at the road's turn where wind
moves among beeches. I know.
I was there. The wind told me.

Grieving the years out.
I have made a room in the wind
where the days grow tired of each other.

It is a weepy sound, my grief
but it is not weeping. Harsh,
it is not anger with anyone.

So wide was my journey.
The moon shines on the sea,
it does not intend to.

For the boys on the wing

They are birds some thought free once
on the wind's swing and air's drop.
Hours perched on the landing railings
to be locked up to be glimpsed
among bars and the meshed stale air,
sometimes singing, their wings tucked.

We are entering silence,
cloud closing the room's light
and the radio music suddenly graver,
each in his moment twoed-up
or threed or alone with the brickwork
hours, nights, years, sinners
whose proper life study is silence.

As ever: half a world hungry
and the deployments continued, the swift
planetary surgery closer, it seems
not a damn thing we can dance to.

Forgive me directness,
and the president his blindness.
And the chairman his bullshitski.

Black and white with my own money.
So far they can't make my space less.
Round and round anti-clockwise my project
silence but who would I say it to?

Between this ear and this ear I'm free.
So tell them, whose task is to despise me,
whose career to contain me, tell them
who call this hell we live here.

Outside I was always
looking round for them –
chancers, dancers, addicts
of the dark. So roundly

all these are cursed men
by their lovers, victims,
consensus of the deceased,
and forever. *Worthy*,

worthy of praising
one sings of his Jesus,
another finding at mass
the priest's hands moving

a moment of beauty,
his vernacular a holy
rigmarole tale told of
bread, wine, blood.

Think of Billy. He'll not wince
past the checkout. Think of John
overdue in the remembering department,
in the red to the last lost quid
hidden in his shoe and that owing
to Veiled Threats Associates. He recalls
a whole ocean cut to a wind and two blues.
He has pictures to prove it: the hills,
the harebells whipped by the first
wind of September. Love I remember:
you were fierce, you persisted
through whatever the weather was.

Born again to the wind's tap on brick.
Born again to the island of the self,
the same giggle in the orchestra pit,
nights when the snake of her dark voice
slides over me. She says all journeys
have no returns. The radio sings
She & I don't go to the laundrette no more.
Here's tansy the dried deathless flower,
roses fallen on roots and I'm Orfus

the man who has everything calling back
from the border and lost her forever,
bringing no light back from the dead.

Think of Az. Az says in the
prison of the self he was born to
he's been here there and Zimbabwe,
the wire and the wall notwithstanding.

What he feels that he feels is always
dissolving. Let's say he matured late
or tripped on the wrong foot, he was
victim victim, his luck never ran in.

Though it's no excuse some days
he's the brain of a squeegee mop,
he says *You make the decisions, so now
You figure it out: what to do with me.*

Don't say guilt, don't say innocent.
Suspend disbelief. Say *the convicted*.
Say *the problem of male violence*.
The problem of abstraction, e.g.
freedom. Some went abroad
to meet a bullet, some take
the tube train's last amendment,
some sleep with the rain and a knife,
spiders caught in each other's webs.

So wide was my journey, like the bees.
We have no wings, our honey bitter,
sour as green ginger, and for so much time
we make little at our trades at the
sewing machine at the sewing machine
with the needle eyes rising and rising.
Social or solitary we're bees, we dance
without partners or sense of direction.
We have silence. We have the many eyes
of mosaic vision. And this herb.
This herb destroys worms. Wormwood.

My footsteps come to the page edge.
I glimpse him again, my violent father,
knee deep in the landscape
till he'd had enough of it. Him
with all the other closed books
whose covers are soil, stone,
the long weeds by the allotments.
I close him again for the last time.

So far to the wall to count bricks.
So we've a rich inner life have we?
What I want is Gloucester Rd Anyplace.
Single. What I want is trains,
and my face angled in wind, my hat
blown away behind. I want to be
in other bars asking what's this game
called *Family Tissues*, what to do
with these blank folded sheets?
I want rain, the lamefoot doves
crowding city monuments, the traffic
and the grainy flush of air in the tubes.

What the righteous don't know

They think only hot and cold
and the dark we fall through.
They don't know life goes on in hell
where there's work painting the brick,
maintaining the fabric, in the kitchens
preparing the devil's marvellous picnics.
We've a roof over our heads,
three squares and it's steady
if promotion comes slow. What
the righteous don't know:
we're their shadows,
wherever they are in the light.

Bodies

Some whose eyes I don't meet,
hands I don't shake, one that cut
NF in a man's back and left him
choke on his testicles, the knife
still in him and ran with the video.

Some with no story to bring sleep
or get supper and no tale
travellers repeat. He can say
I was responsible, can't say
I killed her, shot her, took an axe
and cut her to pieces, sawed her up
with the breadknife we'd used
so many years cutting our bread.

He asks himself over and over
what name her teeth had bit back
in her long coming, her *tsunami*
she called it in the pluperfect.
How when he'd phoned she was
never at home so where was she?

*

Charged with looking at the building.
In evidence a white male in a dark Allegro.
Some with a bottle, some with a needle.

Late afternoon the white meat waggons
roll in the day's catch, remanded
without bail, some misfit, some vicious,
the accused to be numbered.

*

Chalkie White, Metal Mickey, Spider Webb,
so where be they now? Last seen
with Murphy of Shepherd's Bush Boots,
helping Sgt E.C.T. Brainfuck from Paddington Green.
Last heard of on the block, on the book,
on the muffin run to Brixton.

Just helping Bill with his enquiries.

This one's Bungalow: no top storey.
This one's Muzz. And this one
singing in the canteen clatter at noon
I'm nobody's child, I'm nobody's child.
And no wonder another voice calls
down the wing as the neon hush falls
across paperwork and it's two hours
to unlock in the empire of the chinagraph.

Time to reflect:
                    he hit her with a bottle,
a sewing machine, a chair, a tennis racket.
Offered her the easy way with aspirin.
Hit her twice when once was twice enough.

At the centre of the labyrinth: a rose.
At the centre of the rose's labyrinth: a worm.

Timekeeper

> *It doesn't get worse*
> *It just goes on being bad*

As ever on the digital
all the seconds my life
I repeat one by one I
repeat myself: *so wide*
was my journey. As ever
no one to tell it to
whatever lies I write
between the barred lines
on the page in the upright
iron of these letters, who
to send them in any case?
What we do here is count,
count, pencil in, turning
a smooth choreography – arm,
chain, keys, whistle, Whisky

2 on the walkietalkie, slam
of the great gates shut –
a century, more. Oh
you'll see me dance, some
time you'll hear me sing,
truth is we despise as we
count each other, as we
study the clock's time
ticking *knockback knockback*,
the hours one by one on Sir
and as ever it's a long time
to the next number 9 bus and this
urgent news out of nowhere.

> *I threw my blade.*
> *It was a lucky shot.*
> *It got him right off.*
> *It killed him.*
> *Or it was a unlucky shot.*
> *I been here six years.*

How divide how many ways
cut up time, alone, paring
the fingernail, notching
the calendar, shaving
a match to a matchstick
by stick to his Romany cart,
wherein he would sail
any lane as he chose
or the slow wind suggested?
The days anti-clockwise
walking the yard count
how many miles, how much rain
and what names for the birds
which are two being *hawk,*
sparrowhawk, sparrow?
Each man here is a thread,
each man is a needle
stitching his tale told
silently over, already old.
Young as I am in this place

whispers run through me,
nightcries, feet running
and rumours. So I moved
once back in the old life
through cities of women's
remembrance and men's yarns
where my name is a ghost,
face barely recalled. Now
my road's closed I've years
to prepare, to polish,
rehearse my story for someone,
anyone, no one, myself then.

The man I killed. I don't
regret it: I'd kill him again.
But for a long time I'd look
at the stars through the window
and I'd see his face.

Through the judas you'll
see me reading or sleeping
or staring into nothing
at a gesture's midpoint,
all my private dancing
in public. Once more
I free the bird my heart
in the closed 8 by 12
our space is, she and I.
She sings. She wakes me
and flies at the little panes,
the yellow paint, the brick.
Beyond glass and the wire
of razor hair and stars,
traffic and the wind. They
make the sound a sea breaks
on beaches and the risen
crowd's roar in the stadium
up on its toes. This side,
just me and the budgie,
lost as though long steering
by one star quit the sky.

Asleep I dreamed my heart
the dark star far away
I long for and remember,
all the stones between us.
I tell her *no* and tear
the star out of my chest,
don't you ever come see me.

At the solstice

As for me I'm free to ponder the crow
my voice blent in the day's wind
soft grey at my back. To the east
stumpy London humming to itself
blocks spires over the land's hump
distant finger of the Telecom tower
my needle's eye of the city my
marker for Baker Street. Out
on some errand some long ago want
for an open country talking out loud
with no one to hear. My good days
are like this one into another just
getting about with an arm and a leg
two of each if I'm lucky. Lucky I am
with my notes my keys to the prison
I pass in and out I sing for my supper.
It could be otherwise. Years back
in the paranoid self of myself
I recall in the seventyeight of it all
I would have killed a man and been here
meeting myself a prisoner on no road
anywhere a record no one listens to
a book no one reads any more my gear
out of style all the jokes out of date.
Years in the dark mad half mad
what would we say when the weather
no longer matters the time the time
any day what month what the season
what game to play? Spot the psychopath.
Which man kills because he feels nothing

and which when he never felt more
which for gain which revenge to be done
which accident which innocent as charged?

What to say when the fear the blood
down the thickening tunnel the cave
the thump in the head the chest
the heart's labouring pump drums nights
at the temple second by second
systole by dystole its promise
a last *jessica jessica* fading off
on the cardiogram's blipless quiet
unplugged at the wall next customer
caught in the panic that kills
bolting from bed 3.00 a.m. in the soft
city's groan at the window the clock's
even passing of time the birds
before dawn the light's blue glaze
in your sleeping face love I begin
I start saying goodbye my wave of the sea.

Wormwood I grew. Tall in the feathering wind
in my garden all summer taller the next
a pushy green bush small yellow cushions
a dusting of air. Wormwood you drew me.
Bitter plant. Absinthe and illusion.
Beer made in the name of this district
there's none now an oak forest once
scrub clearing last feeding of sheep
before market. The long trains
put on speed west go crying to Bristol
to Plymouth the rocky rainy peninsulas.
Crows rubbery avuncular here in the mist
in the grass small peppermint snails.
Wormwood the name of the prison its wall
a pit dug in men's lives four hulks
four ships that never sail anywhere
moored in time in a dead space
between the wire and the wall.
The name *Wormwood* the star falling
destroys a third part of the waters
the third part of men. Goodbye heartsease.

In the nowhere waiting for a result
hanging on to the empty urine bottle
hoping for anything the bomb to drop
the knife to its tryst in the artery.
In the shadow land. And overhead
a helicopter in the broody air of August
above the keen abstractions and the facts
that are all bricks locks razor wire.
We fail as men where is no centre
to the self, these many voices
failing in first person singular.
I've done two rapes a man whispers
but I'm here under another name.
I'm no father confessor. Here I am
too many shades of blue already
in the three-ring circus of myself
thinking maybe I can hide in here
with all the other confessions
in my study of male violence
but I can't. No more dancing
for this customer. No more
crossing town to drink Campari
with the daughters of the brown contessa.
Time to say goodbye to the dark ladies.
Here is where we leave the shoes.
Here is where we leave the gloves
the hat the 44 the rolled umbrella.
We're pulling in your licence Jimmy.

Bricks made of clay. Clay dug
in the river leas in the Thames flood plain
brick cut fired tapped to the trowel
coursed brick on brick making prison.
Prisoners brickies once labourers
thieves from the bridewell hard men
from the Millwall to dig in the mud
their own quarters the cells
of all who came after men women
convicted walking the yard circles
turning the mill hooded and ruled
by silence. Boxed masked ranked
of a Sunday sly in the cubicled church

passing notes looking always front
at priest and their maker condemned
to brood on their criminal ways
they step in a chained procession
down time cuffed censored banged up
there is nothing to hope for. Bricks.

Worm's Wood I invent. Old dark place
under the treecover of oak and sycamore
bushy scree tangle of briar thornwood
men are lost in. Wood of *straunge wormes*
snagging men's ghosts caught earthbound
in the ongoing assault that is prison
the failed university of time the first
last faith called fear. Everything
sharp blades fists in the recess
a kicking an ear bitten off here's
an edge takes an eye a finger a pencil
a razorblade jammed in a toothbrush.
And no maps no signs again no way out
each shadow casting its shadow.
My journey can end here I can
die be forgotten lie unconsoled
in the brown city clay any time
a fate common reasonable even so what?
I could be anyone the wood-goer Nick
I have almost a name for him *Nick*
who moves in out the nightmares
down the landings of the sleepers
sleepless fingering the dreams
the convicted whisper each celled
dark bricked barred lonely alone
forever maybe lost most likely
I could be him: say Nicholas Wildman
a fox for instance the very same man
John known as Marsbar alias Professor
a.k.a. Jack be Nimble Jack be Quick.

The night whispers

(for John and all the men in the world called John)

1

There was a friend of mine,
used to offer me a cigarette.
On a Tuesday. John was talking.
He was saying what he hears, his ear
pressed along the wall along the wing.
Time's all there is he says, flat,
to one side, every second word
what he'll never do again with women.
He'll take a light off me though.

He's the man that ate boiled ham raw.
He'll take on a sliced loaf single handed.
Time is the crease in his pants I think,
pressed as in the army under the mattress.
John keeps himself neat. He knows
how quick they'll spirit him away
in a bodybag along the stairs before unlock.
He says he heard the screw say *One Off Sir.*

It's time.

Time he looks back from morning after morning,
his face changing in the same mirror.
Time is the razorblade, the comb's teeth
and the measure of the toothpaste. Time he eats,
shits, drinks, is sometimes merry in,
the fallen grey he lifts off his shoulder.

Time scuffs the shoe and blunts all the nails.
If there were no nights there'd be no fear.
Time I could handle but all this dark stuff
either side between the light and the light.

Time is what.
Time is.

He tells me what he hears in the night whispers
through pipework and brickwork, bars and the hard gloss,

and he writes down the messages: *Oddy's on the roof.*
The nurses are having a party. It's in.
All it costs are little pictures of the Queen.

Oh and love he says. *Love Love Love's*
faint echo on the landings, through the masonry
on a thin late airwave *Love* running down the batteries,
singing on a bent guitar
Lost in the saddle again.

Ah, John.

Lost in time both of us talking about love,
a word born over again and again in the prison house
where so many with their hands killed love,
and then the dark came down forever. So now
behind the yellow wall and the yellow fence
where the wind in a scatter of old leaves
beats the wire to security, the dogs howl
moonward and the champion dopesniffer Duke
sleeps on but John when he sleeps never dreams.

Time is what it is. The protagonist is mad again,
lost in some mean southern border town
all barber shops and bars and far too many shoes.
I've been out again beating my heart on the wind,
and maybe this time John we never get home
and the journey ends here and time's all there is.

The idea is don't die in prison John,
in this part of the nightmare.

   2

My brother calls me from the world's other side
and never said which city. He's been robbed,
he's broke, homeless, out of a job and 48,
he's drunk in the wrong house and whose phone is it
and I fear my brother will die in the wind.
He says he's glad dirty money from a dirty job
went to a dirty place to buy a dirty girl junk.
Wherever morning is I hope he'll still be glad.
He'll send an address when he has one.

So now you know the plot. Fox is away
in Australasia waiting for the cops,
and when he called I was thinking about John
and what he tells me: *many things
will never happen.* As for me
I've been too close too long to the damned
and can't leave, lost as they are in time,
on my wordtrack covering the territory,
always in the dark thinking I've a lucifer
when I'm far too near the wire when the lights go up
and I'm lost in the saddle again.

Take me home, love, my scars and all my alibis
and my bad manners and whatever wounds we die of.
If you can find me. My name is John.
Maybe you can love what will be left of me.
Take me out of this prison.

Carteret plage

I came to tell you my feather:
at the marina so many bells,
so many voices coming ashore
saying *listen we have nothing
to say beyond who we are*:
old business the wind works
through the slack riggings
of boats laid up for winter,
each the one note clapped
on the incoming wind, slap
of metal on mast, wave on hull,
rope on the rain an orchestra
of random notes moored where
always this was the river,
for someone the waters of home.

My blue feather. On the beach
so many lives feathered into being
and out of it. And so much
interesting foreign detritus
in the rubbery scourings
in the kelp's piled tripes
weary with flies in summer.
Everywhere a tangle of guts,
crabs, starfish and bladderwrack,
the weeds of abandoned brains,
tumours, dropped masks, amputations
and all the bloody murders ever
ending in string, ripped nets,
hooks, driftwood and the wreck
of the good ship *One blue glove*

Quatre-vingt je ne sais quoi,
Merde de lapin s.v.p. Ce poisson-çi,
c'est une seule nucléare n'est-ce pas?
Mes enfants, ma langue c'est fini,
je suis en vacances, après la guerre,
not permitted to be bored or to work.
Mine is a country of small cheeses,
here I live in a bordello of cheese
and white Muscadet with the widow
of Arromanches, perhaps I'm a man
other men would like to be like
but they keep their distance,
ces enfants que le bonheur oublie.
It's late *et la clef c'est fini*
dans la chambre privée,
et Monsieur Toledo bonne nuit.

My blue feather. Falling.
In the quick wind. If the wind
turn you round, blow you west
down the rowdy Atlantic
and out of yourself, my bride,
my blue feather. By night
on the dark edge of water
I hold you consulting my text

that says here *a wise man*
holds out. Do we think
the rock thinks forming the slow
thought of itself that dissolves?

The wind off the sea, steady.
On the quays faces of Vikings,
on the beach wayward paths
secretly marked by stones,
by the track of a dog,
the snake tongue of seaweed
spelling your name in cursive
in a scribble of wormcasts,
and the doll's burst head,
from her bleached broken face
a single blue eye staring seaward.

THE HEART, THE BORDER

(1990)

In the Evangelical Cemetery, San Michele, Venice:

Sacred to the memory of
Archibald Campbell
Master of the SY Minerva
Who died on board
March 17 1891
Aged 56

*

*The heart knoweth its
own bitterness, and the
stranger intermeddleth
not therewith.*

Dorothea Extempore

I am a citizen of an incurious land. While everything changes, this does not change: we accept the customs of our ancestors. We are born, we are named. From infancy to adolescence it is explained to us, patiently, over and over, what are the three things we must do, and this is our whole education and all our lives thereafter: first we must plant a tree, and second we must begin to make a rope. Thus each of us has a rope, each of us has a tree. For each, the rope's first thread is the umbilical that spun us from our mothers, and as we grow we must gather and plant the seeds to grow the hemp to make the fibre from which to spin the braids of the rope, weaving into it the stray hair of all those we love and some we do not love and some – it turned out – who never loved us. Making such a rope takes many years. Meanwhile we must tend the tree: the roots, the trunk, the bark, the branches, twigs, the leaves, the fruit and the seeds, and whatever birds and animals and insects live among them, the dawn singers and the evening moths, the cicadas in their long cycles down among the roots for 17 years, and whatever plants grow there in the shade. Later, when we and the trees are grown tall enough and the rope grown long enough, we learn what is the third thing we must do: we must take one and hang ourselves on the other. And somehow sooner or later, one way or another, each of us ends up doing just that.

Writing in prison

Years ago I was a gardener.
I grew the flowers of my childhood,
lavender and wayside lilies
and my first love the cornflower.

The wind on the summer wheat.
The blue glaze in the vanished woods.
In the space of my yard I glimpsed again
all the lost places of my life.

I was remaking them. Here in a space
smaller still I make them again.

Greetings from the Winter Palace

Once he'd won a medal, he had a letter
proved it. He'd had a wife and a wedding.
He came and went, talking with his hands,
with all his names and all of them lies, alibis.

Call him Bob, call him Bounce, call him Dodge,
he's up again and down again. He says
beneath his breath *if you want to know the time
ask a policeman*. He has a problem and a needle

and he steals to keep it sharp. He writes
from his next station of the cross
*I'm in the Ville not treading on the star.
I dream of snow, of Acapulco, any fix.*

And then he's fading to a scrawl, the number
that he goes by, gesture of his mouth,
his hands folding on his hands. Then he's gone,
another junkie, another star no light comes back from.

Jack's postcards

Just a line of posts along the baymouth,
and the tide out. And I'm supposed to know
what they mean, this ship, this flag,
both departing on the horizon, this message.

I'm being tested. I'm under observation,
interpreting these picture postcards
sent by the nuns from Inveraray: *wish you
were here. But we pray for you.*

Pictures of cool green woods,
a thirst forever slaked beside the river,
a minaret, a market and a leaning tower,
and in the distance more the same –

the sunset over palms and best regards
from Disney World. You should know
the censor's on my shoulder always,
like the poor, like my angel, striking

what I cannot say in any case: does love
still hold each others' hands, does the heart burn,
or is the universe a glossy magazine
and all the polished girls bone china bright?

The pornographer

Three things the shrink said: he feared everyone,
he invented himself in everyone he met,
he feared sex. He'd pointed a camera at it
and ended up in jail, so much hot dry flesh
on the cold, burned-out eye of the lens.
For himself he loved no one, no one loved him.

They close their eyes, these lovers he's hired,
as if they were alone. They can act
no better than the rest of us, the way
they do it no one ever gets pregnant.

Watching, you wonder what the fees are,
who thought of Mozart by the Rome Symphony,
what they're on, what they say later
over coffee, cigarettes, Courvoisier
washing out the sweet spermy taste.

So this is how it is: flesh hungering for flesh,
fingers and tongues and all the cries,
so much juicy footage and white noise,
the soundtrack whimpering as if all life
wanted to be one and come again again,
smearing itself in itself. Meanwhile,
back at the big house the master with the maid,
the manservant with mother and daughter,
and the plot minimal. Like so many lives.
Sad thing for him this is the real thing.

Figures in three landscapes

One: *Brady at Saddleworth Moor*

Out, this is air, abrupt and everywhere,
the light and sky all one blaze of it.
Count them: eleven clear hours of wind
over the world's tops into my face –

this old bleached-out moon always adrift
through the bad dreams of the neighbourhood.
In my ten thousand days I count this day:
the moor, all its space and vastness

I hear them say I say. I find nothing
in all four corners of the wind
where stones haven't changed, tumps, gullies
one blue blur of heather and upland grass

where one grave looks much like another.
Think how many years the rain fell I felt
my heart in my chest a fist of sour dust
forming in the acids of my discontent.

But it knows one thought: nothing's forgot
though my vision's bad, my sanity debatable.
I can forget, I can remember, I can be mad,
I will never be as free again, ever.

Nor will anyone be free of me. Count on it.

Two: *Hungerford nights*

Before you get through this, before
the next page, before the next breath
you catch is the last breath:
the assassin's device has found you.

His knife of a heart has emptied your own.
Thereafter down the rest of the page: blood,
the book unreadable, plotless,
the tale of a man with a Kalashnikov.

How he soothes and greases it, nights
in the garden shed, a boy with a stick
in the bathroom mirror of his mind.
What he read, wore, saw on the video.

The symbols slip into their metal shoes,
oils groove the mechanism into one
precision-milled moment, rapid fire
along the High St and you're dead.

And you're dead. And you're dead.
Himself he had difficulty with.
It ends with 16 red roses on his coffin,
one for each victim, like any cowboy.

His ashes scattered in an unknown place.

Three: *Murder at White House Farm*

So who am I now, falling nowhere
on my black wing in the black wind
calling my cry: *Innocent Innocent,*
may where was a murderer now grow a rose?

Can you find me, framed in a photograph
in the surf's eye on the world's other side,
riding the incoming water? I'm locked up now
in the grey tide of my heart's only season.

Singing my orphan song *Pity me Pity me,*
survivor of all I slaughtered, my years
closing before, the steel gates behind
I imagine a rose. I think of a kiss.

I consider the indifference of objects:
the knife killed a man carves bread
in his kitchen, the hammer
that clubbed him goes on sinking nails.

Here the clever ones dance and the smart ones
steal their money. We all go to the wall
known as *Anyone else*, and the stars
wander on in their merciless courses.

And no one calls out the seeds, we're all
God's wayward apprentices, miracles once,
thereafter mundanely repeated,
a lie telling a lie till one size fits all.

And all the words beyond this say farewell.

Against the grain

Someone must count them, the bodies that come up
one by one out of the fire, up from
the gloomy cradle of the North Sea
that has weighted and washed them, months.

Someone must number them, name each one
by the fingerprints, the rings, by the teeth,
someone must stare at the remnants of the dead
from Zeebrugge, Kings Cross, Piper Alpha:

more oil there than under all Arabia,
I recall long ago, *that we bought and paid for.*
We're dying of neglect. My country
is a free enterprise disaster zone.

And now someone must count them all: *one, one.*
Someone must zip them into a bag
and bury them, tally the ongoing total,
put up a stone. It goes against the grain.

Three Docklands fragments

1 *The Enterprise Zone*

On my birthday the snow wind
bringing feathery rain, a fine dust
falling on the edge of crystal.

I take the grey road along the river
where pass lives sadder than yours, mine,
slow death in the tower blocks.

These are the Silvertown Blues,
Fight the Rich ghosting out
in concrete, by the flyover.

No one ever gets straight here.
The ego's tale of itself is miserable,
nothing much happens but murder.

Yet that these wastes be repeopled
and the rich inherit, everyone's
moving downriver. This is *the zone,*

carved from the sour and floury air
of London's residuary body,
filling with cranes and dust

and the racket of money being made,
and there's nothing to say but to say
to myself *Thou bone, brother bone. You old bone.*

2 *Of things to come*

Down the Bendy Road to Cyprus and Custom House
where the new cities rise from the drawing-boards
and the ghosts-to-be of George in his Capri,
JoJo in her birthday suit drinking white wine with soda
fly in from Paris for the weekend. Later
they'll gather with friends by the marina.
Later they'll appreciate the view of the river.
Later they'll jive to the mean mad dance of money
between the tower blocks over the runway
amongst the yachts already moored in the development.

3 *Yuppy love*

What he calls her: my little pocket calculator
my fully portable my VDU my organiser my mouse
oh my filofax my cellnet my daisywheel.

What he dreams driving home at the wheel
on the brimming motorway: her electronics
the green screen of her underwear her digital display.

Oh my spreadsheet he groans in the night:
my modem my cursor lusting after her floppies
wanting her printout her linkup her entire database.

The New Management

(after Sean O'Brien, in his manner)

It's best they look tough in blue suits,
like police. They are anyway,
ordering the lights up, the heat down,
and you redundant. *We're letting you go,*

they say, *You're not in our cost centre.*
And you're not. You're out on the city's
skinny peripheries in the landscape
of windy bungalows. You don't live here

and of course it is raining. Entropy
was against you from the start and now
when you can't play the flute there's
only departure's uncountable sadness.

And they're watching. In other times
they marched in with banners and speeches,
read the new rules in their own rough tongue,
shot hostages, put up the salt tax.

Now they wear suits and the leader says
stand up, *sit down* and everyone dances.
They move to the music of money and leave
without introductions. Fact is

they're the missing witnesses to an accident
standing in the shade of the portico
to one side at the victim's funeral
in the Italian gardens, in dark glasses,

where one sniffs the roses, one shrugs,
another fondles a cigar he will smoke
over coffee, checking the till rolls,
later, the printout, the bottom line.

Which is you, wandering the empty quarter,
where you meet no one, you find nothing,
you return with no answers, only grit
in your teeth and a long thirst to slake.

Running on empty

What's it like? they ask.
Lots of space debris I reply: this music
has been written by psychologists.
'My name is Vera Lute, from Truth or Consequences.'

Some wander all their days
and never find the river.
So many lives are wasted and no one knows why.
That sounds to me like a crime.

Tell the BBC in confidence,
tell the golfing correspondent from *Angling Times*:
there were days when my heart was sore
and it always seemed to be raining.

Now there's too much to be angry about,
and no one left to forgive.
I'm the atheist at the bishop's conference.
I'm the fly in the ointment on the wall.

On and on down the dirty decades.
Nothing as described in the brochure,
as promised on the party platform
and nothing but bullshit to listen to.

My country is falling off the back of a lorry
but I bear you no malice, Alice.
What I'm in is chagrin. It's late,
I'm out on the road, running on empty.

And I'm calling you in.
I'm calling you in.

Imaginary confrontations

What a strange world Mother says,
stepping back into the room. We're still
talking about our sons – tall, handsome,
saying *just leave me be now Mother.*

That drink looks like a hedgehog
the cowboy says. Turning to me:
is this your crow? You're as much use
as one trouser I reply, *as half a pair of gloves.*

With that he puts *The Inferno* into his pocket
and gallops off across the map of Colorado,
I'm only here as an observer he announces.
I'm only part of the wiring in the wind.

This phone's bugged I say into the phone,
and this dream's rigged, to the people
living in the fibreoptic I've never met
who overhear us. Who knows who they talk to?

These days we talk funny, on the TV
discussing racket abuse in Latin America.
Suddenly I remember you in the bikini area,
and forget you again, wiping your tape into silence.

After the hurricane: how are things
in your wreck of the woods? Does the censor
know about you or were you educated locally?
Answers on a postcard. Wake me if I'm dreaming.

Intercepted letters: Harry inside

These words with difficulty, friend.
It's been a while. So little happens
through the slow harvests of time,
the abrupt inflexible silence at my door
there's no getting round. I make lists.
I add up columns of imaginary numbers.
I ponder the inscrutability of dice,
cards, horses, men. Maybe in the night
one thought thinks itself in my brain's
slow stunned contemplation of itself:
such a busy machine. It begins one end
of the room, it sweeps inch by inch
to the door then back again, it sifts
the junk, it inspects each matchstick,
finger paring, print, drop of blood,
pollen grain, every other dead roach.
It considers for, against, if, but,
maybe, and all I might have said, done.
It remembers what love was, the wind,
the banners of the seagrass, the old wheat
that was childhood, flesh falling
into flesh and the wars over, a moment.
It leaves nothing out and spares none of me,
the keys, locks, all the bricks, pipes,
bars, years, papers in the wind,
and all there never is to sing about,
to say nothing of the weather. What I do now
I keep my nose clean, a clean shirt
on the heating pipe and every day I work
mopping the wounds that go on being wounds
as the war goes on, day by day, so long now
we don't say *the war* any more.

Intercepted letters: Harry on the road

With one mighty bound I'm free, on the road
south and north, back from the border,
– skint again. I should be glad and am
yet each day I grow heavy, day by day
sinking closer to the earth's core.
Evenings the lights come on in the bars
where I'm no longer in residence
among the sour faces of the whisky drinkers,
men married to their fists, always hungry,
staring after the heels of women,
living in the ventilation system,
in the tape's hiss in the stereo.
That's how it is at the border:
ours an insanity we barely control,
a life all one fit of bad temper.
I saw fiend grab tot says the SUN.
I shall consider the ambivalence of a hat.
Oh I know, I'm all over this story,
I'm in and out the mask of myself.
All these words have been twice lost,
once in prison and once at the border.
They came home like me hungry in the rain.
There's where I met her: the drowned bride
in the bleak water, up from the country
from the deep freeze for the weekend's
brief encounter with imaginary friends.
How she moves I think she's the air
dressed in itself, she's shaped
like good bread, like geography
I'm lost in with other men like me.

Back from Leah's country

It's true I was in love: with the roads,
with the dry river-beds and the canyons,
Joshua trees, mountains, sky, woods, snowline.
And you. We ran away together. Years ago.

It's true long after I'd look at your name
in secret, its winged calligraphy of wind,
smoke riding the air I dissolved in,
vanishing into the dark signature of your hair.

It's true I fucked you with my blood.
It's true later your name was a thought
that ran out. With you I was like you
without plan, without blueprint.

Like the cactus the repetition
of segments of itself, over and over.
I hate maps you said, and went off
into the desert expecting me to follow.

You would have taken me to Spider Mother's House
and filled me with your version of yourself.
You would have kept me in a room below the earth
and wrapped me in your silk till I was clean,

divided in departments of myself. It's true,
I was five parts hot air and no water
in the empty space between the slices of bread.
It was your darkness I was in love with.

Then when I came back I was mad, dumb,
lovesick, still drowning in the dry waterless air
of Leah's country. Now I'm myself
right side up there's even less to say about it.

We are what the rain sees, never
where we are but somewhere yesterday,
some other place we're on the way to,
anticipation turning into memory.

These events are put together backwards
from hints, shreds of evidence and hearsay,
restricted information, bias measured out
into the tight little shoes of language.

And it's too late to learn anything from them.
So there's an end to the affair.
Don't write. It's true this silence lasts
until we die. Let's not be friends.

The spectator's terrace, Gatwick

Maybe I came to consider distance,
departures, the hole in the sky
where plane after plane vanishes
into its promise of exotic arrivals.

On the ground the rain hisses,
the air sings with spent fuel,
travellers, strangers, saying *honey
it's best we both get insurance.*

Think of the miles of wiring,
the valves, pumps, connections,
blips on the radar, bolts
that shake loose, metal fatigue.

Up here on the spectator's terrace,
smug, aloof, not going anyplace,
I hang out with the cognoscenti
on a ten-visit ticket for £2.50.

We inhabit the buffet,
bright city of darkened glass behind wind,
dreaming there's somewhere
to get to, anywhere else.

Here's where the blood clot strikes
and the end of all memory.
Here's where we all go out
in that grey sky the breeze is.

Then the heart

In the spring, working up and down
the enterprise zone, over the mountains
and over the mountains from one sea
to the other: sudden panic, in the chest's
left pocket a sharpness persisting into pain,
fear of more of it: of death's knife
and a surgeon's chainsaw to the breast,
and beyond the old fear it always was –
some moment I will die, and the universe
go on making light of itself.

Such an arrogance night after night
keeps me awake so I hang black hours
on my heart's thump and blood beat
at the sour lip of oblivion, in fear
that asleep I'll not wake to the last star,
the lost dream, the first birds of morning,
another day to write Tuesday's sonata,
Wednesday's epitaph, Saturday's lists
and my cherished Ode to a Month of Sundays.

* *

This pain: a crowbar to the chest. Small men
in black suits at the meeting of my ribcage
are forcing a door, muttering in a language
without a word for *No*. Now I can say
how Tom Thumb felt in the giant's fist
and what the cut worm won't forgive,
what the vampire howls with the stake
to the far side of his screaming. This pain
begins at the horizon, it begins
promising only more of itself, then
down the distance's swift oncoming
takes on the sudden likeness of wolves
in a slick dark river of fur pouring east
through the breastbone, left at the rib,
bunched down the shoulder, the arm, elbow,
wrist, knucklebones and out down the fingers
gnarled all the way, and beyond

more wolves coming.
                    Then it stops
like a toothache lugged all weekend
at last to the dentist, folds to a bat
hanging upside down in the ribs' raft,
a far off murmur of wolves, a snarling.

* *

I have no beginning. I arrived
in a white room of frightened men
sweating it out in white sheets. Here
in my skull I've this voice: the prompt,
pilot and navigator, backseat driver
yelling what to do. And my father
the northern puritan nagging *Work.*
Do something useful, son. It began
being his voice but now it is mine,
the disease of the pale Europeans
with their spades and measuring rods.
It killed him. It will kill me.

Insomniac, all my life a rehearsal,
my heart counting time at its post
not to miss the very last moment –
the trumpets, the strutting horses,
the drums and the brass band's last
Abide with me falling all at once
from the world without one more word,
thereafter part of the dust on the landings,
the full stop any time now where
to cease must at last cease itself.

        hush, now.

Why not here as at the beginning, circled
by these good women, among these pillows
and these clean white sheets, – so much care,
so much love in the scrubbed soft fingers
of the nurses, all of them so many colours
that are all of them blue? Why not here
among these sweet blue lilies?

* * * *

I have no beginning. Each day
is a beginning, an ending, a victory.
Each day a defeat. When I sleep
it is far back in the cave of myself
and I bring nothing back but the dream
of the hollow tree of my own curled self.
Some days I hold one thought, the blackbird
on the chimney singing we say
his heart out across the roofs
and washing lines of London's east,
where I find myself again. This is
the summer of my unfinished symphony,
a life cut back to the domestic bone,
chasing flies out of the kitchen,
the cerebral existence of a sparrow
eating grains, nuts, bits of green.
So farewell to the dancing. No more
getting drunk with the lost boys
telling the old tales: *how I lost my heart,*
how it broke, bled, how I gave it away
you say *easily.* All these years
it was only the proud pump in my chest
signing in moment by moment. Now
it has missed some of its step. Now when I say
I love with my whole heart what you get
is bruised, scarred, some part of it dead now.

* * * * *

There were so many names, so many voices.
Now when I need it where is my voice,
for instance sitting in a train I try
counting my heart among so many beats,
and always my potential to drift off
into some other life and never come home.

Someone was here, where I am, the one
they call *the heavy breather, Sobersides.*
I have parts of his memory and think
he was more fun than I am, muttering
my way through the dark, frightening
the children. As for him he couldn't hear
what his heart said, too busy killing himself

and at the end with one last cigarette,
one last double and one last madman's dance
sang farewell the music. Telling his tale
a life he did not live he was never
at the event, at the feast with the candles.

Now wherever he is that I was, wrecked maybe
on some beach with the rest of the flyblown
plastic detritus, living under a rusty tub
with the name gone forever from its side,
when here I am answering his letters,
paying his bills, signing books he wrote,
picking up his pieces, sitting in his shed
all summer long, writing *Heart*
like the fennel root. Heart
like a great horseradish. Heart
like a loaf of hot bread new minted
from the oven, keep beating,
brave messenger, bearing news of yourself.

First echo

I recall the high trees rocking in the wind,
across the road where the soldiers drilled.
They learned their trades there, and went to war.
Beyond was unknown country, fields and distance
where the sun went out
                                        One day my shout
among the tall trees found its echo there,
bouncing my name back among the elms,
calling and calling at the house back
and a second out of time the voice of *not-me*,
repeating all I said though what I said
was only *I, I, I am...*

How does anyone write anything?
How do they begin, in what gesture,
in what moment of a prayer, the pen
to the paper? What would anybody say?

Braille transcripts

1

Winter comes to the northern plains,
winds tearing the landscape, searing
the leaves then stripping them. Rust
is on the dust, an edge on the sedge
and the party is truly over. Find me
if you can in all this whiteness, in
the cries of birds flying south, the
patterns frost makes on the window's
glass. I'm here, somewhere. Find me.

2

The octet for strings, then applause
like the rain. 'Rain falls every day
here in our lives, with fog from the
river but rain chiefly on this rainy
coast': the barman telling his tales
I listening to what I shall call his
Reflection of a Tenpin Bowler: under
his foot the bone growth and new hip
are one with the pelvic swirl, stop,
foot stamped down and away that ball
went into a full deck, he made money
that way, again turning to the optic
and repeating *but the rain, the rain
on this accursed coast.* St Petersburg
that's where he'd rather be, *one day*
he says. Just switch on the TV, plug
in the phone and the air conditioning
and bet down the line. *That's living*
he says. Away from the endless rain.

3

Simple returns: we plant snowdrops,
tulip, crocus and daffodils, against
spring. Tom-next-door's dead and his
apples sour, and Johnny-two-doors-up
was beaten and robbed, in this quiet
neighbourhood. So where is that song
I sang once, moments a bird homed in
the sky and the river in its valley?
Where did that poetry go to, a shore
of only the waves' long arrivals? It
grows late and darker in the year, I
grow older eating a poor man's feast
of beans for my supper, reluctantly.

4

Indian summer. The road flecked with
gold, the plane trees full of birds,
their songs flooding the sunset. 'My
heart is dying' I say, testing it on
the air's autumn breath. I can't see
myself in these thickets, in so many
voices I've lost my voice. The back-
yard fills with wind, with the odour
of mints, rosemary, a shock of white
heads is the cornflower. In the last
of the foxgloves a last brown bee is
still fumbling his music. Day by day
it grows earlier late, the day's end
is blue, and gets closer and closer.

The furniture game

She's far away, beyond seas and the mountains.
Her easy presence makes her absence difficult,
not my heart more fond. She's the good wood
of which this furniture is made, she's everywhere,
in old sweaters, things made easy with wear,
leaving her shoes around. That drives me crazy.
In old fiddles sleep the sweetest tunes, they say.
Oh my love, my lily, my songs of the nightingales,
my sweet magnolia, come round the mountain.

Epitaph for a gardener

All his life a soldier in the field
at war with the weeds, the grass
rooting back faster than he tore it up.
At peace now it blows over him: *green, green*.

The annunciation

Many have laboured to convey it:
this moment that will trouble
centuries to come.

She was spinning, according to some,
working a tapestry, taking a walk
in the cloister, or as Da Vinci has it
reading a book.
                     A dove or an angel
announces the news in a shaft of light
that is God's impregnating glance,
his most important announcement to date.

Here at any rate she looks properly
sceptical. Just as she might be
under such unexpected circumstance this is.

Venetian pieces

The Chamber of Torment

Outside men groan, caged in the square,
buried with their feet sticking up. In this room
the strappado has heard all their pleading,
the nailed planks have witnessed their replies.

It's all very simple: a plinth and a rope,
a long stem of agony hung from the roofbeam,
and the man drops, breaks, babbles whether he prays
hourly, at nightfall, or to the man in the moon.

Or whatever you wish, signors, I beg you
throw my brother in there behind the curtain,
take my friend Giovanni Giacomo who deserves it
for the money he's owed me these 15 centuries.

Casanova in the room of the Inquisitors

They take the blindfold off: wigs,
courthouse ritual, marble, polished wood.
Underfoot the black and white tiles
confuse the feet and trump the eye.

They will take you through the cupboard
to the rope, the hard boxes under the lead.
Does anyone here know you? Will anyone speak?
What is it you're accused of?

Love, I guess. Love brought me here
to confess all, answering *Yes* the dancer,
Yes the Armenian, *Yes* Edurne whose name
means *snow* and *Yes* the dark witch of Calabria.

But it's not what they want. They want
the names of my accomplices, my secret recipes,
who taught me to play so sweetly my instrument,
who taught me to whisper to make the clowns dance?

Sinistra

Packed arrows, bones in their boxes.
A horned wolf's head. Masks, silhouettes,
always the face behind the face another mask.
Egg white stones in the grass.
In the pine cone a tiny snake.
All over the honeycomb city of whispers
pale saints in wire haloes, rotting
in their boxes, holy arms, holy legs.

Take the left hand, through shadow,
the stopped door of water, the campo
of the church of Our Lady of the Dead End,
the magazine stand a cabinet of darkness
all through siesta, the birds asleep,
the book closed, speech cut in stone.
The city dreams itself on the slow tides,
imagines water that can be walked on.

In my dream I met a girl who said *Venezia:*
it means the place to come to, a dream
for those who do not dream. I believed
there was a time we were each other's star,
lovers in the long water, waist deep
working the estuary among the kelp beds,
rocked in the sea swell, centuries ago,
another life I never lived and never woke from.

Then a long cry ran down the alleys,
a bleak signal through the salizadas
of the window-shouters, generations fighting
over the squares, their shouts riding on the wind
across the Fondamente Nuovo from Dead City,
leaflike, whispering all the tears, howls,
groans and all there ever was to pray for
through the miserable ages: *pray for us.*

Round and around the Ghetto Nuovo,
repeating *our memory is your only grave.*
From here were taken all the Jews of Venice,
from the furnace to the furnace.
This is a cursed place in a landscape

of leaning towers that one day fall,
where men rose from the dumb sea to speak
yet said not much. Only the seabirds.

Only a ship's horn, rousing the afternoon,
thrashing of ropes and metal as the sea
sucks its timbers. Boats slip
their moorings, move on the water's glance.
The gondolas are water snakes, funereal
bent Venetian pricks, at night the shadow
of a shadow, clef of coming music, harness
of the ghosts of horses that they are.

And then a bell tells half the fourth hour
of the afternoon, the day begins again,
– two men at chess, a radio bursting briefly
into dancing music, through an opened shutter
a hand and a jug water the geraniums,
somewhere a piano plays a practice piece,
offstage a woman yawns, a cage bird sings,
an English voice says *but these are wild birds*.

The baron regrets

The light here. Sometimes
it is domes and clouds, sometimes water,
the oar's fin through the ocean's drowse.

I have not painted. Where I look
is everywhere a study in perspective,
the eyes' delight in their deception.

All afternoon boatmen walk to the horizon,
moving on the edge of dancing,
their speech always on the lip of song.

What could I add to this: yesterday
at sunset a proud woman on a bridge
singing aloud not for money but for love.

The wine's cheap. The waiters
flash me their smiles and sleek black bums,
counting the cutlery all through siesta.

I eat late and am steady by midnight,
weaving my way among reflections
home to the same dream: the city

adrift on its rafts, the weeds
in the bright sea choking the air,
fish belly-up and the city drowning at last,

these posts low in the water, clinging
much as they clung together, refugees
on the sandbanks, building with reeds.

Long ago. I've kept up my notebooks.
Otherwise a whole summer wasted in Venice,
the tracks of light across the distance.

Neapolitan interiors

Views around the bay

Far off now a city of apartments, passages
of ducted light the days grow older in.
A city of *why not?* and all the hours
hung bell by bell around the towns,
but the shaky earth is cracked and the core
jets out hot here. Some have little –
a chair on the street, a pack of cigarettes
to sell. Scent of basil, resin,
smell of fish, bread, stink of traffic
always on the move along the bay's eye
losing sight in the blue haze of itself
between the mountain and the bay.
See this and die.
                    Out on the night water
two men fish the dark, one with a light,
one a spear. Inland Orion glints,
clearing the cliff, where the dim lamps
shine all night in the house of the dead:
Giovanni et Famiglia, Rosaria, Longobardo,
all their children folded in the drawers
stacked to the roofbeam, each a candle,
each a bell's intermittent random tongue
counting in the saints, the packed
municipalities squabbling along the coast.

Ercolano's message

Begins father forgive me, today I learned
but one word *oziosamente*, asleep in the sun
among the brown stones, all the guides
to the buried town nagging in three languages.
I have been between life and life, stone
by stone in the rich dust where the lizards
are at home – Papa Lizard, his inamorata,
his busy mates and their many bambinos.

424

Where was wineshop and water gossip, oven,
mark one man left on another man's wall
that he owed him, some inscription to a tart
she's a sweet fig, a vine, a fruity lotus.
Caught side by side in the sudden dust:
old or young with their offspring, a slave
grinding his bad teeth, Pliny the Uncle,
townsmen, dead all as all the dead are.

Buried. Stopped rooms in which to fight,
make love, spin, dream or wake suddenly
to cockcrow and children or the other birds,
the long shush of the night sea, finished.
No one here but an old man with his ruins
muttering in the kingdom of the lizards
spent prayers to the failed gods: *nothing's*
sure nor long sacred. Message ends.

A traveller's question

I have been days, years on the road,
sinking in winter, dreaming of the south.
I am who sets out who never arrives,
arrives though he never departed, the self
always talking to the self. I am one
changed by a journey whose tale's never true.
Therefore who is it crosses the littoral,
the wind faintly with rosemary, at night
glimpses in the cold bouillon of stars
himself? I have grown weary being part
of God's interminable education. Again
the dark sisters whisper in the walls,
and again through the rocks the wanderer
Odysseus mast-lashed and mad unstops
his ears to the singers on the wind,
all the songs on the radio telling him
nothing so well endures as the ruin of things,
a young woman lights up an old man's dark
but it won't last. Not much changes.
Whatever set the slow stars in the sky,
the Plough and the Pole to steer by

and all the blue jewels of the moon
doubled in the sea with the evening star,
more to the point will I ever get home?

Postscript: nunc pro tunc

Roman, I'd retire to the coast from things
public, – greed, power, the grim lusts
of the merely ambitious, all the sad wants
most men have merely to be remembered.

Devious or discontent, our doings
shabby deals in an alley, cutting throats
for loose change, thereafter soon enough
retching up again on the flophouse floor.

I would retire to Ercolano, where I'd be
resident cynic, the large events so far
beyond my notion or my wish. Slowly
to my own design I'd build a good house.

Between the mountain and the sea, my nets
slung under the olives, I'd fish a little,
sleep much, contemplate the grape, take
a long view of the town's doings and write.

The magic of Poland

One:

the coast a long ribbon of string,
green earth, woods. Then immigration,
not user-friendly.

Try to find a bar, and when you find one,
a beer. Try to understand the money
you got for your money. Stay warm.

Take a long tour of the monuments:
these are to all the many years the ravens ate,
the long depredations of the wolf, the bear,
the arrival of the Adam Smith Institute.

I write you, love, from Nova Huta,
from Kraków the soured beauty, another night
at the Palace of Culture I'll get weepily drunk
for you and for the magic of Poland. *Na Zdrowie.*

Two, the waitresses in Old Town

They are discussing shoes, footwear, feet,
limping and clucking like chickens
picking over their patch but too old
for the pot now. He wants her maybe
once a year at Christmas. By now
he'll be home asleep on the couch
or dead drunk on the floor. Her friend,
she had a pair of sandals, perfect,
but they stopped making them, closed
the factory. He doesn't love her any more.

Three, the music of the Emperor

Farms and unfenced fields,
villages, chained cattle,
turkeys, road signs
reading *Muzeum Oswiecim*:

Auschwitz-Birkenau.
Flat grey earth.
Pits, drains, factories.
The machineries of death.

Work will make you free,
Anna Sophia from Hamburg,
Jelena from Kraków,
tenants of the Ghetto Nuovo.

So close, far away as the moon,
as all the lives all the dead lived.

An offshoot of the rail,
tracks ending in grass, chimneys,
a tangle of old wire,
a pond of white human ash.

Four, the photograph

Time stops here.
And I am not in it. These chipped bowls,
piles of clipped hair, tangle of spectacles
are here for no one.

Beyond this moment nothing ever changes
but the yellow light across the fields,
bleached in the snapshot, fading out, the corner
of the picture turning inward where it burns:

a field of brick chimneys, the horizon
dirty smoke. Nothing beyond this:
a deathless landscape
with the heart burned out, the smile intact.

Monument

In which the bronze mouth forever opens,
a stone calling for stone, flags,
marches, bullets. *Freedom* he calls it
in the black metalled letters next his initials
chiselled into the bottom left hand corner.
The date. A handful of old flowers.

In which his raised arms are the hands
of the ventriloquist forever talking to himself,
the ego telling itself the same lie:
palm out in the signal to be still and listen,
the other a fist and a finger pointing
into the future, which completely ignores him.

Zoo Station midnight

Drunks glitter in their liquids, fish
far down water where the light dies
on their armour of metal plates and crutches.

Outside in the city flowers of smashed glass,
the faithful in black spider armbands are back,
and the firestorm raging these forty years.

The animals wander the trapped streets,
furiously wounded. Here comes the midnight train
from Friedrichstrasse, from Warsaw, from Moscow.

It arrives in a flurry of flags and snow
with wolves howling, taking the width of the night
to get here. It arrives dragging the sheets

of its landscapes, – peasants, fires, shoes, no shoes,
speeches, snags of barbed wire, bayonets,
the apple blossoms of spring, the marsh air.

Late again he says, the stranger at my elbow,
bastards, sucking on a beer. In his black coat
and white hair he may be my double, my dark brother.

He knows a bar, a taxicab, a place to stay,
a woman, it takes a little paper money,
a word from him and we'll be out of here and into history.

Katja's message:

> 'This sentence has no meaning,
> but what are you going to do about the crocodiles?'

In Berlin, attempting sleep, this sentence
without meaning keeping me awake;
one by one the hours climb the clock,
labour as slowly down the other side.

The silence at the border is absolute,
full of watching darkness, wire and neon,
the dark trees either side without wind
or weather or the baying of dogs.

It goes on and on, the silence, a lake
without a name where legends surface:
a bead of air, a log of wood, a skin,
an eye blinked open in the dark.

It is the crocodile, easing down
into another sleepless night
along the border, here beside the wall,
where still this sentence has no meaning.

The Wall

There is the one side and the other,
and between there is the wall. Each side
has its monuments, its flags, its currency,
its bulletholes, its notions of the other.

Over here we say *the beaten in the lobby*
of the crestfallen. Some days we pity them.
Over there they watch us through binoculars.
Over there they call us fascists.

There, here is *over there*, and their maps
of where we are are coloured white,
as ours are of them. No one
over there can fall in love over here.

Here the street ends and there's wall,
and on the other side the same street:
tramtracks, kerbstones, streetlights
coming on, pedestrians about their business.

They do not wave or look back. It is
as if we were each others' ghosts. Either side
history comes with a wall round it.
We are each other's terra incognita.

Somewhere there's a piano playing boogie,
and on this side a late-night argument
strung out with booze and bamboozle
till the word gets lost in the many

qualifications of itself, and it all ends
in tears. Over there the long silence
broken by dogs at each change of shift,
some border guard on his two-stroke.

And everywhere it seems a night bird
fills the dark with long pulses of his song.
He doesn't care to be one side or the other.
His song is all of him.

I understand where this late night music
of a sad piano is coming from.
I understand where that long
leashed baying of manhounds is coming from.

But I don't understand where the nightingale
in these long pulls of music through himself
and the buildings and the trees
or from which side of anywhere he is singing.

Passing through

Travellers in a new country, arriving
without change for the phone, between trains,
just passing through. *You should have called*
distant friends say. *Ich verstehe Bahnhof* I reply.

Then we meet, drinking in another doomed city,
down streets named for dead soldiers,
victories understood only in the vernacular,
and we with our own debased currency another history

glimpsed in the driving mirror, central Europe
on fast forward: printout, flags, bullets,
disbelief on the faces of the tyrants,
end of system without escape clause. Walls fall and men.

As ever we're struck by odd presences –
six porcelain urinals in a row, their mouths open,
the white tiled wall, in the half-open door
a brush waiting to be used, our faces in the glass.

There is a perfume called Sorrow.
There are bars, twilight, the sweet dark music of the city,
blossom, the faces of women, but is there time
to write the book of deeds before it's out of date?

Chinese whisper

I am a labourer on the Chinese Wall, one of thousands. Far from where I was born, I do not think of it. I was brought here with my neighbours, and set to building the wall. Our life is work, rice, sleep. All day from dawn to dusk I take my place in the line of men labouring up and down the mountains, heaving one by one the rough chiselled blocks of stone from the man on my left to the man at my right shoulder. I am indistinguishable from either one, my thoughts could be either of theirs. When one of them dies he is replaced, when I die the line will move up in my place, and the stones go on climbing the mountain, assembling into the wall. Only the wall grows, but we will never see it. Ahead of us, empty country; behind us the wall, perfect, new, cresting the ridges, enclosing the wastes, dividing the farmlands from the desert. We eat, work, work, eat, sleep, moving over the country with our many arms and legs like a long dragon. When at dark we sleep, exhausted, our sleep is the hard sleep of the same heavy stones moving up the mountain, down the other side. And memory. Asleep, still handling the stone blocks, I sometimes glimpse far away, impossible now, red willows by a river, a fish leaping, white lily flowers in the water.

After Brecht

In the end it is Joachim with his maps,
Thora in her garden: roses, lilies,
the scents she desires so she grows them.

It is the sunlight, high
through the tall evergreens, the birdsong,
the afternoon wind in this place, and our voices.

Telling our tales. We grew up on the other side
of a long long war we all lost.
Years have gone by. All our lives have.

With songs, sometimes music, children,
some love in this old cold world,
years of many letters and a few kisses.

It will always be so: this moment,
the sunlight, the long afternoon, the blackbirds,
Joachim with his maps, Thora in her garden.

FROM

TENDER TO THE
QUEEN OF SPAIN

(1993)

Tender to the Queen of Spain

In the foreground there is the large row boat upside down on
trestles, being scraped and repainted by two men in the working
sunlight of the harbour, a spring afternoon, in Weymouth. Seen
upside down, so that my head must tip to read it, its name says
it's the tender to a larger boat, not visible anywhere amongst the
other boats of the small port – lighters, trawlers, coastal barges,
fishing trip and pleasure boats, yachts, old coalers painted up with
their brown sails slack in the intermittent wind, sail boats tinkling
like a mad orchestra of only cymbals. Our boat is not amongst
them. She is out chugging on the huge sea, with an unknown
cargo for unknown destinations, for who knows how long, and all
we know of her is her name: *The Queen of Spain.*

Milly's end

She died. Worse was her undoing,
the tongue's unravelling, the memory's flat battery

coughing in the night *someone has taken my orange juice,*
someone has stolen my shoes. Up,

down, either was difficult, *it's not*
her any more I hear my voice say again

through the narrowing months of her vision
that could see bright clear to a winter day.

There was a war, she worked in the harvest
of wet beets, soldiers came in and out her gate,

in and out of her kitchen, hot white mugs
in their hard cold hands.

Where are they all now? she asks.
How many ever came back?

The other elegy

...i.m. Asa *(foolish enough*
to have been a poet) Benveniste, the tall
skinny tree of you felled in the churchyard
at Heptonstall among the Queen Anne's Lace.

It was a Friday, it was the thirteenth,
sunset, Easter, and you you would have
timed it differently, you would have sat
right down and writ yourself a letter.

This is for all the lives we did not live,
mooching in old harbours with the tides,
driving home across the rainswept moorland,
drunk, remembering Brooklyn, Amsterdam.

At the border will be stones and again
white birches, the one magpie of sorrow,
you in your black cap surprised and amused,
you with two flowers where the road runs out.

The painter Mannfred Otto

He is a painter, time indeterminate. Europe.
Then. Also a husband, father, neighbour.
Burgher of the town he was born in, a citizen.

Self-portraits, mostly. Masks, in various light,
shadow so, various moods, different stages of his life.
Certain moments he was drawn to paint:

his message to the woman he'd marry he'd not met yet,
in his hand a sprig of rosemary. A flat faced boy,
the young soldier, a wanderer, mid-life, old age.

The day he won the old quarrel with Sartorius.
The years of invasion, famine, the great death.
Mother, wife, children, all at once gone.

What he couldn't paint: the black rump of night
where there's no point to the dawn, no purpose
for him in the sun's ever again coming up.

And the outrage of birdsong, the dawn chorus
a panic in the chest, acid on the tongue.
And who let all this sudden white light in here?

Self portrait in shadow. Self portrait in sorrow.
Self portrait with fruit and flowers.
Self portrait with instruments and cats.

Slowly: outside events: astrolabe, compass,
half finished block of stone, the texts
in the vernacular he lived by, a white bird.

Sheaf of gathered wheat. A stuck pig.
Baskets of dark grapes. Like so. On the hills bonfire smoke,
autumn woods, towers of the city. Cloud etched to rain.

Jack remembering

Out walking the hill's side, the wind here
smashes the saplings, no trees,
no tree cover, nowhere to hide now,
the old stones taken for walls and roadwork.

Above these grey towns, streets I don't know,
a corner the road goes where trees gathered
that are gone now. So much sky then,
the stars scattered milk, the silence.

I lived beyond this, in my own house,
with a yard and garden, trees, chickens, a pig,
two goats and the white doves, all my days
I made a rough worsted, the same gun metal grey.

Home from the wars I was handsome and workshy,
a green stone on a ring was mine once,
that came from the Nile. Another took it,
thereafter into the ground with him.

I was a good soldier, bright buttons,
bulled webbing and boots, knife crease
in tunic and trews, I was always on parade,
on the march, on manoeuvre, on a drunk, or asleep.

No, I'm not mad. I have this wound, Doctor,
I call Ivan the Terrible, it bleeds when the wind's
from any direction, winter and summer. It weeps
but I don't know for what grieving.

What else I recall are tiny white roses
growing in the Basques' country of the tongue.
And wayside herbs: feverfew, yarrow,
soldier's wort, all good for something.

Brother Scratchwood

Where I am: in the far black of the cave
of my self, in the dark that was never lit,
which is to say nowhere, among the unwritten,
the *agrapha*, who live in the mountains
and pay no taxes and therefore do not exist.

My life an alphabet of edges,
smoke around a taper, my eyes are not good,
only a vague ache now where I used to be.

I've hung out in the empty spaces between lives,
through slow winter dusks, decade by decade
through seasons of nothing but patience patience,
in the nowhere wherein I imagined *nothing*.

And went mad with the thought of it.
God knows there's not much of me,
light enough to be someone, anyone by,
peering into a name *Brother Scratchwood*, for instance.

Who waits the way iron waits, and the stars,
the way flame sleeps in the wax, the cast
in the dice, mumbling my interminable prayers,
kyrie eleisons to my own wayward heartbeat.

Night after night, all night long,
my arse crossed on the misericorde's edge,
where Moses crossing the Red Sea sniffs
the wind of thin farts come of piety's porridge.

And that's all there is of me, stoney hours
left and right of me my brothers on our knees
calling à cappela in the empire of the dark
crowding to one candle's flame. Amen.

One of Milly's gifts

Sometimes one of Milly's gifts gets drunk,
makes a fool an absolute asshole of himself,
comes home late and stormy and breaks things,
mostly his own things. And next morning

can't remember any of it. He's sorry
but he doesn't know what for. He can't tell
who the enemy is and he doesn't have any friends.
There's a list hereabouts and he's not on it.

His subscription's cancelled. In the dawn,
sleepy, bladder heavy, the first of the birds
waking in the blue light of his brain,
he gets up, discovers just all the books

floating in the bathtub, and the kitchen
covered in broken blue and white crockery
and the wife of those years saying *Why?*
Why do you do these dreadful things?

Three in a play

Three cardplayers
in a game of three:
Stick, Twist, Bust.

Three lords of the dance,
Thump, Boot, Headbutt,
rough tongued and tattooed, three liebknechte.

Freelance, hitmen, anyone's.
Anyone: that huddle at the door,
three fiddlers about to play the Fire Hose Reel.

Three men in a tub.
Three drunks in a pub.
Three dark eyed assassins.

The three gold-tongued knights of the court
of King Arthur, three horsemen
who are Dürer's knight, death, the devil.

Umbilicus, the young naval attaché,
Scrotum, the wrinkled old retainer,
Sputum, a Flemish outcast.

Three separate faces
on the night bus, that follow you home,
and know where you live now.

Woman without a name

Passing on the stairs, what to say to her,
lost in the blue hazy spaces
of the beautiful distance of herself? Say:
You're very kind. And very beautiful.

Decades ago, in an ill-lit guttural city,
where I, exiled, cold, smoking my black cheroots,
stalked the winter park, feeding the water birds,
my academic study life at the water margins.

And that's the whole of the affair, her heels
clacking up the stairwell, the elevator
out again, the winter night, the corner
where she turns clockwise out of my life forever.

It's late, and this is where the door turns in.
Her name her name if I could think of it.
The luxury of a name, and through it swifts,
in the high trees the rooks squabble.

Coffee, little cakes. I take her picture out
remembering her as she was not, forget-me-nots
knotted in her fingers, frowning
into the old box brownie, so long ago.

Part of something else

Turalura she sings to herself, breathing
in, out, him staring into the fireback
numbering his grumbles, his what he now
only wished he'd said then but thought
too late, later, the moment gone.

Turalura, turalura. As for her
the bread she bakes is soon stale,
his side of the bed always lumpy,
her sex cold dry inhospitable, then
his inventory of misery begins, *cunt cunt.*

Turalura, lureia. She knows the moment
he's wound himself up and the wire hisses out of him,
taut, barbed, edged, and it's thereabouts
she'll go up, go to sleep in her white sheets
mumbling *Is there any wonder? Turalura.*

Later in the tea-room

I could believe, a moment or two,
there in the cathedral with the candles
and soaring through the tall stones
the music of the choir and the organ.
And all those dear dead battered bishops.

I think Heaven must be like this:
feathery quiet and old flowers,
weightless light and long webby nothings,
stones made of cloud, soft rain and warm snow,
ice cream you'd never get sick of.

Consider John Longland, 1521-47
Bishop of Lincoln, Confessor
to Henry the Eighth. And consider
what griefs what regrets what bottomless bragging
he must lie with, centuries thereafter.

The blue time

Saturday the storm. She left early,
in her pink shoes skipping down the road.
She'd dreamed of candyfloss, roses,
her mother's wild chrysanthemums.

Time for a walk and a stare at nothing.
Time for tea and hot buttered scones, a turn or two
through the wild wind of the garden
savouring lavender, thyme, angelica.

It's the blue time in the season's swift changes,
flagged once by the first cornflower,
twice by the first blue star of the borage,
a message to foxgloves and the tall white daisies:

solstice and midsummer, harvest then winter,
when the alphabet will have run out of letters,
and the year that's halfway over
still has no direction. And the bank won't wait.

Accounts

The noose tightens. How much for each foot of rope,
each inch of neck, and the boxwood coffin,
who paid for lunch and was drink taken,
and how much to pay the hangman's wages?

Sir: my business was slow, my cash flow
sluggish, my credit withered long ago,
my only product in these words that light me
dimly through the dark not in much demand.

And I've no other skill. Words, figures: cold,
untouchable and abstract, logging receipts, payments,
goods in goods out, plus, minus. I might have been
bookkeeper in some distant trading station,

Reykjavik it will be called, forty years
shivering in the tight mouthed service
of the Northmen, entering and tallying,
and that because I was a boy who wrote.

Meanwhile to one side, late, through the long north light
I write the plot later called *Hamlet*:
a brother's poison and a wife's betrayal,
the son's dilemma as to vengeance, justice, silence,

and the last act always bloody carnage.
Then back to the profit and the loss
of journeys, dreams, chance encounters
with the other strangers, till all the words

that wondered at the world came down to this:
final demands from the Department of Wishful Thinking,
the bottom line, the exact amount now due
I cannot pay.

Brief encounter on the Yellowdog

Our man is sitting at a bar among reflections,
bits of himself he glimpses in the mirrors,
mopping the spilt drink of all his life,
rings on his fingers, keys at his hip, labels
in his lapels and maybe one day he'll be one
of the many tales he tells, he'll settle down
in far off Aberdeen and write a paperback,
he'll call it *Lost in Space* by Justin Thyme.

Outside: Aldgate in the rain. In here the music
is some song of a lost love, the barman says
ask me what you want, ask me if I'm working.
Dry Chablis she will have, he a half a bitter.
The trains are late, the signals on the blink.
They talk of distance, valleys of bells.
The deep sleep of wine and woodsmoke. Figs.
Apples. Vines climbing the Tuscan sunlight.

Nothing's happening as usual with everything.
Everyone as usual is somewhere else, these two
exploring each other and the Algarve,
the bartender back home on the Boyne,
the music somewhere on the road and our man
Curleytoes is rafting down the river
with the painted hostiles all around,
and that's the moment all their eyes meet.

It's called the here & now. He belts out
Oh the times we had below the snowline,
we lived the life of the river there,
women sharp and skinny as the reeds, our kids
spooning up the boney soup of winter.
Oh I was never sober, I was never drunk,
I stayed out of the army & out of the nick.
So don't collide with me I'm a solid object.

On the Yellowdog it's winter again, the music
in his brain wolf and coyote, a wheel spinning
round and around in its rut. *Oh Billy*
can your drool, can you sit up on a stool,
can you piss into the pot Little Billy?
This customer has eaten too many tomatoes.
He is no longer in touch with his despatcher.
What he has is a bad case of mad social worker.

Let's call it failed author syndrome. He has a dream.
He can see it all the time on the big screen
in his head. He'd settle for a dry goods store
somewhere at the edge of town, day by day
adding up the takings, home by 6 to the wife
and the Yellowdog River but it's time,
friend, time to go now, in the piddling rain.
Time to disappear to Planet Zero.

The bad news

And so it comes to this: didn't get the job,
didn't get the loan, didn't get the fifteen quid
my brother Novak owes me nine years now,
and don't qualify for the dole, so I quit.

Never a lucky ticket in the state lottery,
never me shouting *bingo bingo bingo*,
and once again I didn't win the pools,
and I'm getting old for this, too old.

Everyone here is dreaming of somewhere else.
Everyone here works at the heritage museum,
visited by people they can't somehow like
and their bossy knowledgeable children.

Not a lot to dream: age & Sir Death,
farewell to the stars, the swallows and the afternoon;
the young are swarming in over the beach stones,
dispossessed, impatient. And that's the good news.

So all the treaties are off and I'm mean as muddy water.
This is bad news day, this is a no deposit no return day,
and though I'm prudent as the Kings of Prussia
truth is I'm an act of desperation turning grey.

Film noir

Titles that are more properly stage directions. Then glimpses, snap-shots, faces on streets, in doorways, in photographs and magazines, in films, in dreams, in shadow, in broad daylight: the occasions of their faces, what they say.

We're still sifting the evidence, bits of film, pages from books, manuals of instruction, catalogues, documents that have all been through the shredder. With their customary revolutionary zeal our students piece them together, patiently, haphazardly, matching letter with alphabet, line with line, a grand spaghetti of internal memoranda, minutes, shorthand notes, requisitions, letters, rosters, countersigned orders, demands, receipts, lists of stores. Ours is a strange archaeology, often inaccurate, barely articulate, the meanings of words forever shifting in translation, frame never matching frame, page page, so there is often no continuity, no sequence, no satisfyingly continuous narrative, indeed, sometimes no apparent meaning at all in these activities other than our persistence, without which nothing makes any sense at all.

Beginning again with a line heard in the street

Beginning anywhere at all with anything,
overheard on the underground: *Birth control?*
She never had any. A note taped to a window:
lost keys ask inside or *just get me a taxi*,
and the door smacked shut. Words found
on water I ferried home, subject to scribble
and sea bile. Yes I vaguely remember Amsterdam.

Today begins my letter to the Galicians,
dated this day on the Greenwich meridian,
Lord Alfred older now home from the grand tour,
confronting at last the blankness of the page,
an empty blue whose sky will surely fill,
a mouth wide open saying anything at all:
last seen by the river talking to a man.

Another day another dollar

Rails and their stations, nights, trains,
home again home again to this sweet black coffee,
here in my own small corner with my pussycat.
Let me tell you why I don't like this music.
Ah to be in England, the sweet impossibility
of communication, all this English babble
babble babble: *bad dog, keep off, no ball games.*

I recall the quiet Amish in their buggies,
carpenters who paint their front doors blue
for their marriageable daughters, living
along the borders of states. For them exile
is just across the river at Auntie Mattie's,
and everywhere the same elegant white birches,
through the mist the deer on delicate tall hooves.

Scenes from metropolitan life

I have been conversing with my old mate,
Andrew-by-the-Wardrobe, one day they say
he'll be a saint among the saints, mumbling
through the traffic and the office blocks
with all he owns in fifteen plastic bags,
and he the curator of abandoned churches,
his simple prayers the sounds stars make.

And yet with me all he ever talks is horses,
horses and beer. And women. How he loved
dancing with strangers, how he covets them still,
their sleek loveliness, knowing they won't last,
won't stay, roses in the rain, laughter
at the stair-end, leaving their shampoos
in the bathroom, and their pink aromas.

The lives of the saints

This one with the tight eyes, *Lorenzo*
he calls himself, *the Magnificent*,
chewing at the inside of his lip,
keeping his act up. All day on the bridge
in the alcove built for a saint he's there
with his singsong *change, cambio,*
wechsel, drogga, wearing Dante's face
and the comic's wall eye leading off
into the sky as he lifts your wallet,
and it's your own fault, tourist.

There is the long life of the window,
the interminable history of a doorway
that opens into poplared distance –
the Arno I had dreamed of, the old light,
some comfort in the furniture of time,
a little continuity perhaps. And there's
Lorenzo, sharp eyed and finger quick,
here where he's always been upon the bridge,
believing as he does in shorter odds
and a free market economy. Him I don't trust.

The maker of fakes

He opens his hands, shrugs. He says
What I make is all fake, there's no
song and dance. Let's say it's a Thursday.

We are walking down into the city
through the late night cars, drunks,
the cleaning squad in yellow dayglo.

Let's say the ambulance is wailing
its two notes *poor boy, poor boy,*
bleeding, dying. Let's say his name

is Leonardo, the maker of instruments,
all fake, a man I seldom meet, for both us
this is how it is here: grainy, fleeting.

He continues: *As to this instrument*
by which I am accused yes it is my making
though how became it a Capela, so sold
and listed, why that I cannot tell you.

Johannes from Dresden

A tall lamp. My face I bear high
through the strange world, a standard.
This face from the Thirty Years War
it is ordinary, a copy of thousands.

The only one I have to look out from.
Faces like mine framed in this yellow hair
died in thousands in the firestorm of 1945
sent by your Bomber Harris. They died

the deaths of the snails, of the ants,
the woodlice they shared the space with.
The flies. Thank you. I will not take a drink.
Not now. Not this time. Perhaps again.

Insomnia 1, 2, 3

Sometimes you can knock yourself out
taking whatever it takes to get wherever it is
and you do it, for hours, and for hours
you try out the trick called not being there
and maybe you sleep and maybe you drift

but you wake anyway on a dead chicken pillow
with a rat in your brain and a bat in your mouth
and though you clean each one of your teeth,
paste on a face that will just about do,
you still can't remember still can't recall
the numbers and names of each drop of the rain.

Something is missing, something is wrong:
that stain on your shirt, is it yours?,
that dark in your face, that trace of a voice
overheard at the moment you dived into silence
out of the clock-driven bird balmy universe
back of the Nostar Hotel of night plumbing and thumps –
that voice that said but what did it say, those words
those beautiful shards, they won't be back now.
Think. Drink hot black tea, black coffee.
Think of the sea. Think of the sweet shift of wheat
with the wind gone through it, just as the sea is.

The emigrant

A hundred miles from home, by the road
the crow's heavy alighting, the first buds
of spring yellowing towards the south.
My name is Stickincraw, my black looks
a mirror of the landscape, all around me
the same rain-stippled misery, northern uplands
I have prowled grinding out my excuses,
my fury at dumb rocks, sheep, bracken,
my short and stocky people, always a wild
mad strand of hair in the long east wind,
all my days it seems. Oh I worked,
mending wall, hedging and ditching
with my father's tools. But the worm
is in them now, and I am leaving.

Filmclip: Leningrad, October 1935

Dark comes early, and wet snow.
The citizens hurry from work,
scarfed, buttoned, thinking of supper,
the tram clanking and squealing
in whose glass an arm has wiped
a V of lit space wherein smoke,
old and young wrapped for winter,
eyes focussed somewhere ahead,
dreaming perhaps of a sausage,
of bread, coffee, a warm bed,
a bullet in the back of the brain.
Then they're gone. Next comes
the future. It looks like the past.

A survivor's memoir

(after Jerzy Kmiecik)

Another day on the slow trains south,
yellow sand to the sky's distant edge
then the River of Mystery brought us
to *Ak Metchet*, the White Palace, called
after the comrades came through Kazakhstan
Kizil Orda, the Red Capital, its names
at the station painted one over the other.

Here nothing to eat therefore nothing to steal.
And so to Tashkent that means Stone City,
Samarkand biscuit yellow, still in my dreaming.
I was by then again without shoes, a hole
the wind poked. That was 1942, the spring,
years from home, prison wire, prison trains,
a few necessary words the heart remembers.

By the Master of Jakabfalva, 1480

It is a wild place beyond the town wall:
the moment between moments when the blade
slits these two in their shifts into saints,
one already to his eternity of *Hallelujah*,
the other, Josias, James, brave before the blow.
Their faces say they thought as much.

Hooded, the two officials barely look,
each the shamefaced witness of the other,
come to see the job done, sign the paper,
make their report and turn into stones.
At the centre the executioner in black,
the ballet of his legs dancing to the blade.

No reply from the East

The mail addressed *Occupant* returns *Gone*,
all night the phone rings, no one answers,
at the stair's end again laughter, thuds,
then *Christ Almighty* they were saying

in those upraised fists of stone. By morning
they have renamed the streets, the wings
are missing from the statue of Victory,
the currency abandoned. And no bread.

So who were they to be in any case –
sour children forever in the blighted garden,
sweet innocents the others laughed at,
an embarrassment to their grandchildren?

I send you these letters I get no replies,
I tell you my secrets they're all of them lies.

His epistle to the Tatars

Friend from a distant country,
Asia and its horsemen. Elegant,
the white birches, through the white mist.

Last night I dreamed of Russia,
snow and a slow train to the mountains,
the taiga cluttered with plinths,
empty pillars, monuments to the empire
of electricity and state power and concrete.
In the high cold a man suddenly said
in plain English *but we're always alone.*

So now what, mon ami, now the planet's broken
and the People's Republic of Paradise kaput,
now the frontier is everywhere and everyone
on it a stranger? In my case I suspect
I have come to the end of my saying,
whatever that wildness was, and doubt
what I saw when I saw in such moments
lost itself in the photograph, faded out
among the vocabularies.

      Inshallah.

God willing we'll be here when God willing
you return. And if not, when this face
I wear won't be my own may you think of me
sitting in a café, some place the lights
burn late till someone blows them out.

Poem ending in frogs

Meanwhile in the lands to the east, business
or no business or no business at all, no work
and the bread and jam factory closed down,
its redundant angels shaving their skulls
and it's Siegheil season again, old footage
with its soundtrack of broken bottles.

As usual it's raining on one side of the road,
there's forty years of ruin on the other,
and an ageing man is leaning into the wind
walking West with a dewdrop on his nose
halfway on the long road to Paris
from Novisibirsk, halfway through his life.

Here nothing and silence and listening to blackbirds,
the window blinds shuttering, wittering
in the hot wind of the time of the clowns
with Kalashnikovs, whispering *staatsicherheits
sicherheits staasi staasi*, still listening, adrift
in the pollen heavy air. Or they're hiding in the swamp
with the frogs, and round their necks bells
that don't ring, whistles that don't blow any more.

Here the Plough swings overhead and all night
in and out of the water of moon and mosquitos
the frogs make frog speech, soliloquy and chorus
of *You. Yes you. Oh you. You you you. You. You.*

You and you and you and you and you and you and you.

Essential Serbo-Croat

Guraj	Push
Pomozi mi	Help me
Boli	It hurts
Boli me	I have a pain
Boli me ovdje	I have a pain here
Bole me grudi	I have a pain in my breast
Bole me prsa	I have a pain in my chest
Boli me oko	I have a pain in my eye
Boli me stopalo	I have a pain in my foot
Boli me glava	I have a pain in my head
Hitno je	It's urgent
Ozbiljno je	It's serious
Boli me ovdje	It hurts here
Boli puno	It hurts a lot
To je jaka bol	It's a sharp pain
To je tupa bol	It's a dull pain
To je uporna bol	It's a nagging pain
Večinom vremena	Most of the time
Vrti mi se u glavi	I feel dizzy
Zlo mi je	I feel sick
Slabo mi je	I feel weak
Nije dobro	It's no good
Izgubio sam sve	I have lost everything
Ne mogu vam pomoči	I can't help you

Lovesong for Kate Adie

Wherever it's bad news is where she's from –
a bronze leathery sort of lady, dressed for disaster's season,
a tough mouth woman, and like me a nighthawk. Ah, Katie,

reporting from the barbed wire rims of hell,
Katie at the barricades I dream of nightly, her voice
a bell in the desert wind, her hair blown which way.

It's true she loves it out where the disputed air
is vicious with shrapnel, bullet stung, the night's
quick stink of sulphur, flies, dead camels, terror.

But I don't mind now if she never comes back to me,
so long as she's happy. The night in her is enough,
that long-ago voice sets my gonads galloping.

Sure I'm afraid for her and pray every evening at 6
for her flight to some quiet place, cool nights
and nightingales between earthquakes and insurrections.

There we meet again, the night bright with stars:
Plough, Pleiades, Pole Star. She drinks, laughs
her special laugh, turns to go. We fall into bed.

We fuck all night, Katie & me, I never flag,
she never wearies, we're drunk on whisky and each other
and sweet fresh rocky and who cares it's Thursday?

She's there for me. I'm here for her. Any day of the week.

The fat man's movie

I can see it now: a story about rich people,
a saga of three cars and two swimming pools,
the brother with too many wives, too many kids
who hate him already and all of them too much money.

Everyone else is a walkon, an easy sucker,
protagonists played by bad actors, a soap
that will run and run through prime time,
a blockbuster: plot, title: *The Fat Man's Tale*.

He starts out a poor refugee, an orphan
running before old grey footage of the war,
singing to himself *one ball, two small, none at all*.
He is a hero. He is given a medal. And so forth.

He goes bad, lives a swindler's life, a conman's,
a liar, a bully, a cheat, steals everyone blind.
At the end of his twisted rope he takes to the sea
in his private boat, calls up his private jet

for one last salute to his fat greedy vanity,
one last flypast, one last upright two fingers
to the universe and to you and to me. Remember
he's out there on the ocean and no one is looking,

no one to envy him, none to impress. And then
he slips off the boat and bobs off on the sea,
a fat drowned crook winched out of the water
and bundled offstage, swiftly buried in the holy city.

Probably in three parts. Coltrane for the lead,
to be played with deep integrity. Faye
to play the woman who tries to save him, the angel
weeping in the last reel, on the Mount of Olives.

Task 17

1 Remove webbing
2 Release smock waist velcro fasteners
3 Decontaminate gloves
4 Raise smock hem above trouser waistband
5 Untie braces
   Pull clear of loops
   Tie ends together
6 Release trouser waistband velcro fastener
7 Pull trousers down to knees
8 Decontaminate gloves again and remove them (inners included)
9 Store gloves in pocket
10 Adjust inner clothing
   Crouch and reach round behind to pull braces to one side
11 Defecate
12 Stand up
   Adjust inner clothing
   Decontaminate hands
13 Replace gloves
   Adjust nuclear biological chemical clothing

Practice
Read the study notes

Practise the procedures for urination and defecation wearing the full kit

Urination and defecation should only be attempted in areas set aside for the purpose

Women should follow the procedure for defecation for both bodily functions

Toilet paper must be protected from contamination

There are modified procedures for urination and defecation in the Arctic. If you are equipped to operate in the Arctic check with your NBC instructor for details of the modified drill

Tasks 17 and 18 from the British Army Nuclear Biological Chemical Warfare Training Manual *Survive to Fight* (D/DAT/13/33/18, Army Code 7133)

Task 18: The unmasking procedure

What you have to know and do

You have to:

- Know the general procedure for unmasking

- Carry out the sniff test

Positive identification

Their eyes they were grey blue they were black nothing.
One had a scar a burn a birthmark one an earring one a tattoo
dotted across through over his neck and the legend *cut here*.
That makes two were there two was it 3? One with the headbutt
one with the fists and the finger rings one with a fancy blade.
One a white male one a girl one something quick I didn't see.
One a bully one a sissy and one who was an absolute bastard.
One with a knife one a razor one with a baseball bat.
One that wept the other one screaming and screaming
at the same time someone someone else laughing out loud.
I found pain pain however when wherever it comes hurts.
They all yelled the same kind of words you know them
the same mad anger the same eyes the same dead smile
the same fury at someone long ago dead yesterday perhaps.
One was white one black one some other shade of human.
I recall as I fell for the umpteenth last maybe time
my thought here in this great multi-ethnic society
you can be beaten and robbed you can die by all sorts
for all sorts of reasons for none by all sorts of exotics.

The Chicken Variations

Chicken calling:

Whisky Oscar Chicken. Whisky Oscar Chicken
calling Foxtrot, come in Foxtrot.

This is Whisky Oscar Chicken
calling Foxtrot, come in Foxtrot.

Chicken faith:

The word was let there be chicken.
Before the chicken was the chicken,
before the egg was the egg,
from the beginning of the word the word was chicken.

And before that the word was egg.
And before that the word was still egg.
And before that the great sky chicken
who is the rooster and hen mother of us all.

Phrases for translation:

Excuse me, parlez-vous chicken ici?
Please, where is the cambio for live chickens?
Is this the fast chicken for Bratislava?
Bitte, do you have a place I can leave my broody hen?
I am married with a roost and three chicks,
I live in Little Red Rooster Town, Minnesota.
I was born in the Year of the Chicken
under the sign of the Chicken, have a nice day.
I would like chicken en suite, por favor.
Chicken on the rocks, chicken all round.
It's my turn for the Lakenvelder meine Damen und Herren.
S'il vous plaît m'sieur I want the Chicken Cab Co.
I would like a bottle of this Chateau Poulet Blanc.
This chicken is too loud, take it away please.
Entschuldige, I have to go buy a chicken now.
Pardon me, I think my chicken is on fire.
I have a one way ticket to Chickenville, goodbye.

Let us consider the chicken:

Lately I've been thinking about the chickens,
clucking their peevish lives out in the long batteries,
where the lights shorten the days, nothing changes,
it's hell on earth and every one in here is loo-loo.

Even in a yard they fret, always at the edge,
suspicious, laying the great egg, staring, watching,
wary for the cockbird or pecking at their dinners
or asleep dreaming worms, slugs, fat maggots.

And then they die, all of them without names,
numbers, without biographies, votes, pension rights,
their throats routinely cut, stripped, chopped up,
cooked in a pot with onions and peppers and devoured.

Chuck. Chuck. The Hungarians, who got them
from the Bulgarians, they say *tyuk. Tyuk tyuk tyuk.*
Comrades, clearly this is not in the chickens' interest.
Our feathered friends are manifestly at a disadvantage.

And no one protests, no one gives a Gypsy's gob
for all their aspirations, dreams, their brief itchy lives
scratching and complaining, part of the food chain.

    Save the chicken. Save the chicken.

Chicken lore:

For a start there was the Miracle of the Cocks and Hens,
there was the Parable of the White Leghorn,
there was the Cockadoodledoo Revelation at Alexandria,
there was the Exemplary Lesson of the Rhode Island Reds,
there was the Sermon on the Flightless Gallinacae,
there was the Bantam Capon Culture of the Po Valley,
there was the Black Langshan Khanate of Kiev,
there was the Coxcomb Dynasty of the Mekong Delta,
there was the Teaching of Salvatore Stefano Cacciatore,
there was the Red Rooster Crusade of 1332,
there was the Most Noble Order of Jersey Black Giants,
there was the Barred Plymouth Rock Declaration,

there was the Constitution of the Andalusian Blues,
there was the Divine Sisterhood of Old Poultry Lane,
there was the secret conclave of the Orpington Buffs,
there was La Flèche, Crèvecœur, Campine, Faverolle,
there was the whole mighty host of Gallus Domesticus
migrating out of the east, crossing the windy steppes
clutched in the armpits of savage horsemen,
and there was blood, there were mountains of skulls.
We were at Marathon, at Agincourt, on the Somme,
we were the Wild Chickens who fought at Malplaquet.
We too had our epics, our ten year return to Ithaca
only to find strangers clucking in our compound.
We too had our blind poets Homer and Milton.
There was Chaucer's *The Dream of Fair Chickens*,
there was the Last Lay of the Fighting Cocks,
there was the Black Virgin of the Chickenshack,
there was Shakespeare's famous Chicken Soliloquy,
there was the patriarch Chicken Joe Bailey,
there was the saint and martyr Adolphus Chicken,
there was the inventor and explorer Gustavus Chicken,
there was the hero Lieutenant General Gordon Chicken,
there was Captain Bingo 'Chickenwings' Benson
who saved us again and again from foreign invasion,
there was the gunfighter Roaring Jack Chicken,
there was the horn player Willy Bantam Chicken,
there was the Ode to a Chicken and the Air on a Chicken,
there was the Chicken Sonata, the Chicken Symphony,
there was Chicken Blues, there was Chicken Boogie,
there was the Chicken Domesday, the Cockcrow Manifesto
the Chicken Coop Oath, the Last Address to the Chickens,
there was the chicken round dance and chicken chants,
there were chicken fiestas and chicken olympics,
there was Chicken Rococo and Chicken Gothic,
there was the Colegio Pollo of medieval Florence,
there were the *Chicken Études* of Guillaume Apollinaire,
there was the School of Contemporary Chicken Studies,
there was the Distressed Indigent Chickens' Benevolent Society,
there were the Thoughts of The Cocksman Chairman Charlie,
there was the Theory and Evolution of the Chicken,
there was the architecture of Frank Lloyd Chicken,
there was Henry Ford's Chicken Mass Production System,
and it says here much else besides, all of it now best forgot.

Saith the Sky Chicken:

Woe to those who sell guns
amongst the warring states.
Woe to those who shell the wounded.

Woe to those who take another's house,
and say *this is my farm, these my chickens,*
who pick up the photo album and say
why these are all my relatives.

Interim conclusions:

What is a mere chicken to do?
Everything you see belongs to the Fat Man.
The true commonwealth of equals is now very far off.
The Dark Ages begin again any time now.

I'll tell you this: the Hundred Years War
did nothing for those who eat worms.
What use was the Renaissance?
The Revolution's been and gone.

Last bulletin:

The barbarians are at the city's throat,
their tanks moving down the great ringroads,
the anti-chicken forces are all around us.
Any second now there will be no more electricity.

This is the end of the Chicken Road.
This is the last hour of the Chicken Republic.
This is the final demise of the Chicken Revolution.
This is the end of all chicken civilisation.

And this is Radio Free Chicken signing off.
Goodbye Foxtrot, Goodbye Tango Charlie.
We of the Chicken Coalition salute you.
We of the Chicken Millennium bid you adieu.

Her mirror

Sideways it always was along the long wall
and I still see her in it though she's gone now,
combing her hair, setting her face right for the street.

I fixed it upright by my door to watch who comes,
who passes. Things are not so easy in this neck of the woods.
The neighbourhood's gone crazy.

But in Milly's mirror all the world's reversed –
car numbers, faces, turned around as mirrors do,
and the mad didikais raging in the street all night.

They beat each other up, they're selling crack.
They brick each others' cars and windows
and they scream through the night furnace.

Milly's mirror watches.
Milly's mirror watches all.

The road to Henrietta's house

Well there's a lot of ways to get there a lot of ways to go.
For a start you can stop off at the Rainbow Café and drink
drink yourself beyond yourself into silence through the jukebox
through all the chatter of the pinball machines till its *Time*.

That would be the end of it that would be the tale. But suppose.
Suppose you have the one drink leave set out across the city.
You take the bus you take the tram you take the train you walk.
You come to the river there you wake the sleepy boatman.

For sure for certain he's sure in a foul mood, and sore drunk.
And when he's rowed you over there's the marshes and the wild beasts.
There's the vipers and the soldier ants and the roaches and the flies.
You have to catch your own wild horse you have to tame it, ride it

at last at long last down the long road to Henrietta's house,
and just because all hell has broken broken loose broken loose
you're thinking someone something in the universe doesn't want
the two of you to meet, ever. Suppose you just keep going

to the end the road makes in the door that opens into light
water in the kettle wine in the dark red bottle and her beads.
And now she wants to dance she wants to click her fingers laugh
fling out her braids flying in the window in the candle's flame.

In praise of vodka

The taste they say for they must
or they feel that they must so they say
so they say they say *it has none,*
there's no taste, just water.

Water: the glassy lake Christ trod,
a bowl Herod rinsed his fingers in,
the rain falling on Troy's ruins,
last word last balm of the living.

The same water, over and over. They say
for they say for they must so they say
we're running out running dry but there's always
the same amount as there's always been.

It's we who are more. As for myself
I've spent all my days working out
just what little Miss Peaches might like
and I'm due a day off for the rest of my life.

So out of the freezer the bottle, the green
frosty bottle, its label iced in cyrillic,
the glass and the water beside the glass.
Russische. Moskovskaya. Stolichnaya.

So this is the taste of nothing:
nothing then nothing again. Nothing at all.
The taste of the air, of wind on the fields,
the wind through the long wet forest.

A stream and the rain. I lie in my yard
and open my mouth to the moon and the down falling rain
and the rods of its words speak over my tongue
to the back of my throat and they say

Voda
Water
Vodka

Voda
Water
Vodka

Voda
Water
Vodka

Voda
Water
Vodka

Voda
Water
Vodka

The carpenter's confession

All these years something grew in me, measuring,
cutting good wood, stitching my own sweet way with a dowel,
a nail, a joint, reassembling the forest into chairs
and cupboards in a room swollen with wood dust.

This was the page of my life. Then I was redundant.
So I come out to Wanstead most days, to the Flatts,
brooding briar and star moss, lichen, the ways of the ants
and the birds, if the day holds the rain off.

Most days in the city's diet of sound I'm deaf in one ear,
in the other intermittently lucid on the left hand channel,
clairvoyant and amplified, the system working at last,
both speakers straight to the brain's right side.

So today.

Today I lay watching a red kite rise and fall
in the shimmer of the updraughts, hearing
the far away laugh of the boy at the string's end:
to him everything an amazement, like new made money.

And the wind through all easy. I pondered the weather,
and what waterlogged secrets the gravel ponds keep,
what guns and what corpses and why, when the day's good
and nothing should wreck it some fool always does.

So today, I brought my Kalashnikov.

Away to one side sunlight was moving on towers
in Leyton and Leytonstone. Gulls, crows, one then
two magpies in the scribble of weeds. And the city
tuned itself out, its traffic a distant barking and child sounds.

As usual as ever I was taking a last backward glance
at the world's green spatter of leaves, wind
haunting the grass, high up and invisible the larks'
rusty twittering, overhead an incoming plane in descent

where the captain had just flipped the no smoking sign.
Traffic noise began rolling in, sirens, then the buzz
of some model plane's toy motor round and around
in the slow light that but for him would be bliss.

So today I put in a clip. Today I took off the safety.

The man who ran away from the circus

That one with the haircut round his ears,
the one that grins with the teeth and the glasses,
the little man holding a long umbrella –
or whichever one he is he's the shorter of the two.

It's been a hard road he says. As a kid
he remembers they were always on the move.
He'd sneak away to do his homework in the Fat Lady's tent.
He remembers ropes, sawdust, llama spit, camel stink.

And he remembers how it was with his dad
on a bad night of muddy rain and a hatful of unsold tickets,
the takings slithering off into expenses, the books
unbalanced on the table and the whisky bottle out,
the dogs howling in the yard. Lenny the lion's sick
and the liontamer out on the razzle with the man/woman.
The ringmaster's run off with the cashflow
and the clowns are demanding a payrise and a pension
and Christmas is coming, it's all they can do
to find hay for the horses.

He's at the end of his endless tether again.

About then the old man would straighten up, pour a drink,
fix his bow-tie and collar, clear his throat,
look you right in the eye and say *There are signs
things are getting better. We're beginning to see
an upturn in our fortunes at last. The confidence rate
is well up this month. There are indications the worst
of this long bitter recession is over.*

That's how it was then. It was either that
or close down the zoo, sell the elephant,
auction off the tigers and the freak sheep,
the sideshows and the performing monkeys,
turn the zebras into handbags, the horses into glue,
lease the big top and develop the site, retire to Brighton
to sell takeaways, become a deck chair attendant,
watch the cricket and the bowls and the grey swilltub sea
from a window in his favourite seafront pub
and reminisce: *ah the good old days of the classless society,*
the world of every opportunity where everyone
could get to crack the whip. That again.

And he's away. Again the horses prance into the ring,
the pompons and the big drum and the trombone's oompah oompah
and the girls glittering in fishnet and sequins.
Here come the stiltmen and the clowns, the jugglers
and the human cannon ball, the rubber man, the singing dog,
the giant and the dwarf and the thinnest man in England,
JoJo with her instruments and Suzy's little tricks,
the man who throws axes, the man who swallows knives
and the one who breathes fire, Manolito's highwire act
from Andalusia, the Russian pyramid, the invisible American,
the drunks, the grand finale of the troupe of South American pickpockets
that did him in at last. Them and all those women.

Interrogating the egg-timer

Born?

I was born in a paper bag in the basement of a shark,
in a windstorm in Arizona, in a Turkish shebeen,
in the cold blue corner of an isosceles triangle.
I was a child of the union of rain and whisky.

How much of my beginning can I remember?

Why, isn't this it? I remember nothing and everything.
There was a blue sky. For once my father was happy.
My mother was a test tube but more fruity.
I find the world fairly round, roundly and profoundly unfair.

You ask about my last life, the one before this.

As I recall I travelled in the suitcase
of a man always stopping to call long distance.
I was the ashtray of a perverted monk,
I was alone I was always alone.

You want to know how long this road I'm on is?

Listen, 60 minutes is the end of my attention-span.
Anything beyond and it's head-over-heels
I'm in love again with someone's juices and aromas.
You've read Lawrence. You'll know what I mean.

My favourite food is anything.

If I stopped eating altogether I'd be a very slim hourglass.
I'm so tired of salt with everything.
I'll just go on being turned over and over,
living out my life in quiet three minute orgasms.

Where did I spend last night? Pass.

Am I capable of transformation? Well,
I can turn energy into raw mountains of detritus.
I am capable of anything. Everything again.
Again nothing. I want to go back into my box now.

Ailments? I catch cold when I need to.

No tobacco, no alcohol, no drugs. Up at dawn,
jogging on the spot, somersaults. I keep myself neat,
ready for action. *Intrepid* is my middle name.
In my job down at the harbour I guide the boats in.

You want to know how I work?

First I have to be turned over. Then
I walk up and down staring at nothing,
thinking of nothing in particular.
Serendipity. A certain aimlessness. Theft.

Betimes I am madde as anie hattere.

Certainly I get sick of the company of Young Smartarse
and his mates, I am a morose and solitary drunk.
I take this ambience from a man called Waits.
I take it and I give it back again.

No, I never watch old movies. I am one.

At what time do I burst into blossom?
Whenever I dance, when I grow up.
Actually I'm in bloom now. Can't you see?
All these pink buds will be shiny green apples one day.

My favourite position is 90 degrees upright.

How did it feel to be taken away by thieves?
Terrific, I love travel. I adored them,
they were all excellent dancers, good talkers.
They taught me advanced kleptomania and secrecy.

When did I masturbate? I could ask you the same thing.

I'm old enough not to be daft enough to answer that.
You want to know what happened to my seven sisters?
That would be Melissa and the others, Sugar Plum,
Stanley Knife, Consonant, Tin Can, Marzipan

and the other one that was never called anything.

They're the Sisters Pleiades now. Can't you see them
all around me? They were all abused by Father Time.
As to my future life I just plan to keep busy.
Busy and useful till the salt runs out.

Then I expect to be a hand or just a finger.

When I speak to the police what will I tell them?
All these questions. I'll say I'm no stool pigeon.
I'll tell them how unbearable you've been,
they should lock you up for life. I'll spit salt at them.

So how would you feel after a thousand nights without sleep?

What does freedom mean to me? My favourite tipple,
the same as my religion: everything I see.
Taking longer to change. When there's
nothing else in the world I can rape.

And what do I mean by 'I'm in love again'?

Well, I was bored in the supermarket.
The top half of my glassy body loves my bottom half.
It's my normal status. In any case
I was dried out, I'd drunk six cups of coffee.

I don't know I'm no intellectual.

I was in love before. She gave me a ring.
That ended in a jackdaw's nest. She gave me white crystal.
I gave her only my time. And what now?
Well, I could write a cheerful book about graveyards.

I could start a small war.

I could drive the peasants out of Thuringia,
lob mortars onto hungry people in a Sarajevo bread queue.
I'd rather dance though. I'd rather the company of books,
candlelight, unaccompanied singing. Fact is

I'm an officer and gentleman in the SAS. I kill people.

I can mumble the Lord's Prayer in Anglo-Saxon.
And the riddles: what am I now, pray? Answer:
a long falling through myself into a pile of whiteness,
the cone of ashes of the dead at Birkenau.

What do I expect of strangers?

That they keep close to the walls. Water, bread, a small fish.
Just slipping in and out of time. I'm content
passing the salt from one half to the other of myself.
This time the answer is *Edelweiss-Piraten gegen Nazis*.

And who would I run to? Who indeed.

The mad. The imprisoned. The condemned. The dead.
Anyone who starts the day without a good breakfast.
There are four of us in here you know,
one for each season. And more to come.

What are my dreams? Wanderers. Other dreamers.

By the end of the week I'm more a smell than a flavour.
There are those to whom I bear the debt of time,
guttural people. I myself am clear glass,
falling white crystals. Drop me and I break and that's *Amen*.

What am I weary of? I'll tell you.

Eggs, for one thing. Quotations from Shakespeare.
The Books of Exodus and Leviticus. Answering questions.
Flying the Atlantic. All of Disney.
The words *arabesque*, *fraught*, and *binocular*.

I'm weary of a life without legs.

Unaccompanied singing

À capella: unaccompanied singing, as in a chapel, from Latin *capella*, a diminutive of *cappa*, cape, referring to the chapel built to house the relic of the cape of St Martin of Tours (316-397?), Patron Saint of France. Born in the Roman province of Pannonia, now in Western Hungary, he was forced into the army at 15 where he became a Christian and an early conscientious objector. Thrown into prison, he was discharged at 20, and shortly thereafter came the incident for which he was to be revered, when, at Amiens, he split his cloak with a beggar. Later he became a hermit at Poitiers, and was unwillingly chosen to be bishop of Tours, to whom miracles were ascribed. It seems everything he did he did reluctantly, but for the matter of the cape. After his death the cape was adopted as the symbol of the Merovingian and Carolingian kings, and carried by them into battle. At the accession of the first of the Carolingians, the illiterate Peppin the Short, the task of drawing up royal documents was assigned to the *capellani*, chaplains of the *capella*, whose original duty had been to look after the cape and the chapel that housed it. And so from the name of a covering against the rain to the name for its sanctuary and its guardians, *capella* comes to stand for all chapels, for their servants, then for the singing that took place in them without music, the music only of human voices.

Sharing the same name is Capella, in the constellation Auriga, a binary star at 50 light years distance, the sixth brightest in the night sky, its name deriving, like the constellation Capricorn, aka the horned goat, tenth sign of the Zodiac – from Latin *capra*, nanny goat, in Greek myth a she-goat (or nymph) that nursed the infant Zeus.

So now we have a story of a star, a nanny goat suckling an infant god, a saint, a cape, a chapel, clerks, and singing.

Let's take the goat track.

Considering the various derivatives of the projected Indo-European root, *kapro-*, goat, leads on to Latin *caper*, goat, *capra*, she-goat; *caprifig*, the goat fig; *capric acid*, so named for its goatlike odour; *capella gallinago*, the common snipe; *capelin*, a species of smelt; *caber*, pole, from Gaelic *cabar*, from Vulgar Latin *caprio*, rafter, though the shift from goats to rafters as yet escapes me; *cabrilla* a tropical sea bass, presumably goat-looking, Spanish dim. of *cabra*; *cabriolet*, a two wheeled one horse carriage, from a French diminutive of *cabriole* from Latin *capreolus*, wild goat, referring presumably to the carriage's motion; *capriole*, an upward leap, all four hooves off the ground, made by a trained horse, through French from Italian *capriola*, leap of the goat; *capriccio* (Italian: *capo* + *ricchio* (hedgehog), literally 'head with hair standing on end' hence horror, or caprice); *chevron*, badge of rank, in heraldry an inverted V, in architecture a V shaped pattern, in Middle English from Old French a beam, a rafter, and so back to the caber and the capering goat once more, though I don't (yet) see how. But then *capreolate*, tendril-like, again from Latin *capreolus*, wild goat, referring to the wooden prop supporting tendrils or vines – and (here it comes) the V shape cut at the top of the prop suggesting horns, a goat's horns, hence rafters, turned downward to support a roof, just as the letter A is the inverted diagram of the head of an ox. And might a cape be made of goatskin?

All this is speculative, the outcome of night-grubbing in the dictionaries. It reappears here and there as motif, hints at recurrent themes, lone voices, a chorus of unaccompanied singing that becomes an opera of fish, birds, leaping goats, vines and rafters, striped sergeants of infantry, kilted cabermen, horses and their trainers, the rattle of many tongues in capricious symphony. As for the parts the performers of this work will play, more night sifting throws up the Portuguese instrument maker, Antonio Capela, born 1932, a leading European maker of violins, violas and cellos. It reveals Sir Arthur Capel, beheaded in 1649, Royalist leader in the English Civil War, 'a man in whom the malice of his enemies could discover very few faults', whose escape from the Tower of London was betrayed by a boatman for 20 pounds. And so now we have a Judas. There's Andreas Capellanus, a 12th-century French writer on courtly love, there's Martianus Minneus Felix Capella, an early 5th-century advocate at Carthage and writer on the rules of prose and poetry, there's a 17th-century Huguenot theologian and Hebrew scholar, Louis Cappel. There's a 16th-century Venetian noblewoman, Bianca Capello, beautiful, passionate, intelligent, the focus of intrigue and scandal, mistress and later wife of Francisco I de Medici, by the ruse of a fake pregnancy and a borrowed baby to deceive her lover into marriage. So much for romance. Soon after the marriage both died suddenly in their beds, of poison believed to have been administered by the Duke's brother. There's Luigi Capello, Italian general of World War I, and

Giacomo Capellin, born 1887, a Venetian glassmaker who revived the glass industry at Murano, there's Heinrich Kapell, a 17th-century gun-maker of Copenhagen, and there's Johann Capeller, of Munich, around 1811 first flute in the King of Bavaria's court orchestra. And for the scenery, tempering the wild Italian with an ochre northern sobriety, there's Jan van de Cappelle, 1624-1679, Dutch painter of calm seascapes and silvery winter landscapes.

And so we begin with voices in the starry night singing without accompaniment. Then a flute, then a quartet of instruments fashioned by the Portuguese master, a chorus, characters, a plot that begins under a bright star with a suckling goat and the splitting of the saint's cape, rain and lightning and horses, scenes amongst the glassblowers and the gunmakers and the horse trainers, to one side the storming of advocates and grammarians and theologians, and all proceeding to betrayal for mere cash, despite the passionate temper of Bianca, the comedy of the baby trick, the mad speeches of the Italian general, resplendent in his plumes and braids, amidst the sombre Dutchman's winter roads and water, ships always in the offing, one of them perhaps *The Queen of Spain*.

WILD ROOT

Eddie's Other Lives

Absent

The other half of the conversation
has flown off in a jetplane
to the country of her own tongue.

And maybe she'll come back to me
or maybe not or maybe she was all a dream
I had in the blue garden in the dusk.

In the house the TV is watching itself
and the stereo listening to itself
and the fridge with its running commentary.

She's out there. And I'm out here
among the moths and the last light,
the blackbird at her evensong.

Country music

In my other life in another country
on the world's other side I get by, just.

A little fishing a little hunting perhaps.
Maybe I'm a professor of aluminum siding

at Pork Chop U, an aficionado
of the beauties of felt roofing.

Let's say I drive a dusty brown pickup
with a roofrack and a rifle in the back.

What you're up against here is decay,
that in the system that makes it break down.

And anyway it's Friday. In all the arguments
for one more drink the ayes have it.

Therefore I'm on my way to the Captain's
to fill up the hole I've made in myself.

She's bored with me, I tired of her long ago.
We get by with the kids and the payments.

All the radio stations sing the same song:
love goes away, it's a sad tune

coming in over the airwaves and out
through the light years to the stars,

the same miserable message
to the whine of the same miserable guitar,

for forever or the next thing to it,
if anyone out there is listening.

Chief

On the one side my great great grandaddy
was Timuquana, chief in these parts.

A great hunter, woman chaser,
fighting man, joker, dreamer,

whose country was this where I work now
up and down the fairways and bunkers.

Look, here's his picture on the matchbook
from the country club of the same name:

the leathery face in the braids
and the one feather that breaks

out of the ring round him like a seal
on a document, his motto underneath:

Close cover before striking.
For safety strike on back.

When that cop come

Old Red we call him to his red face,
Hey Mister Red, Yes Sir Mister Red,
you see the heat rise to his head,
and that's what makes him crazy.

So then he's writing inside his hat
like he thinks it's New York,
Pay now pay later pay forever he says:
Gimme your name or I'll break your face.

Seems I remember him in school,
snot running down his white trash face,
a pimpled adolescent chewing toothpicks,
beating his meat behind the bandstand.

Now he's just a dirty cop in Meatville
writing my name down in his notebook
telling me I'm booked, hooked, cooked,
and I'm telling him *this conversation cut.*

Joy #1

*Come down here this mornin Madson Wisconsin goin home Denver.
Husban's up there inna Vetrans Hospital Madson, s'real good
hospital.*

*He got hit by a truck. Half his face smashed in, one eye hangin out.
Couldn't look at him.*

*Had to make myself. Asked me how I look Joy? I said OK Sonney.
It was a goddamn lie. Looks like shit. No wonder I'm smokin like
they goin outa style.*

In the next street

There's only ever one argument: his,
bawling out whoever punctuates
the brief intervals his cussing
interrupts, something unheard, reason perhaps.

What you never get is silence,
always some groan on the horizon
out on the borders of attention
where would be quiet if they let it.

Always some conversation far away,
foreign, banal, dramatic, translated
it means *my wife's name is Judit.*
I am an engineer from Spidertown.

What to reply? *Your Majesty*
my name is Smith. All lies anyway,
all we do is get drunk, the evening's end
collapsing loosely into gutturals.

We drink to silence, where the stars think.
We drink to the music of rain on the roof.
We drink to mothers, brothers, lovers, kids,
to the candle burning down its length

till someone blows it out. Distance
makes no difference, the same want
for love and money, the numbers of the winning line
in the state lottery like a needle in the brain.

And then I've had enough. I want
to go home now, far away, plug myself
back into the sockets, the blackbird,
the evening humming stories to itself.

Everything in its place, the moths,
the mouse in the mousetrap. And
in the next street the same old argument.
He's sure he's right.

Joy #2

> *My mother. She was killed onna street. Had t'go home to Livpool*
> *England bury her. That's where I come from, ways back. She was*
> *killed right onna street, hit by car. Knocked down hit an run. She*
> *was onna crossing. She was dead. She was inna right. But she was*
> *dead.*

Poem to which the answer is no

This music you're listening to –
let me tell you why I don't like it.

No.

You with your pretty little Doris Day wife.
She's been buying and selling in cyberspace.
She's looking at Jesus through the eyes of Bugs Bunny.

And *yes*. This could be me here among the glittering cities,
Eddie the Unsteady glimpsed travelling in the opposite direction
on an Amtrak out of Toledo, last heard from in a motel room
in Moon Township, old curmudgeon on a stick
limping aimless in America, through all the other zones
of time and distance and the self, beautifully lost
somewhere in the great riddle of nowhere, my double,
carbon copy, fax, living on my wits, conjuring
something out of nothing and taking that to the bank.

I'm sorry sir, we're not connected to that service.
Your call cannot be completed as dialled.

Eddie's on the hoof,
Eddie's off the bone,
Eddie's getting drunk
and won't come to the phone.

More stick

Here he comes again my man Eddie,
making his way downtown on some cross street,
the rain and the cold wind in his face
down past Jerry's barber shop and shoe shine
on his way to the invisible liquor store.

Like me he is of the brotherhood of men
with sticks. *East Wacker to West Wacker*
six times a day and back again, I was
a messenger then my foot got sick.
It collapsed goddammit. Eddie on the edge

of everything, Eddie on a freight train
to a heart attack. He can say
you're the one who was here, always will be.
He can say only time I refused a drink
I misunderstood the question. Oh he can talk,
he's the epicentre of any conversation,
it runs all round him but he's not here
and tomorrow won't remember. Any of it.

And through it all the dead music
of the buildings, airshafts and ventilators
and the electrics, the sirens hunting down
the streets of the trashed neighbourhoods
along the lake shore, scruffy trees
standing in black water, then just the gleam
of cities shining in the night, blur
of conversations over the Earth's rim.

This is a fugue that is a dream of the world
that's a bad dream anyway. *Fool:*
what's this fist for, this automatic
in your guts, this knife? Fact is
in this bar he's come in from the rain to,
waiting for a train or a bus or a plane,
fact is there's not one not two not three
but four talking TV screens competing
for his anxieties. All this infests his brain.

But Eddie no crazy. Eddie sick, he in trouble
but he no lose it. Eddie no mad.

Joy #3

> Name's Joy, an that's my nature. But I swear to God it gets
> harder. Don't much get on with Sonney's two boys from first
> marriage, 16 and 18 years old, both of them crazy, crazy as
> lunes, out half the night raisin hell, come home, switch on TV
> stereo high as it'll go.
>
> Sonney wants me to move up there with them, thinks he'll be there
> a while. Says he wants me with him but I don't know, sella house,
> move our stuff, get those boys to help an I don't know they will.

Joy #4

When I married my first husban Elliot I was a GI bride. Those days I was an entertainer, I was a stripper, clubs inna north, Leeds, Manchester. I thought he was the sweetest thing. We didn't last. People don't I guess. His business went broke an he took off, took a farm up in South Dakota, took the boy. I said I wouldn go, said I didn come here to be no farmer's wife out inna wilderness, so we split.

The geography of clouds

It all happens so fast, in the long grass
looking up, or staring from the bus
going West: the stately kingdoms of the clouds

collapsing into violent republics, empires
forming and fading on fast forward.
The cartographers never catch up,

the mapmakers turn broody and suicidal,
the subtitles in an unknown tongue,
white on white and all too fast.

In a half an afternoon the history of Russia,
in an hour the discovery and conquest of the New World,
in minutes the development of moveable type.

The late bloom is on the sedge
reads the soundtrack. *And the blossom
no sooner flowers than it falls.*

East of here, west of here

the days are the great flatlands,
long arc of the earth's curve
falling away on all points of the compass.

And what the light presents: barn, tree,
girl in an orchard, an old woman
peeling apples, glimpsed as you go.

The nights are the mountains,
to be got through in the headlights
east of the river or west of the watershed:

the same: speech that makes sense
only of essential things: bread and salt
in greeting, a glass of wine, farewell,

some place to lay me down to sleep
to the tick of the same bedside clock,
the battery wearing itself away.

Noises off

Some dream or other, the moon wash
through the window blinds, the night city
with its night sounds. I'm on the road again
in my other life, the lights glittering
in the late distance, the wind
broken out of Canada and laced with sleet.

So here I am in this little town
between ocean and ocean with my bag
and my out of state cheques and no cash.
I'm rich in bad paper and dead currency
and they say *money never lies idle*
but what do they know of it?

It's always this aching hour of the night
in some place called French Lick
or Mud City Indiana, the connection
half a day away to some unhappy town
where the furniture is made of neon
and sings in praise of K-Mart and the 7-11.

And there is always racket, machinery
that bleeps to say your dinner's done,
your laundy's dry, horns, talking trucks,
the chatter of the video arcades
and the low murmur of the soaps
and the endless wailing of the cops.

Alarms no one ever answers, bells
that ring till the electricity runs out,
and then a door opens on a sudden blast
of heartbreak music, betrayal's beat,
the same old blues of separation,
men's inconsistencies and women's.

Joy #5

> Don't know what I can do in Madson. Waitressin I guess. Just
> when I was thinking to live and die in Denver now I have to do
> the same for Wisconsin. I don't know.
>
> Sonney was driving to Canada, got hit up there by Green Bay.
> Hit by truck. He looked awful, don't know how he's gonna look
> when it's over.
>
> Kept askin me How do I look Joy, how do I look? It's real good
> hosptal.
>
> He was smashed up before. Photographer. In Veetnam got a grenade
> in his back, thirty seconds get it out with a fish hook. Goddamm
> Veetcong.

Speech

Now America is one whirled fire,
one babble of speech, the captions loosed
from the cartoons, the sentences
issuing out of the wrong mouths:

fuck you says Chief Joseph,
throwing down his spanner, fired
within six months of his pension
from the Milwaukee Cutout Corporation.

One more nightshift, leaves the bar
and torches the factory. Out in the wind
that picks at the stone face of the city
for the last time in this life

Schroeder stomps to his pickup:
from where the sun now stands,
punching the radio to country,
I will fight no more forever.

A dream of disaster

Now where we are we will always be,
the moon high on second hand light,
her dark weight lugging the tides
between ebb line and nepe.

We never got there, driving through Ohio
when the brakes failed, someone
pulled a gun, or in the airspace
of the wide Atlantic some instrument

gave in to entropy and heaved us seaward.
We are the names on the lists.
This is our baggage floating in the sea.
We are the percentage of the reckoning.

And the moon up there is our crazy sister
who just never got started, and we
are on our way to join the angels
in their interminable barbershop quartets.

Dead trousers

Old trousers that were best once, now
they never go anywhere, mooching round the house
doing odd jobs, paint and varnish stains,
urine and spilt coffee where once was beer,
whisky, the faint aroma of sex on the hoof.

So the centuries flash by: all those handsome women
in pretty dresses that turn suddenly black.
And the impossible jobs: making a whole
of the hole in yourself, slamming the door
on your discontent and out into the rain.

489

You're on hold, in the queue, listening
to the *Nessun dorma* song on the line
and the *sorry-to-keep-you-waiting* voice,
faint electronics at the world's rim.
Please speak after the tone.

Please leave your name and number. Speak.
Get it all off your chest: love and love's
bereavement and how short a term of office.
Make your confessions, all the bloody times
you were a bloody fool. So speak.

To nobody out there.

The theft

I am a thief and this my thiefwork,
here in the rare book room in Toledo
rummaging the works of the dead professors,
examining their boxes of effects.

It comes to this: a stout carton
in which the late dean's ashtray, gown,
seal of office, rotary inscription,
pipe, golf trophy and cigar-cutter.

Amen.

Joy #6

> *I guess I'll do it all just like he says. My friend Marlene, she
> waitresses with me, real good friend, she'll help me I know.*
>
> *When my mother got killed onna crossing she said she'd come with
> me, help out, I said no. Strange goin back there. Hadn't been in
> 40 years, hadn't seen my mother since don't know. But she was
> dead, so I just buried her, came away, nothing else to do but come
> on home.*

The telephone is in the key of C

she says, breathless, home again
from the long corridors of air and traffic
over the ocean's curve, where I have prayed
to all the gods of wind and water

for her safe return, keeping the stillness
still for her. The stories tumble
over each other, interrupt each other,
all she's met, ate, heard, trembled at

in the country of endless explanations
and too many sudden noises, the freeways
and the announcements yelling in her skull
from the continent of her own tongue.

All falling away, almost in her grasp,
a word forming in the ear of her hearing,
glimpsed in the moment that's gone now,
the stray bullet snug in its target.

In the year of the comet, with vodka,
phenobarb and plastic bags on their heads
39 grownups went off to board the UFO,
each with a roll of quarters for the shuttle.

The telephone is in C. And the dryer,
that's just a basso profundo klaxon
that won't quit, that and the microwave,
that and the cuckoo clock and the planes.

Sleep is what she needs, and a dream
through which geese on the inlet,
near and then distant, fading south
beyond the night swamps into summer.

The rustle of magnolia in the wind
and the stars over all, a nightbird
calling over water, the oncoming
of the great trains' wild concertos.

Before the Lisbon Tribunal

They asked why I came here. I replied
to hear the rain falling in the street,
footsteps running into the wet dark.
To consume fish and more fish, drink tinto,
branco, verde, secco, make love, sleep late,
waking to the calls of ships on the Tagus.

And the arrival of what ships did I wait for?

I described the *Alfama* winding on itself,
a heap of washing lines and lemon trees,
sardine scales underfoot, children tumbling
down its alleys. In the cold empty cathedral
what I felt was *cold, empty*, a barn
built by the thugs of the Second Crusade.

What could I tell them of this?

I spoke of *Guincho*, its name that means scream
for the Atlantic wind rushing through, days
watching the slow shift in the quick sea
arriving in walls of water, the sea's change
and the light's change till the round bowl
of the earth's rim's lost and the light gone.

And where did I think such light went?

They were amused, patient. Those were early days,
I was not yet accused. At my second examination
they were seven, young, clever, soft spoken,
a clerk scratching, his tongue between his teeth.
There were no charges, the questions random:
could a ship of armed men be hidden in a fist?

Did I believe their mares sired by the West Wind?

Did cheese produce mites, bad meat blowflies,
did a closed box of old rags generate mice?
I was to help clear up certain allegations,
they as anxious as I, and so forth, to be done.
I have pen, ink, paper, candle, a writing desk
and this white room wherein to write my confessions.

Poem without a title

The borders are open,
the borders are closed.

I stood in a long line of suitcases
in the Hall of Tears. Each
they inspected in leisurely detail,
quartering the face, solemn.

Sullen. *Open please.* I recall
a pair of blue women's underpants
held to the grubby satin of the neon,
and the paperwork, the paperwork, I thought

this time they will empty out
the entire suitcase of my heart
when Bang went the rubber stamp,
and Klik the Ausgang. *Go now* they said.

Into the gold light. Into the birdsong of the dollar,
into the constellation of the milkshake.
Go be the little boy that lives in the lane,
this is what you get for your sack of apples.

Still he was there, my father,
at the stair's end these twenty years,
back from the shadow country saying again *I told you so*
I told you so.

*

The salt in the shaker,
pepper in the pot, everything
in its place here at the Terminal Café:
eggs on the skillet, coffee in the cup.

Outside the river traffic on the river,
the sky as the sky is, blue if you will.
I can stroll in the Italian Gardens,
I can relax in the Sicilian Colonnade.

Here in the city I'm at home.
This is what I get for all my apples.
There's a bar I go to.
There's a woman I see.

There's a bridge where I watch
dusk after dusk the downgoing sun
lash the water to fire, and go home
content in the dark and recall nothing.

*

Years go by

Father I say. Dad? You again?
I take your arm, your elbow,
I turn you around in the dark and I say

go back now, you're sleep walking again,
you're talking out loud again, talking in tongues
and your dream is disturbing my dream.

And none of this is any of your apples,
and even now as the centuries begin to happen
I can say: go away, you and all your violence.

Shush, now, old man.
Time to go back to your seat in the one-and-nines,
to your black bench on the Esplanade,

your name and your dates on a metal plate, back
to your own deckchair on the pier, your very own
kitchen chair tipped back on the red kitchen tiles

and you asleep, your feet up on the brass fender
and the fire banked, your cheek cocked
to the radio set, this is the 9 o'clock news Dad.

It's time. It's long past it.
Time to go back up the long pale corridor
there's no coming back from.

Part of the crowd that day

They watched the pilgrims leave for Santiago
gawping by the roadside. In the harbour
watching the boats gather they knew something
was afoot, so many horses and these armed men.
Mostly it was all too difficult to believe.
They watched the stones rise in the cathedral.
They watched the stars. They watched winter
follow summer and the birds fly south again.
They watched the thieves carted up the road
to Tyburn and the beggars whipped through town.
They were townsfolk, craftsmen, shopkeepers,
the labouring poor who came in from the fields.
They watched the witches burn, the heretics.
They watched the ships leave for the Americas.
They were on the bridge at Sarajevo the first time.
They saw. They wondered. They shouted
burn her, hang him, slaughter the Albigensians.
They were the onlookers, the crowd a gasp runs
mouth to mouth down the grumbling street
as Marie Antoinette goes by, and this time
they are shouting for her head. There goes
the Iron Duke, there the beaten Corsican,
and this the little father of all the Russians,
this the firing squad. They were on the hills
looking down on burning Rome, and still around
when Il Duce came to town, and how they cheered.
They gawp at the hungry, they gawp at the dead.
In the end they are not spared. In their turn
everything happens to them. Of any half dozen
one has a secret vice, one an incurable disease,
one a deep faith in God and the rest don't care
one way or the other. But they see it all happen.

With a name like Spratt

Imagine at their dinner if you will
Jack and Mrs Spratt, whose name was Martha,
may she rest in peace and all the saints preserve us.

Née Robinson. Sole relict Jeremiah Bethia Robinson,
a man that was never any fun at breakfast,
a life from start to finish without meat and 2 veg.

You will recall his long face spouting God's holy word
at every spoonful of his pudding, an upright
exclamation of a man much given to kneeling down.

As was Martha. When Jack took her he would take her
from behind and call it prayer, wondering the while
what's for supper, wondering if the stars were edible.

He loved her for her bones. He did this or that
and one died then the other and they're long gone now
to where there's nothing in the cupboard but the dark.

Theirs was a tale told to cheer the poor
and promote thrift among the lower classes.
Written on their stone *They licked the platter clean.*

Suspicion of reporters

Help she was howling over and over,
a long call in fire and he:
he was scribbling *help me
I'm burning*, his mind's eye

setting angle, speed, distance,
closing the shutter, the bright
ring of strangeness around things
forming the frame of her burning.

He wrote *Nor could I save her,*
he that was chronicler, eye
of events at their centre. As she
in her death was, as this is.

White noise

Late night watching TV till it stops.
The hiss silence sings to the ear
carried in on the electron blizzard
patching into uneasy sleep.

Slow panic of walking columns
tents blown on the wind
shifting the lost villages
in shoes those who have shoes.

Bringing the desert along with them
its seeds in the mattock's edge
in the hoe's angle those who have hoes
bringing their hot rainless weather.

Call me Shrug I know nothing.
I'm like distant trouble. I may be
far from your door but I know
your name and address, alias and alibi.

Will our children bear children
and will they be anyone like us?
Will the great stream shift south
will the rain come will the ice?

You say one day but name it: *Tuesday
the fifth sixth the fifteenth
October November December.* Your life flies past
like a train and you're on it.

Body Cakes

(for Aggie, recalling Asa)

Öländska kroppkakor. Kroppkakor.
He liked to say it, aloud, over and over,
reciting his recipe of white flour,
barley flour, potato flour, potatoes,
onion and allspice. One of his ceremonies
that end to end made up a life: his.
Or just what he wanted to eat.

I never cooked them but the once,
the same rainy day I watched
his tall skinny body into the narrow grave
dug too short so they must tip him,
I thought his black cap perched on the coffin
would slither away, but it stayed.

We got on with the bitter ritual
of burying the man I loved.
It rained all that day and that night
we got drunk, and we sang *please
keep me in your dreams*. He was
gone from me, my viking, *vicarunga*,
my long lover, whose boat came ashore
here on my life so long ago now,
and from there I was stilled.

The body cakes weren't a success,
grey, a mush, wallpaper paste,
that the next day early, before anyone
rose from their beds, I took out
and buried, deep, in the garden.

Archive footage

The film is jumpy in the sprockets, bleached
in black and white and all the shades of grey.
The memory is dying. Look: this is Jack,
in the fading photo cracking at the corners.

The seaswell, the old grey swilltub
filling in the first milky light with grey ships,
so many manoeuvring in so much silence. Jamey?
Jimmy or was it Jack? The sky another grey.

Jammy we called him for he was lucky.
He'd been in Africa in tanks, the one man out
when the magazine blew and all his mates gone.
They put him back together. Jerry.

George? He'd gotten wed, they had 36 hours
of Withernsea passion in a mate's caravan.
The sky bleached out. Here the shoreline
of dune and shingle, flat country over the seawall.

John? Joey? Jim? Home the last time turning
at the back kitchen door, his handprint
pressed into the wet blue paintwork. That
she kept thereafter, that was all of him.

Photographs say nothing. Cheekyface
she called him. And he liked his beer.
Years from now she'll sing again
she'll dream again we'll meet again.

And there'll be bluebirds. Jess. Jeff.
5th East Yorks wet and seasick off La Rivière.
Shot or drowned, face down in the sea,
his white enamel mug drifting after him.

Years from now the wireless becomes the radio,
the gramophone the record player
and the record player the stereo, she'll sing along
songs he sang her then, his lily and his rose.

Josh. Johnny. Jock. The memory is dying,
the battery running flat. Before it fades
let's say this one is for Jimmy and for Jack,
and all the others who are never coming back.

First and last, Alderney

Nights with the sea's mouth at my ear,
the moon at the window. Each day
the beach flushed twice over,
newly minted with footprints.

All day walking, Platte Saline,
La Bonne Terre, up the Zigzag
to Giffoine, to the Four Winds
and La Vieille Terre and the town.

Gulls. Distance that's one side
Normandy, the other wild Atlantic
pouring itself in, the northeaster
that rips up all our words,

all he said and she said
and all they meant: the tale
that's merely you and I my love,
weary and adrift and wordless

at the light's end, at supper
in the First and Last where we are
sole audience to some tipsy crew
wondering aloud whither the weather

and whether the weather wizard works.
She says it's all too blue out there
and all too blue in here. She says
I wish to God I'd never fallen down those bloody stairs.

He says he rather likes the idea of a ratdog.
And so forth. And as for me
I was getting my voice back from the wind,
trying to keep it to myself, I was

thinking how we could be nothing much,
grass in the restless air, a high bird
rising in the baymouth in a landscape
with the light bleeding out of it.

I want to sit here in this moment
of the quick world and watch
the light fall over the long seawall,
the sea beating at the harbour mouth.

I want to be who I want, the wind
rocking me to sleep till I'm still.
I want to be in love with water
and seaweed and lost shoes and you,

taking serious interest in the tides
and the moon's battered face, the gale
banging at itself, the casual dramatics
of the way the world works out.

The way each day the tide makes
a clear heart's shape in the bay's arc.
You the gulls mutter overhead
their cries rising in the last light:

you, you. I can be glad anyone
makes anything at all of anything,
in whatever space there is,
any shape on the delicate air will suffice.

Poem for translation

He loves a woman. If she lived
on the other side of the street
he would cross the traffic to her.
If she lived on the other side of the city
he'd take a bus, take a train, call a taxi.

If she lived on the other side of the river
he'd take the ferry, row a boat, he could swim
to her, waiting on the riverbank as he arrives,
dripping wet, with a flower in his teeth,
his tongue working at the first words of her language.

If she lived on the other side of the ocean
he would work, beg, borrow or steal,
and fly to her. But it's not like that.

She lives on the other side of a closed border,
in a country without visas or passports
or any kind of paperwork. They would be
closer if she lived on the other side of the moon.
She would be more alive to him if she were dead.

It's as if she exists on the other side of music
or birdsong, on the other side of the mirror,
close but far away, like an echo. She's the song
he doesn't have words to, the words he has no tune for,
almost the melody he can almost hear.

For Julia, 1910-1996

Tears, like the rain falling, like
the first pale flowers opening in spring,
oh such a surprise. And then
the full riot of tears, beauty, weather,
before the leaves begin falling again.

But this time the whole tree has fallen
with a great echo and scurry through the forest.

That's the way she went: with wind and stormclouds
and nine days of rain, and over East Ham
Town Hall a double rainbow, and no doubt
at each foot of it a whole crock of gold
for anyone foolish enough to look for it.

There's always an end, has to be,
an end to everything, to summer
and to rain, to love even.
And to the endless sketch of the conversation
in the head – if you remember it aright,
if it ever took place, ever happened at all –
even if it's just a conversation

you only imagined, longed for, for years,
with this woman everyone loved.

Dead now, and so far beyond all our desires,
said or unsaid, all of it the same now
in the broad length and the long breath.

All I can say is: let the heart fill,
let it flood with love, till it bursts.
What else is there?
                    Death, my friends,
is a dark blood red wine, that comes
in a tall green bottle, a Rioja from Spain,
or a Merlot from somewhere abouts Balaton,
with a label that is but one small corner
of a Csontváry painting: Mary at the Well,
circa 1908: women come for water,
on their elegant heads great clay pitchers
borne aloft with such tall, timeless, eloquence.

Looking for the constant

(for Alan Sandage, astronomer)

It was the best of all possible lives,
much spent lying night after black night
in the hard cold cradle on the mountain
under the 200″, gawping like a boy again –

the same boy with his ear to the telephone pole,
listening for the singing through the wires
of words in the wood – staring into the stars,
further and further out among the jewels of time.

The life of an eyeball. A life of measuring,
allowing angle, age, velocity and distance,
the black dusts, warps, city haze, and all of it
in motion, afloat, aloof, in orbit with itself –

and with whatever else lies out beyond the faint
limit we can barely see where for us the lights
aren't lit yet, on their long tether to infinity,
watching the far galaxies breathe into the plates.

It was an honourable life, a long tradition
fore and aft of those who wondered why
and what is all this stuff? It was a dreaming,
seeking a measure in the unforgiving distances –

crouched in my cold cage among the stars
from which we're all of us made – and I was
part of that becoming, nothing endeavouring
to be something that could understand itself.

The rest was cold calculation: maps, papers,
surveys. I sought a constant, the ratio
of speed to mass that meant creation
thinned forever to grow dark and silent –

or collapsed and blew apart again,
the breathing out of breathing in,
a symmetry. There might be reason there,
if not a god of love a god of meaning.

At any rate that's the scenario I go for.

No one

Let no one be surprised at what we are about to relate, for it was
common gossip up and down the countryside that after February 6th
many people both saw and heard a whole pack of huntsmen in full cry.
They straddled black horses and black bucks while their hounds were
pitch black with staring hideous eyes. This was seen in the very deer
park of Peterborough town, and in all the woods stretching from that
same spot as far as Stamford. All through the night monks heard them
sounding and winding their horns. Reliable witnesses who kept watch
in the night declared that there might well have been twenty or even
thirty of them in this wild tantivy.

– from the *Anglo-Saxon Chronicle*, 1127

Voices in empty rooms, in the time that is no time
beyond midnight, a shape in the milky moonlight,
a pattern of shadow, the chill column of air
on the landing. No one there. No one.

Thuds in the dark, and from the locked room
a groan, whether of pain or passion, then the nothing
we go on listening to. Cats. The building sinking
into itself, dry rot eating the timbers. Spooks.

No one's here. Ghosts. The dead who are dead
and for nothing, tangled like smoke.
Ghosts of the barbed wire that persists
long after the rain and the rust has eaten all its teeth.

To all this the stars pay no attention.
To each came the night of the last syllable
and its endless pointless repetition,
a water that remembers all that's passed through it.

Ghosts of my grandfather's white shirts
on the wind through the washing lines,
his voice that still says whenever I visit him
I hope you've had your tea we've just had ours.

Misty ghosts of the rain falling in the last of the forest
up by Theydon Bois, the dead ferns and the weeping birch,
and the old voices rubbing through like stains,
the same refusals spinning down the cortex.

The ghosts of meaning in the mouths of politicians.
Ghosts of the job I don't have, every day
I go down and clock on though I never get paid
still it keeps the hands and feet busy

and you know the monkey likes to use his hands and feet.
I have become the upturned hook at the question's end,
the maker of one syllable at a time: *moon moon*.
I am the ghost of the actor who only ever played ghost.

Ghosts. Vanished peoples consigned to the hedgebacks,
their gods demoted to the production of sour milk.
There are countries that don't exist any more, citizens
with their wines and their sauces and their music

where are now new people with their different names,
the Road of Brotherhood & Unity become the Avenue of Victories.
Of the language of the butchering Huns a single word remains
and that *strava*, meaning funeral, all they left behind.

Ghosts.

Half mad and half wild, there are times if I don't go crazy
I'd go crazy, so I'm walking in the dawn and the traffic
all the way to Barking asking where has the silver river
of my voice babbled off to? Calling in the ghosts.

Whoever they are they will not go down the river,
they drift like the drowned bride in the water eddy,
returning over and over to count the takings,
scraping their knives across the doorstone.

Ghosts.

In the new minted year 1091 the priest Walchelin
taking his customary homeward path through the woods
was assailed by the howling of the homeless dead
led by a man with clubs, *exercitus mortuorum.*

Familia Herlechini, Gabriel's hounds: the wings
of the wild geese overhead, mist shapes, lights on the moor,
then the onrush of the wild hunt, soldiers and women,
the parson and the clerk, the lovers who will never be satisfied.

Ghosts.

Once on Alderney I glimpsed through rain and sea-squall
where their miserable burials had been the graveyard
of the slaves who were whipped there and were all called *Russ.*
Nothing there. No one. That side is all golf now,

bunkers of one sort or another, rainy emplacements
where the field lines were broken, gun turrets
knotted in briar and seagrass, the road curves away
through the few trees it takes to make a wood there.

Years ago a young man in blue across the porch, a clear
afternoon in Pennsylvania, solid, adolescent,
loping by the long windows, and then he jumped
into the bushes and was gone. No one there,

at the rope's end the dog flailing the empty air.
There had been such a boy, sulky, slamming his machine
into the oncoming traffic on the turnpike. Once.
And this was his short cut, mooching into town.

Another that stepped tread by long heavy tread
down the stairs of my father's house, and the door
slammed so the house shook and we woke and we looked
but the bolts lay home, the key snug in its socket.

We agreed, my father and I. No one there.
It was all we ever agreed. Now he's long gone
into the dark, to whatever answer to whatever question,
incommunicative as he ever was, and still angry.

Dead and buried, there was the cut glass bowl,
its silver rim cracked all the way around, the sound of it
high in the air of Sunday afternoon tea and that because
there was no place at the table for him, he was dead dammit.

That and two words that came clear, roundabout, devious,
distorted on the telephone, garbled in translation –
and a knock, once, at the back kitchen door,
the shape of him as if he would come in from the night.

But no one. My mother stands at the door looking out
and he's not there, the kitchen light scatters outward
on the path and the dusty leaves of the blackcurrant bushes.
And now she's dead, little Milly, but of her not a glimmer.

Not much at all of her: the ring she wore I wear,
her button box, thimbles, pins, a card of hooks, a grey
length of cotton threaded through a needle's eye,
a white china shoe with the arms of the city of Blackpool.

Goodbye she says, rouged and pretty and pink
in her stout wooden box. *Goodbye.*
She'd say *I've seen better on a card of buttons.*
She'd say *You make your bed you lie in it.*

Sometimes I almost hear her, where the stair turns,
or I almost see her as I pick the bright black berries
year by year on the cuttings from her garden by the sea,
few as they are each summer there are more of them.

Countryside Around Dixton Manor, *circa* 1715

Now strike up drum
cum harvest man cum.
Blowe horne or sleapers
and cheere up thy reapers

Layer under layer under the paintwork
England is making its Midsummer hay –

the dancing morris, pipelads and drum,
scythemen and rakers, cockers and carters

and centrefield my lord with his ladies
riding where now the pylon hums

with its wires over spring wheat
through the morning's early mist.

These are the same hedgebacks,
same lie to the landscape, Mickle Mead,

Barrowdine, Harp Field and Sausage
still here though the names are gone now.

* *

In oils, unsigned, anonymous, a jobber
moving through landscape, used maybe
the wide angle lens of the *camera obscura*
for this sweep of a corner of Gloucestershire,

back when all was thought well enough,
and nothing would change beyond this –
these peasants sweating in harvest
content dreaming brown ale and a fumble

among the haycocks, and the dancers dance off
to their drink and their shillings. My lord lies now
and since and soon and thereafter in Alderton
in St Mary of Antioch, long dead.

* *

Long gone, nameless maids in a row,
long curve of the back of 23 men
in a Mexican wave of swung scythes

to their lost graves. Two gossips
by the gate that is still a gate
maybe went for infantry, and the pipeboy

shipped out to the far world, most
stayed, went hungry, died anyway.
The painting's a lie, the landscape true

where the field keeps its shape. Everything
beyond this moment is yet to happen.
Everyone here is part of the dust now.

* *

If my heart aches it's for this
though none of it's true:

the world we have lost never was
so we never lost it:

glitter of horse brass, bells
rolling over the evening:

all my lord's dream of himself
in a hired man's painting:

same tale then as now
and this has not changed either:

the enriching of the rich –
impoverishment of the poor.

None but the reaper
will come to your door.

The Great Hat Project

(for JHW, may he thrive and with him all his ilk & tribe)

Hats I have known: the broad brimmed,
the beaked, the peaked, the high crowned,
the aviator's leather helmet with flaps,
the beret cocked at an angle to the brow,
the hat at ease with itself, the top hat,
the hard hat, the clown's cap and bells,
the Homberg, the silk, the stetson, the straw,
the Derby, the wide brimmed curé's hat
that drifted away from me from the iron bridge
long ago; the hood, the helmet, the ten-gallon,
the sou'wester, the rain hat, the sun hat,
the biretta, the busby, the bearskin,
the Sherlock Holmes, the Napoleonic full fig,
the beanie, the porkpie, cutiepie,
paper hat, party hat, kiss-me-quick hat,
the mitre, the flat cap, the black cloth
worn by the judge sentencing a man to hang
by the neck and may God have mercy on his soul;
the blue baseball cap worn brim backwards,
the bobble with a badge *Georgia Bulldogs*,
the pith helmet, the shapka, the turban,
the tarboosh, the fez and the liripipe
all of which I must wear when I want to be invisible.

And oh the fedoras of victory, the trilbies of shame,
the kerchiefs of desire, the beavers of lust,
the cloche, mantilla, chenille, chaperon, Phrygian cap.
Hosannah to the panamas of innocence, hallelujah
to the bonnets of bliss, aloh al-akbar
to the cachic and the bashlik and the burnous,
hats off to the scarves of the babushkas.
Did you know Lincoln wrote the Gettysburg Address
sitting on a train using his stovepipe hat
as a desktop? What do you think of that?
The hat as mine-of-out-of-the-way-information.
Signor Know-it-all. Magister Clever Chops.
The hat's bona fides. Hat's old bones.
The hat public enemy number one, pariah,
persona non grata. Hat the subversive.

Hat the arbiter of impeccable taste and discrimination.
The stocking cap treatment. The hat puzzle.
The great sombrero scandal of September 1895.
The hat tax. The War of the Seven Blue Bonnets.
The hat nightmare. The everlasting unforgiving
memory of hats, their absolute refusal to compromise.
The nine lives of hats. The transcendence of hats.
The hat's birthplace in Galilee removed overnight
by the physical intervention of angels, deposited
lock, stock, stall, manger, halter and harness
in the grotto at Loretto, according that is
to Pauline theosophy, can you swallow that?
Night of the long hats. Hats in outer space.
The hat worn by Those Who Do Great Works.
The polkadot hats of the Sublime Insurrectionists.
The pointy hats worn by professors of pontification
at the university of Chapeau Falls Wisconsin
in the Department of Missing Headgear,
Faculty of Hat Studies. Hat and mouth disease.
The flora and fauna of hats. Hats Rule OK.
The hat in the poetry of Andrew Locomotion.
A Short Treatise on the Hat, by Harry Novak.
The It'll-be-all-right-on-the-night hat.
The hats of God. The Great Hat of Versailles.
Imagine the hat made of water, the hat made of snow.
The people's hat is deepest red. Electrification
plus hats equals the revolution. The silly hat brigade.
Give me liberty or give me hats. Hats off to Larry.
Into the valley of hats rode the six hundred.
Two acres and a hat. We take these hats to be self-evident.
The hat soliloquy: Whether to take up arms
against a sea of hats and by opposing end them,
that is the question. For every hat a season, a farewell.
For every hat there is an opposing hat. Hat=mc^2.
The silly girls' night out hat. The pig's hat.
The lumpenproletarian hat. The great hat famine.
The heroic hat. The destabilised hat.
The deconstructed postmodernist hat.
The hat as a concept just at the edge of meaning.
Yawning, he wonders if it's time for bed yet.
And can he please have his dinner now?
Portrait of *The Hat with Fish and Apples*.
Painting of the hat in robes of the Bishop of Durham.

Hat in the role of Lear. Hat son-of-a-bitch.
The hat visits an ailing relative in Caerphilly.
Suddenly the hat sits bolt upright in his rocking chair.
The hat on the wintery Haf drinking mulled wine.
Photo of the hat in his garden by the runner beans.
Hat, star of stage and screen. Hat son of Hat
who was begotten of Hat from a long and noble lineage
reaching back into the Bronze Age, the Neolithic,
who knows? Hat's escutcheon, his entire dog and pony show.
The hat realizes *Jesus I'm somebody's father.*
The hat fights in the Spanish war on the wrong side.
The hat's nemesis. Sometimes the hat makes love
to his sister and later is devoured by guilt,
this despite the fact hats have no genitals.
Adolf's hat, the goosestepping *Sieg heil* hat.
Nacht und Nebel hat. Ein Reich ein Hut.
The hats of the ethnic cleansers, caps worn
around Pale by some calling themselves poets,
their manicured haircuts that are also hats.
Hat bastards. The hat in the underworld,
realising what he's capable of in the name of hat.
The hat as envisaged by Dante in the 7th ring of hell.
The hat is a Dutchman far away from home.
The hat asking the whereabouts of the red light district.
The hat smuggling in a little hashish via his hatband.
The get-stuffed hat. The go-boil-your-head hat.
The am-I-making-enough-of-an-asshole-of-myself-yet hat?
The fall-over-and-get-chucked-out-of-a-taxi hat. The hat
rubbing his left ear and complaining he's misunderstood.
The hat saying *Go from here. Go home*
to Little Miss Sugarplum who loves you very much
despite the constant smell of burning in the room.
The hat orders a red wine and a red stripe.
Hat's name shouted from the top deck of a 57 bus.
The hat a voice in the night saying *I'm lonely.*
The hat considers suicide but it is not yet
his last resort. The hat transformed, redeemed
at last by the all healing properties of love.
My kingdom for a hat. Le hat c'est moi.
The ageing hat. The hat on a park bench
in the autumn of his days. The hat with a habit.
The hat studying his profile in the mirror.
The hat awake, aware, conscious, a sentient being

contemplating all the other mysteries of the universe,
wondering to himself *do you suppose there is*
a finite number of stars? The hat as holy writ.
The hat feels disinclined to go to evensong.
The hat rushed into hospital for emergency surgery.
The hat fallen on hard times, the hat with the blues.
The hat suffering from a hefty dose of paranoia.
The schizophrenic hat off his trolley,
out of his pram, two cups short of a tea-set.
The hat's seasonal transhumance through the Alps.
The hat helping the police with their enquiries.
The hat that died in the service of his country.
The hat brought down by insurrection and shot.
The hat sentenced to life for bloody murder.
The hat handing in his keys to the desk clerk
saying *c'est la vie mon cher ce n'est que rien.*
The homeland of the hat, green rolling hills
and the far river sparkling in the sunlight,
the hat remembers, the hat is in love, he says
I promise I will take you there, my beloved,
my woman of the hats, you who are my dream,
my gift my vision all my inspiration my love
amongst the white tongues of the arum lilies.
The hat's dream life. The hat's dark secrets.
The hat's prayer. The hat at his rutting.
The hat's occasional sexual peccadilloes.
The hat gets his rocks off. The hat purrs
with pleasure and pours himself a large Glenlivet.
The life and times and further adventures of a hat.
The hat dressed to the nines and going on the razzle.
The hat's programme for reform of the judiciary.
The hat's codicil to his last will and testament.
The hat's last territorial demand on Europe.
The hat as the currency of the Common Market.
The ghosts of dead hats. The hat in exile.
†I.M. Monsieur Hat. Requiescat in pace.
The hat gone to his just reward in hat heaven,
joined the great architect, kicked the bucket.
The wild hats hooting in the woods.
The hats that have no homes to go to.
hats who have changed their names for immigration.
The alienated hat. The blunt-spoken hat,
the ey-by-gum hat, the bugger-you-anyway hat,

the hat calling a hat a hat speaking his mind
and doing as he would like to be done by.
The hat sleeping it off in the ditch.
The last hat on the Yukon. The hat's death in Venice.
Superhat. Hat's last ride. Exit hat left.
The hat's memories of an idyllic childhood.
The hat will now reminisce for fifteen minutes.
The hat considers his options and draws up a plan.
The hat wins the Nobel Prize. The hat gets the OBE.
The hat packs his bags and moves to Amsterdam.
The hat going into a sulk. The hat in recession.
The hat swears innocence on his mother's grave.
The hat sitting down to a fine fish supper.
The hat saying *so who's been sleeping in my bed?*
The hat saying *I spy with my little eye.*
The hat switching channels. The hat movie.
The hat in a bag. The hat lost in the city.
The hat going down the pub to get drunk again.
Hat's story: I was married once, my sunflower
I called her, *come in* I said *under my broad brim.*
under my high crown, come in love and I will warm
your cold innards. She was pretty, we were madly in love.
So much for my perception of reality.
She ran off with the captain of the Woolwich Free Ferry
singing *sanfairyann my hairy little spider*
leaving me weeping bitter tears into my billycock.

The hat was no longer in my court.
The hat was now firmly on the other foot.
The hat was now put before the horse
that was now of a very different colour.
The hat hit the fan. The hat with egg all over its face.
The hat up hat creek as we say hereabouts
without a paddle, or *that hat won't hunt.*
Gnashings and wailings. Salt tears.
Lamentations throughout the Republic of Hats,
Beethoven on the radio, state mourning.
I learned the watched hat never sleeps,
to let sleeping hats lie, turn the other hat,
never count my hats before they hatch,
and that every hat has a silver lining.
Heyho I say who needs the aggravation?
Time to say *goodnight Comrade Vodka.*

I guess I made my hat and so must wear it.
So now I walk on the sunny side of the hat.
And I say plenty more where that came from,
there's still rivers and music and birds,
sunrise and sunset, sunlight and moonlight
and the sunstruck wind dabbed water on the mere.

Go tell the honey ant

The scavenger ants trek through the forest,
each day an exact slice of the compass.
They eat everything and they spare nothing
in that sector. They are out there,
I hear them with their black flags.

There are the slaves and there are the slavemakers,
toughs who spray propoganda substance
turning their victims onto each other,
and they make off with the eggs. These are the slaves.
They do all the work around here.

That's how it is in the ant universe.
Nothing can change it. But how would you like
to be pumped into a bag of glucose and water
hung from the ceiling against lean times?
Upside down. That's some career plan.

As for the bear grubbing in the bleak winter
of the bears, he's not interested in this
but in the rare sharp sweetness on his tongue.
He blinks. If I were you the bear in me says
I'd stick to sweet things, especially honey.

Columbus to Isabella

Every man is a master of disorder...

COLUMBUS, Letter to the Sovereigns of Spain

My ships are beached at Guincho,
furthest west into the ocean
and alas we are at war with the neighbours.

At the far limits of the sea
islands rose on the sky's edge,
where we landed, sea sore,

myself wearier than the rest
in all that muttering crew
eager to unship me and turn back.

200 nights I did not sleep
in my bunk nor change clobber,
bad meat and wormy bread

and all on my own dead reckoning
shortening the miles in the log,
reading birds and weeds in the sea

out where the pole star wandered
and the earth's shape was a pear
such as may lie before you, Lady.

The natives are mild and naked,
fit to be your servants
and receive Christ's Blood.

The gold is always further off,
west towards the falling sun,
silver as it pours into the sea.

Days on Dog Hill

A season of loose connections, bells
and weddings through the rainy summer.
I woke with my head in a crock,
I had dreamed of nothing.

I'm into town and out, down the hill
and up again, muttering *waggontruss,*
windbrace, through the tall woods
along the old pack road that no longer goes anywhere,

and like the windy leaves never still,
always on the way to some thought
lost in the traffic and the chatter,
the town below fading into voices off,

a hammer's knock travelling beyond itself,
a man shouting his name over and over,
lives made from the sounds they make.
These things do not connect:

a yellow flower from a far off country,
linked hearts cut in a tree's side,
sussura of pigeon wings, an animal threshing
the undergrowth, scribble of bird song

here, here, and your secret names for me –
Old Paint, Wild Root, Scissorbill. I dreamed
the ridge and these massed dark roots of the yews,
anger like a sudden wind. Wild root.

Here

I point to where the pain is, the ache
where the blockage is. Here.
The doctor shakes his head at me. Yes
he says, I have that, we all have.

They put the wire in again, on the monitor
I watch the grey map of my heart, the bent
ladder of the spine that outlasts it.
How does it feel? they ask. Here?

I am moving away down the long corridors
of abandoned trolleys, the closed wings
of hospitals, rooms full of yellow bedpans
and screens and walker frames, fading out

into nothing and nothing at all, as we do,
as we all do, as it happens, and no one
can talk of it. Here, where the heart
dies, where all the systems are dying.

Night at the Blind Beggar

Easy-peasy they said, a simple job,
money for old rope. Here's a drink.
Go to the Blind Beggar in Whitechapel
between this hour and this hour.

Sink a slow thoughtful pint or two,
a tough young bucko in his suit and tie,
out for the evening on a mission,
the bystander with the job of seeing nothing.

A quiet night, the light fading, traffic
on the High Street, music on the jukebox.
Then at 8.30 Ronnie walks in with a Mauser
and blows a man's head all over the room.

Hadn't bargained for that.
Not that sort of drink.
Our man sees everything and nothing.
That's it he's out of there.

Jumped the District Line, at Paddington
the first train anywhere took him west
into an ordinary life: job, mortgage,
wife, kids, the years becoming more years.

Except the long days and longer nights
of all the rest of him are spattered
by the bits of brain on the wall
and blood over his white shirtfront.

This is his tale of how he got lost.
Dogget he says into the strange silence
he inhabits, the question mark as ever
slung around his shoulder. *Dog ate my dinner.*

The gracenote

Saturday night I'm on the Broadway,
round my own neck of the woods
listening for the numbers knowing
I'll have none of them that win.

Fourth pub left of the tube stop,
I'm in Murphy's where one of us
has a very bad cough, my mate says
she left me with just one chopstick,

I was one chopstick short of a pot noodle.
Most times it's like this, a strange
normality where I'm agawp, always,
a good listener is all of it, mimic

with an ear cocked for the gracenote –
always a nice touch though you don't want
too many gracenotes in any one place,
and I tell you all this for nothing.

I'm the starling on the wire, giving it
with all his harsh repertoire of cries,
some of them his own, some borrowed,
some blue, none of them ever repaid –

bits of magpie song and blackbird,
owl's voice, sometimes in a tone
recognisably human a single word:
habitually, habitually, habitually.

Narrow Road, Deep North

From the northbound train
white flecks on the brown ploughland
like flakes of fine snow –

they are birds, gulls,
suddenly flying. Across
winter fields somehow

I missed the white horse
on the hill that was boyhood,
all of it gone now.

Playing fields some place
that was some place once, goal posts
moved and again moved.

I'm on the run, hours,
days of the one bitter thought
on the narrow road

to my life's deep north,
in my pocket a ticket:
ADULT. ADMIT ONE.

Ah this long rocking
as the landscape turns to frost,
lulling me to sleep,

weeping and weeping
over the north, for my dead,
for all my lost ones,

they who will not come
my way again, them we won't
see again, ever.

The dry northern air,
the white wind will sort it out,
and the rain, the rain.

And everywhere birds
in a glitter of flying,
the landscape dancing.

At Culloden larks
that are dust in the tall air,
black flags of the crows.

Barefoot some, kilted,
charging through juniper, thorns,
thistles, their faces

set to the wind, sleet,
shrapnel, grapeshot, bayonets,
Cumberland's well trained

Hessian butchers –
hungry and down hearted, fell
all the wild flowers

of Scotland. Exeunt
clansmen, croftsmen, fishermen.
Bonnie Prince Dickhead,

says Billy, days away
on Skye, in the old mates' club,
and a dram to go.

Ah, water. The sunset
a riot. The far islands
where clouds are mountains

under deep white snow,
and the Hebridean *yes*
begins *no, no, no,*

and *no* again *no*
till the *yes* of it at the
sentence's finish:

aye a wee dram then.

This is for you Jim,
whose garden is the battlefield.
This is for you, Con,

that you stay upright
and vertical in Tarbert,
this god forsaken

hole. That the Wee Free
tether the goat, the rooster,
that the seventh day

is all cold meat, is
fact friend, *in the Good Black Book*
you will find mention

of boats but never
a bicycle. Things the heart
will no longer hold,

and bursts with, thoughts
on the waves and the west wind,
the long birds overhead,

heron, Brent Goose, swan,
their distant migrations,
continents their shores.

The light off the cliffs
climbing out of the dull sea
into rainclouds.

The best monuments
belong to the defeated,
and always anyway

and after a while
all the bartenders look alike
and your man goes off

the rails, *refreshments*
sounds in his ear like *fresh mints*
and on the rolling

bar on the rocking
boat asking for chewing gum
what he hears: *tuna.*

Let the light bleed out.
Let there be me and the landscape
and the moon, dreamer

when the dream goes out
into the next and the next,
following the tongue,

the eye, lone white house
on the hilltop, why don't I
live there?

I ran away to
Scotland, the people there to
see, and found a pound

was as round and soon
spent, home again home again,
jiggety-jig.

Ah but the cold clean
air of the mountains, water,
Callanish sunlight.

And again gulls' cries,
tern, bittern, the heart's last blips
on the monitor.

Time to go home.

The yellow dock gate
comes down and the town bell rings
two, two. From the dock

a woman calls her farewells
to her man and a voice shouts
Kenny, Kenny, but

it ain't me Sunshine,
we roll in the water's heave
on *The Isle of Mull,*

on passage, the land
fading to mist and distance,
on the dark water

black snouts of dolphins,
up from their own deep places,
breathing in ours.

Blue Prague: the worst you can say in Czech

It's true I desire to go far away
and mutter to myself in the wind,
taking the long train of myself off,
lost among strangers and distances.

If I called myself now on the phone
my voice would say I'm not at home just now
and what I then called now would now be then,
every moment its own in another time zone of the heart.

But no I was never in Prague, never lost
in its blowsy statuary, never visited
the House of the Bell, nor drank the absence of absinthe,
never ate the Executioner's Special.

I was never the King's Jew.
I was a limping man on a stick
with a broken eyeglass, just
an old *dědek* with his tobacco.

Nic moc, no big deal. The city
a blue rainy haze of lights, *Strasne dobry*,
awesome, a wolf wind howling over the tiles,
crack of flags like gunfire, bells.

Někecam. I met a tall man walking
with a tiny cactus in his fist.
The chambermind will bring the cattle.
Would you like grilled meat on the needle?

Messages: among the scrambled stones
and bladed upright Hebrew a folded note:
let the hatred cease. Crows overhead
sawing the air, the souls of ancient rabbis.

Do prdele, the worst you can say,
lost in blue toothy Prague.
*Sere medvěd lese? May all your sons
be bartenders. Noší papež legrační klobouk?*

Journey without maps

1 *Night train*

The moon's wide open mouth, its
thin light over fields and woods
that could be anywhere, distant names
of cities chanted on the speakers –
their two notes *born free, born free.*

Outside the same night: lit windows
flying backwards through the dark,
the streetlamps of little towns
lighting empty roads no one
is walking home, late, tipsy.

And in a flash of sudden neon
a tall crane in a field of wrecked cars.
It is the night of old shoes, their mouths
slackly open: *where now brother,*
how long ago was yesterday,
how many days until tomorrow?

2 *September distance*

A blur of birches. Borders
that are more than what you feel there,
wind rushing the reeds, long wing
of wild geese flying south, sunflowers,
poppyheads and milkweed, forest,
mile after mile the tall fields of maize,
the long plains measuring the distance,
west to east autumn yellowing the leaves.

It is a place called Russian Horse,
a place called Shoemaker in Iron County,
a city of bells and crippled Gypsies,
the Gold Boys in and out the bars.

The streetsweeper sifts his broom
for flakes of fallen gold.
The dancing whore in Goat Town calls
oh tonight I want a man between my legs.

3 *What Feri said*

In the far distant relation
between Finnish and Hungarian

one sentence is the same
and only one and though

we don't know what it is
we know it is about fish,

a live fish swims underwater.
And in Vogul a sentence

the same as ours it says
twenty women's horses go on ahead.

4 *Glimpse*

of a man tapping his finger
on a map: *here, I live here,*
not much of a place, a crossroads
with a light that doesn't work,
a store that doesn't sell much
and a closed petrol station,
nowhere in particular but we think
it's the centre of the universe:
Podunkstadt that was before the wars,
thereafter called Amnesza.

After the changes the beer is better
but still undrinkable. Things are not good
but they are not unhopeful. Here
we have the best of everything
but you can't have any of it.

5 *Flatlands*

This is another place I won't remember
somewhere on the great plain
of long byres and tall wells and sky
where I have been travelling fast
with that far shine on the road ahead
and the wind over me, at night the cars
with their lights trembling on the highway,
as if the stars were passing through us.

Moments that are snapshots, coins slipped
in a beggar's cup, a one-legged man
on a bicycle with a broken umbrella
waiting at the crossroads that are
always unlucky places, the burials
of lost travellers and victims,
beside the memorial's unreadable epitaph
eaten over by lichen and rain.

6 *Closed border, Slavonia*

Over there the flag of one country
blowing in the wind of another
beyond the closed checkpoint:
fields, river, birchscrub, the same.

This is the border where the road runs out
into a tractor trail of snowy mud
to the last house by the wire,
and all the dogs are barking.

Nothing between me and the wind,
tall reeds and border fences,
here to say I've been here,
take a snapshot and turn home,

a traveller with his keepsakes –
a man's bone from an old battlefield,
a bent bullet from Mostar,
weary with the weight of my self.

7 *TV in the East*

On SKY and SAT late night images
passing for desire and its flesh,
the play of light wherein they kiss
and soft things flutter to the floor,
a mouth begins its snail of a descent
to the promise of a breast and cut
to the commercial: all the lives
we may not want and cannot have.

And on the Russian channel mirror script:
mountains, a place far to the east
of open sky and early snow, a swift
upland river and slow drummers,
chants, horses and horsemen, women
in a long line through windy smoke,
led by an old man wearing skins,
on his head the antlers of a deer.

8 *Waking in Heroes' Park*

Too many days counting coup on the borders:
countries sucking on their stones,
some gone rusty in the rain,
another sulking on its wounds.

Markets and stations, crossings
where the police jump on the vagrants
and the fugitives, everyone's a suspect,
everyone an item in their career moves.

In Heroes' Park I wake to white noise
and the world sailing its ocean of dirty air,
across a bridge men carrying planks,
copper pipe and scaffolding, tea kettles,

sheets of clear glass. And through
the autumn trees a line of bright
schoolchildren, babbling like a river,
where I wake, dreaming of chickens.

Moscow dogs

Sasha says:
all the chairs in here are broken
though some are more broken than others.

Outside over the garbage cans visited
every few minutes by the old and the poor
a white plastic bag drifts on the updraughts

so delicately, riding the air,
settles on the new leaves of the cotton tree
just above the steps to the door that never opens.

The only reply:
three legs good, four legs better.
I want the words for dogs, huge, loose on the streets

but the only Russian I know is *da, niet, voda, pivo,*
vodka, spasibo, dosvidanya: yes, no, water,
beer, vodka, thankyou and goodnight.

Horrowshow: very good. *Spiceybar*: thankyou.
Watch out for the dogs.
To say *I love you* say *yellow blue vase.*

All the old fear lurks on the stairs
all the way down the elevator shaft
in this Stalinist wedding-cake block of flats,

it blows on the dust of the streets,
on everyone's shoes, in everyone's bones.
Watch out for the dogs.

Georgia, Georgia

sings the market radio, *Georgia on my mind.*
They sing a lot here, in the underpass
three in four part harmony, wail of a saxophone.

Glimpse of a woman crossing herself over and over
before the locked door of the cathedral.
Bulletholes. The dusty south. Tbilisi.

Spectacular storms are breaking far away
over the mountains, no one but a few shepherds
are out in it, and they may not live to tell the tale.

Driven on the storm the sudden wind
through the thick black night of the city
shakes the walnut trees. Here they dance.

Three things a bride must know:
to cook, play chess, and recite Rustaveli.
There's a lot of Rustaveli.

Dumplings and dark wine, a balcony on which to sit
and contemplate the evening, lightning on the mountains
and suddenly short bursts of automatic fire.

Tie a note to a wishing tree. Sleep,
in the morning woken by the cockbird's cry
without a shadow of a doubt: *Cau-ca-sus. Cau-ca-sus.*

Hungarian quartets

The night anywhere

is just a car choking into life and idling
as he nurses it to warmth, the window ice
melting as he buckles in, the flare
his lighter makes in the inner dark
and she chiding his late drinking,
hoping he will drive slowly on the black roads,
and he will let her sleep tonight.

There is a man's far away shout, a woman's cry.
It could be anywhere: the cold night stars
burning overhead, the silence of the snow,
a horizon of dogs recalling how they ran in packs
long ago though this flat border country.
It could be here in the Bácska running south
with the great river down to lost Vojvodina.

It's late, after palinka and fisherman's soup.
Then for hours the thump of the bowling balls
the local skinheads and the Serbs downstairs
roll half the night between long telephone calls
to somewhere far away. It could be now.
It could be anywhere in this northern winter
before sleep. It could be anyone's song.

Sándor the poet

Meet Sándor the gypsy. He is a poet
in his own kingdom, under the reeds.
Today he is building his winter house.
This is his pig. Thankyou he says.

Thankyou for coming to see me.
Would you like to marry my daughter?
You are a rich man from the West. Be kind to her.
Buy her chocolate and pink champagne.

Someone is shoving a wire through a pig's nose.
Someone is revving a motorbike
up and down the dusty alley. When the screaming stops
you hear water pouring from the pump,

you hear the wind over the waste and the reeds
where his people live by the old Russian barracks
at Kiskunmajsa. They could move in there
but the government, the government.

The bitter eyes of the Gypsies,
empty pockets, empty glasses. Soon
it may be time to go to jail again.
Soon again winter, when some will die

in this village without a name.
A special tribe he says, their leathery
wee women are blue eyed yellow haired
daughters of the Red Army, 1944.

Nem jó he shrugs: doesn't work.
He waves at the flies, complaining
you see how it is here with us
the Cigány? Look at the flies on the bread.

And picks up his instrument and plays
a lament for the ancient distance,
at night a sky burning with stars,
every one of them Hungarian.

Alma the apple. *Róka* the fox.
The leaves are drifting from the trees.
Soon will come the bleak zima of the puszta.
Thankyou for coming to see me.

Misi's song

I will sing one song
from Novi Sad. But this
this is not a song.

The words: difficult, different.
I can't remember: la la la.
Oh my love.

My beloved landscape and the landscape of my beloved.
I was born to it.
I should die there.

Each night the phone rang.
Sometimes silence, breathing. Or a man
cursing in Serbian:

why don't you go?
You have a wife, children,
we can kill them.

You we will impale.
Land I was born to.
This is not a song.

Dmitri's song

I will sing now the lost song
in the lost voice from the lost time

if I can find it
if I can find where I left it

the old song from the old time
of an old man who is young again

ah but always

something is wrong in exile
and the heart is bloody always

The Shadow of God

*

I am Suleyman, sultan of sultans, sovereign of sovereigns, distributor of crowns to the lords of the surface of the globe.

I am Suleyman, the Shadow of God on earth, Commander of the Faithful, Servant and Protector of the Holy Places.

I am Suleyman, ruler of the two lands and the two seas, sultan and padishah of the White Sea and of the Black, of Rumelia, of Anatolia, of Karamania, and of the land of Rum I am Rum Kayseri.

I am lord of Damascus, of Aleppo, lord of Cairo, lord of Mecca, of Medina, of Jerusalem, of all Arabia, of Yemen and of many other lands which my noble forefathers and illustrious ancestors (may God brighten their tombs) conquered by the force of their arms and which my august majesty has subdued with my flaming sword and my victorious blade.

I am Sultan Suleyman Han, son of Sultan Selim Han, son of Sultan Bayezid Han.

I am Suleyman. To the east I am the Lawgiver. To the west I am the Magnificent.

*

Suleyman. In his dream the far world
is a basket of heads at his saddlebow,
sunlight's flash on the edges of blades
raised in his name to the dim horizon:
I am Suleyman. At the end of Ramadan,
in the spring of the year that will send
his quarrelsome soldiery north again

Suleyman rises from sleep, consults maps,
glancing up glimpsing the evening star
low in the cobalt canopy of the day's end
caught in the thicket of the new moon's
upturned horns, and takes that for his omen.
That year as every year war is a season,
war is a fetva, a jihad waged on all
the unreconciled world of unbelievers
beyond the gaze of the Magnificent.

That year his beard points west again
to the domain of war: glimpse of far hills,
country scoured flat by the rivers, the beasts
are deer and wild pig leaving their tracks
on the soggy waterlands, on the scrubland
thistles, milkweed, juniper, vines,
the eyes of the tall white birches
glimpsed through the pines. The birds
are swift, hawk, crow and kingfisher,
the little seedeaters, the buzzards
sentinels on his way, the storks
from their round high nests in the wind
glance after him, the pheasant's stutter,
the owl's stare in his tracks, the woodpecker
tapping in the dark light of the woods,
the shrike pinning his dinner to a thorn.

The Lawgiver, Suleyman, whom the Prophet
favour and posterity long remembers,
goes out of the city to his war camp.
He hoists the six black horsetails of his flag,
unwraps the forty silk shawls from the black
sacred banner of Mohammed and raises it,
and from all the heaven protected empire
of dur ul Islam come the levies, sipahiler,
akincilar, seğmenler, tüfekçiler, azaplar,
topçular, yeni çeriler, tribesmen and the wild
bowmen of the steppes, the half naked dervish
not counted into the muster, one hundred thousand
dreaming of loot, calling his name, *Suleyman,*
taking the roads north, Constantinople to Belgrade
and the rough tracks beyond into the wastes
of the unbelievers, the mire of the infidel.

In his journal there is rain, endless rain,
day after day the grey slanting downpour,
vague cloudy horizons and the sky's flood.
And bitter winds. 80 days on the march
in the downpour on no road that is a road
driving the great train north, 80 nights
pitched in the sheeted rain, slithering
with horses and camels and weaponry
in the black Balkan mud of the flood plains,
left of the river between the rivers
in that year of the rain. The beasts
are deer and boar and wolf, the birds
hawk and butcher bird, black cormorant
low over his black shadow on the river,
crows in a black storm overhead, or perched
on a stump, watching the way God watches.

Ropes split, the big guns sink in the bogs,
the cries of horses and men no one hears,
merely the dead born to die in the muck
for the enlargement of empire and the word
of the Prophet, may God's smile ever rest on him,
for the enrichment of some, enslavement of some,
somewhere in the mapless country of the rain,
crushed by the wheels, some lost in sinkholes,
the ropes falling away from their hands
and last of them the O of their upturned
mouths calling his name: *Suleyman, Suleyman*.
The names of the days are rain and wind,
the names of the rivers run into each other.
Up the Danube day after day 800 boats
weigh upwind upstream on the downcoming
agua contradictionis beyond which the barbarians.

Under the six black horsetail standard,
under the sacred banner the horse army
lugs its stores and its guns northward
into the oncoming rain and the clutter of mud
and the wind in their faces: cavalry, artillery,
sharpshooters, musketmen, soldiers, raiders,
shaggy Tatar horsemen, all dreaming of rape.
300 cannon through the marshes, some lost,
the horses straining, the whips, no roads,

no bridges in all this nowhere of mud,
tracks that run to dead ends, watery graves,
roads running off into water, marsh paths
learned at a blade's edge and goodbye
the quick blood, always eager to be off,
goodbye the names hawk and buzzard and heron,
the names Sava and Drava mean nothing now.

Suleyman. The bared teeth of the horses,
their necks rear from the reeds, screaming
as horses scream, men scream, the rain falls.
Imprint of reeds on the sky lances on the wind,
lancemen and horsemen. The birds are shrike,
buzzard, crow, the owl falling on its shadow,
the harrier's underspread wingspan two skulls
on the grey light rising on the sky, the rivers
Sava and Drava and Danube though the names
mean nothing to him. Problems with stores,
problems with water, questions of powder,
fuel for the cooking pots, meat, some warmth
in the long shivering rain, shaving the rust
from their blades, sword, knife, sabre, spear,
matchlock and carbine, guns lugged down roads
built of reeds, the stores rotting away.

The sodden saddlesore army of divine light,
fractious and lice-ridden and chilled to the bone,
crying *Suleyman Suleyman*, those running before
crying *Suleyman Suleyman*, the Magnificent.
He is crossing the Drava on a golden throne
from the domain of peace to the domain of war.

                              To Mohács
in the marshlands, still in the pouring rain,
August 29th, 1526, where those summoned
and hastily gathered died in thousands
in the space of a moment the chronicler
scribbles, in the safety of distance,
cruel panthers in a moment to hell's pit.

That day the guns chained wheel to wheel,
smoke and the cries of men and horses,

the knights shot from their saddles, armour
dragging them into the mire, the hooves
stamping them in, the infantry butchered,
in the space of a moment the swift
routine of retreat, slaughter and rout,
the space of a moment. No prisoners,
the wails of the wounded, the dying, becks
brimmed with blood, and the young king
thrown from his horse, drowned in his breastplate.
Thereafter Suleyman recalls he sat on the field
in the pouring rain on his glittering throne
to the long applause of his army: *I am*
Sultan Suleyman Han, son of Sultan Selim Han,
son of Sultan Bayezid Han. The Shadow of God.

And they butcher the captives, dig the pits
to bury their own brave dead, horses and men,
30 thousand whose last rainy day was this,
and the other dead lie in the rain, or scatter
their bones in the wetlands and the reedgrass.
Whatever birds pecked out their eyes
their names are no matter nor the stream
they drowned in nor the name of the planet
whose soft brown body they shovelled in after.
Thereafter the land burns and the churches,
thereafter women and slaves and silver.
And thereafter, pronounces the historian,
his quill's tip brushing his cheek, his point
squeaking over the page, the lamp's glint
on his inkhorn: *the long Turkish night,*
the tomb of the nation, dug in the rain.

In the space of a moment, in the centuries
moments pile into, leaf over leaf,
season by season as the winters pass
and the wars roll over and the borders shift
it is ploughland, old bones surfacing
at the hoe's edge and the plough's iron,
scapulae and vertebrae rising in a flat
wide fenced country laid open to the wind,
prowled by the tractors of the collectives
and the same wandering birds, black earth

through white snow, wind beaten scarecrow
and the white silence of another winter.
It is a museum of bones in the thick boney
stew of each other, where some bird sings
in the evergreens and a boy rings a bell
in the long white silence that follows.

It is a field of poles upright at a pit's rim,
carved into cruel faces, chiselled in grimaces,
spiked, helmeted, horned, a ragged line of posts
that are totems of men straggling off into trees,
some aslant, the long necks of horses
rearing from snow. They are flail and bludgeon
and battleaxe, calvaries of yokes and the bows
of the swift horsemen, the trailed arms
of the willow tree. They are the crescent moon
and the star, the cross, the crown, the turban
and the tarboosh, gnarled glances of soldiers,
the figures of dead men rising from the earth,
Suleyman with a basket of heads at his pommel
and the dead king Lajos in his blue bonnet.

Overhead the high jets in the clear blue
corridor of cloudless sky above Serbia,
flying the line of the great rivers
whose names are the same though the names
of the empires and the nations shift
on the maps. South of here, not far,
in the debateable lands of the warring states
the bones are again rising in the mud.

The wooden cock crows from his wooden post.
In the clear dry air a bell rings.

*

A bell rings. In the town the dogs bark
and all night again the banging of boats
on the river and the thud of drifting ice
on their hulls and the slapping of waves.

Always dogs, beyond gates, over walls,
loose on the streets, howling to the far
flat ring of the world's edge of woods,
rivers, barns, border posts.

Wolfhounds, manhounds, pit bulls,
mutts, mastiffs and mongrels bawling
at cats, cars, bells, footsteps, wind
in the winter trees, the yellow moon.

Each with his patch to scratch, each
his yard to guard, each with his own
view of the world, his own particular opinion
he will not give up easily.

Wars begin with this and end whimpering.
They begin with the squabbles of neighbours
and end in the baying of men: what's mine
is mine. And yours is mine also.

And someone has backed into the lamppost again,
someone has knocked over the empty bottles,
someone has burst into drunken tuneless song
on the late street and set all the dogs off.

Someone has been beating his wife again,
broken all the crockery in the kitchen,
woken the kids and the curs and the old wounds,
slammed the door shut, kicked the gatepost.

And gone off to the river to think it all out,
contemplate drowning himself at last
as all round in his reeling skull
in the great dark the dogs bark.

*

Very fast very slow this music
a lament from the villages
a music come down from the mountains
called across rivers across plains:

ah no joking and no joking
a gift for the kolo, bridegroom
the thieves they are singing
dance my love dance faster
faster till we fall down.

The reedgrass that will be thatch
first snowy fields turned in the plough.
a line of trucks in a white field
waiting for grain not yet sown:
end of the winter quarter
end of the season of craving
the river's ice drifting south
snow collapsing from the buildings:
the days of the death of King Winter.

The *Busójárás.*

Time to take to the streets
wearing the skins of beasts
masks years in the making offspring
of the old whisperers in the hearth
kin to the devotees of trees
and certain stones and all rivers
lord of the vines and beasts
our lady of the wild things the old gods
who never made it into heaven.

Busós.

They step out of the unwritten
the unremembered out of Illyria
out of the south the dark the flight
and the distant remembrance of panic
the horned hoof footed hard drinking
god of the shepherds. They step out
through the winter streets in masks
horns in sheepskins and old bandoliers
with their bells and their rattles.

Busós.

With their antlers tall in the skins
of beasts belled shaggy moustache men
huge with their clubs and horns
wild in their tall wooden masks
coming on from the distance
all the years they have travelled
out of the unlettered the *agrapha*
the history of the forgotten
the long shadows of the lost gods.

At noon they have crossed the river
they have taken the streets
filled with organised riot
the ruckus of men in the male dance
the clatter and rattle of flails
the interminable clanging of bells
rain clanking into buckets
in mockery taking their ways
through the orders of anarchy.

Busós.

Fierce and yet not fierce
joking and yet not joking
this is the management of chaos:
the war of the great ratchets
the battle of the bells upright animals
striding through the streets
through the cold falling sunlight
in a wild skirling music
bearing the skulls of animals.

Busós.

Others come as veiled hooded women
a brown friar another the devil
a joker in a Russian tank mask
a Groucho Marx an Austrian helmet.
And these others ghosts in dirty sheets
rags sackcloth and ashes and stocking masks
bunched in knots of impudent silence
young men scattering the girls
the dead risen from the dead.

Centuries ago the traveller
Evliya Çelebi warned his far flung
wandering countrymen of the masked
madmen of Mohács in the marshland
in their shaggy jackets and bells
and their faceless faces:
they are devils devils
in the place of devils
no one should go there.

In their own legend of themselves
they chased the Turks out of town
in terror. In the ill-disciplined
shaggy masked half drunk ranks
among pitchforks and whirling clubs
the carved severed head on a stick
of a janissary, moustache top knot skull
goes round and round in the racket
and the gathering fire and the dusk.

How years ago they were fearless
in the place of defeat and rose again
how years ago a pig's blood painted
a cross in the town square and how
the masks stained in animal blood
and the wild cries and the kolo
was their resistance. How once
they were one with the beasts
one with men one with the gods.

Rutting and butting as beasts
sticks for pricks bells balls
and under the mask is another
and another they are Busós
three days of the year Busós
parading their ragged squads
to the square where the cannon
from that year of the rain
thunders mud and rags and smoke.

Busós.

Come nightfall on the third day
of marching and mayhem and music
that is Shrovetide the fire's lit
in the square. King Winter is dead
carted off in a coffin and burned.
On the coffin in flowery
Hungarian script: *it's sold,*
our country, it's sold, we have
nothing left but our fathers' pricks.

Where does this music come from?
an old woman asks. From all round her
from everywhere from earth
from the wind from the long turned
furrows of defeat the old sorrow
the old joy the songs
of the long gone into the dark.
It's sold, our country,
and all the thieves are laughing.
Time to march one last time
on the town and burn winter
with bells and cannon and fire
round and around the tottering square
masked men and horses the music
round and round the kolo
the dancing of the hairy men
and winter goes up in the flames
the tall smoke climbing the sky.

Busós.

The sliver of moon the first star
on the pale blue flag of the sky
as the sparks flare and die. At the edge
of the embers of memory the borders
of hearing: bells laughter a child
a cough girls singing the swift music
in the ashes of the evening
wisps of voices at a distance
in that far off language.

Wire through the heart

Where the scythe has been

This is the music of no music.
You have to listen hard if you're listening at all
to hear it out on the wind through the aspens,
faint as far off bells, as birds
on the edges of hearing, dogs in another country,
wolves working their way across the horizon.

It begins among the smashed stones
of some old Jewish graveyard glimpsed
in passing on the long roads somewhere,
some star in the window of a place
selling auto parts, a faint air
round the bare brickwork of a dead synagogue
in some town whose name you no longer remember,
where is no schul any more, no Sabbath,
no dark sidelocked men arriving on carts
with their shawled women, their solemn
children in long coats perched
like chickens, where is no kaddish said
for the millions who never came back,
where isn't ten together who can say it.

The music of where music has been:
only the tall windblown grasses
in the abandoned yard that will fall
to someone's else's scythe
to the descant of bird song
before the summer's over –
the soft sigh of the blade.

Signed sealed & delivered
(for Erzsébet, Kisszelmenc, Ukraine)

This is your permission.
Your licence. Keep it safe somewhere,
these words will get you through.
You will need them to pick herbs
by the border wire, and a handful of flowers
to put on your mother's grave
in the village where you were born
in the other country whose steeple
you can see from your yard's end.

To get there you will need this paper,
and again when you come back to say
you have been there. You will need
these words to say you have read them.

This is your permission to be someone,
anyone, a person called Kovács
who says it's all right to love someone,
to excess even, to go crazy,
to piss in the street, go to jail,
to one day die and briefly be remembered
best for the side of you that stood in light
at the gate of your house in spring
just before the sun went down, considering
the acacia blossoms and the onions
and your own diminishing options.

This is your permit, your passport
to the other side of anywhere.
Signed, sealed, delivered,
dated this day vaguely in May.

Of course, the signature's illegible
and on the wrong side of the paper.
And the rubber stamp cut from a bar of soap
was stolen long ago. And in any case
as to delivery there are no stamps,
the post office became a nightclub,
and the postman if he's been paid

since January, and if you still
have a letter box, he might just deliver it.

Maybe.

The Secret Police
(for Zelei Bori)

They are listening in the wires,
in the walls, under the eaves
in the wings of the house martins,
in the ears of old women,
in the mouths of children.

They are listening to this now.

So let's hear it for the secret police,
a much misunderstood minority.
After all, they have their rights,
their own particular ways of seeing things,
saying things, cooking things,
they too have a culture uniquely their own.

       And we think
they should have their own state
where they could speak their own
incomprehensible tongues, write
their confessions, their unknown histories,
cultivate their habits of watching
by watching each other, and fly
their own flags there, at attention
on parade in their medals at their monuments
on their secret anniversaries, making speeches,
singing praises to the God of Paranoia.

And at the end of the day
bury their dead, publish their coded obituaries
of each other, and rest at last
in their own kind of peace, forever.

Intermezzo, Sub-Carpathia, May 97

There is a bird in here, an oriole perhaps,
a nightingale trying to get out still singing
across the border between sleep and waking,
bringing the dream along. Sometimes
a solemn joyful music from the church
in some village of black widows clutching
prayer books, the black crows of sorrow.
Then a high chant from the music school
in was it Munkács?, and round the back
the strings tuning up, and once
in the muddy street of the Gypsies
the boy's high soprano above accordion
and badly tuned fiddle.
                              Wind
around the small sandblown hills, the reeds.

In the vaults hacked deep in the rock
the cold wine sleeps, that will become
a sharp memory on the tongue, the cold
tug of the air on the body. Elsewhere,
István the First sweeps bees from a honeycomb
with a long grey bird's wing, the bees drink
at the watertub and fill the air with sound,
honey spills into jars, one the beekeeper
gave me to sweeten my mornings, its gold light
shining here now on my windowsill.

In any case

The lives we live, always taking us
over some border, we spend our years
trying to get there, in the tracks
of the old migrations through the passes,
west and out from the land between the rivers
down the broken roads of the armies.

Everywhere old borders, countries slithering
on the maps, on their rafts of magma
never still for long. Everywhere memorials,
the dead of wars and Stalin's Terror
in these parts, the starry graves
of the drunk heroes of the Soviet Union,

and others unknown. Along
the roadsides crosses for those
who hit the brakes too soon, swerved,
hit a bus, burst into fire, went over
into the brown flood of the Tisza,
a bunch of fading plastic flowers.

We took the river road into the mountains
through the towns of closed factories,
where even the salt mines were shut,
a stork preening her ragged nest
on the tall brick factory chimney,
up through the high villages of the shepherds.

Fleeting: the fast river full of rain,
plank bridges hung over the flood,
wires and watchtowers over in Romania,
halfway up a steep impossible hill
a man in a blue shirt climbing to the sky,
the villages shifting into other tongues.

To the Tatar Pass of savage raiders
with no place to go back to. To the
Verecke Pass, where the seven tribes
of the people of the ten arrows came,
long ago though in any case the date
is debatable, the stone monument
lost in all the paperwork in far Kiev,

in any case unfinished. Up here the air's
foreign and thin, the first flash of lightning
among the peaks, the misty distance.
What of the 18,000 driven through here
in August 1941 to be shot on the other side
just for being Jews? What of the thousands

dead at Szolyva of cold and hunger,
typhus and TB and dysentery for being Hungarian?
For half a century no one could speak of them,
put chisel to stone. *Here* it says
on the boulder over the mass graves
Here one day will be a monument.

The materials in any case have been stolen.
I hear one man reading from the stone,
another say *here should be a monument
to the unknown thief.* Then wind again,
the mountain river rushing to its meeting
with the ocean, half a continent away.

Hucul

Villages in the high valleys, a tall
long legged people, come early summer
they walk off into the distance,
grazing their sheep among the clouds,
making cheese in their high solitary huts
over the old tracks of the transhumance.

This must be one of their jokes,
this busted flush of a country
with its government of shadows
in leather jackets and shades.

This is another:
                    from peak to peak
across rocks and fast water, birdsong
and bleating and the far glitter of bells,
one Hucul is asking another for news.

Haven't you heard? comes the voice
carried on the distance the sound travels:
The Russians have gone to the moon.

What, all of them?

No, just one of them.

So what's to shout about?

Heaven's dust

I would have sent you a postcard, love:
view of the castle on the river
that is all the names of this place:
Ungvár/Uzhgorod. Dusty streets
hosed by rain, scrawny horses,
the market, old town, old doorways.
Faces of shepherds or a long shot
of the mountains, Gypsy women
in red flowered dresses, the footbridge
over the river. A few snapshots
of desolation: an old woman selling
two toothbrushes, a lightswitch
and a heap of shrivelled radishes,
empty plinths where Lenin stood,
the biggest wolves in the world,
the old synagogue across the river.

But there are no postcards.
No stamps, no post office,
and in any case it would never reach you
bearing its message Oh I love you
from the collapsing country
across the shifting borders.

It would have said *Furthest point*
Europe from three seas/ the pole
of continentality/ 670 Km. equidistant
Adriatic Baltic Black Sea./ Oh
lovely River Uz/ thou givst me such a buzz/
Oh gorgeous River Ung/ thy praises we have sung
in good Slovak beer.
                    And who
would have thought in all the

siftings of the stars I'd be here,
an old man with his tobacco?
Surely we are all heaven's dust. All's well.

Border theatre

No, I am carrying no contraband,
no firearms, Kalashnikovs, missile launchers,
no drugs, no coils of copper wire from Minsk,
no nuclear materials, no body parts,
no bodies, no bullion, no known diseases.
Yes, I would like to leave your country now
and put its broken roads and rusty monuments
behind me, and Yes I'd like to leave
in less than the 36 hours it may take
for this performance on the border at Uzhgorod.

Act One: *The first gate.* The actors
are police and tough leather men
who shake each others' hands, swap
cigarettes, their parts and uniforms
interchangeable, short of speech
and not much eye contact, men of few words
and blank faces and all they say is No. Wait.
What's happening is difficult to tell,
some drive up and drive away,
some wait hours, some straight through.

This for the first hour when suddenly
it's action time, we're in the cage
and in the second act called *Wait & See*
at the soldiers' gate where we wait,
wait, where nothing happens much, money
changes into money, a blue beer truck
passes for the second time and back,
guards mooching down the border strip
through vines, the watchtower watching,
flags snapping in the wind.

Hours more until it's hurry up and wait again
down the long hill of traffic, uniforms,
exhaust gas, another hour to the last act
and the exit and the exit stamp.
Yes, this is my own face, the one I usually wear
to these occasions, Yes this my bag,
Yes this my emergency tin of sardines.
And then we go. Not recommended.
A seven-hour performance all about itself,
and we say we're lucky. There's no applause.

Malenki robot
(for János, Nagyszelmenc, Slovakia)

'Over there in the other country
my sister had daughters I've seen once
in forty years, nor visited my dead.
It's too late now, they're poor there,
and here I'm just an old working man,
and the only thing left for me to do is die.

'These are my blunt carpenter's hands,
and this on their backs the frost
that gnawed them at Szolyva, three winters,
two years I was a prisoner there.
Monday I build doors, Tuesday put on roofs.
Roofs. Doors. My life. Vodka.
It was the priest told me to go,
three days he said, a little light work,
malenki robot, two years building roofs,
and that because I had a trade.
I survived wearing the clothes of those who died,
after a while I survived because I had survived,
and then came home and here the border.'

The wire runs through the heart, dammit,
therefore we will drink cheap Russian vodka
in János' kitchen, and later take a walk
down to the border and look back
into the other world, the village in the mirror
that is the other half of us, here,
where the street stops at the wire
and goes on again on the other side,
and maybe the Gypsies will come to serenade us.

SHED

(2001)

Trillium

(for Kosovo)

There was a girl screaming on the mountain
over there. All night. She'd gone crazy.

Columns of those driven out. Clips of film.
Photographs of the world's unravelling,
the scattered dead, a city of crows and collateral damage
and dust. And the silence.

I was in the woods, they shot at me,
I didn't know my way.

Snatches of speech on the airwaves: *help us*.
In such times only hurried notes,
moving to no conclusion, a fool's work
to make anything of them, a liar's to make nothing.

I didn't know my way.
Screaming on the mountain.

The shorthand of death and desolation –
estimates, statistics. Not a song,
not a poem, not a melody, not a fugue.
Not a single note of any music.

They shot at me I didn't know my way.
There was a girl screaming on the mountain.

Among the trees the wandering white trillium of her headscarf.

The Millennium near Barking

The state I'm in, another fugue somewhere
south of north, not far off by the sexagesimal reckoning,
though all that is just another pair of trousers
in another order of events, and this where I am now

is already the other side of that. Here is where I'll be,
living near Barking wherever Barking is, at midnight
on the moment as the arbitrary settings of time
tip us out with a bad hangover into the next thousand years,
a device designed to get us to forget ourselves again,
waking in a new dawn with a new minted identity.

In the last words of the sailor king *bugger Bognor,*
let me die in bloody peace. Are you sure it's safe?
the last utterance of Will Palmer, hanged for murder
in 1856. *On the whole I'd rather be in Philadelphia.*
It's true much of the time it is very boring,
sitting in some place nursing a gutsache
so yes I'll have another drink, and think
of all the pretty bottles behind the bar
I'll never taste, all the bars in all the world
I'll never visit, all the blue skies, all the women.
You know it's funny how you forget heatwaves,
and what was the name of that distant country
of which we knew little, whatever went on there
is a fictionalised account by now, the answer
to all these dusty answers is just dusty.

So let the last night begin, in the deepening blue
the blackbird and the evening star, the other stars
winking on, their messages across the distances that say
here, I'm here, still here, out here, over here
in all this enormity, that is to say nowhere
in particular, this speck among the tides of vast dust
spread out across the time it makes up as it travels.
Whether the machines cease or no on the midnight
I'll be here, no doubt as usual engaged
in my inconclusive experiment with alcohol,
speculating this red ten takes that black jack,
this black pawn that white bishop, muttering
aloud these words I've made to be the last words
delivered at the last minute, ending in a dream of flying.

The other shadow

I make lists of things: soap, soup, batteries, film.
And piles of things: socks, maps, passport, compass,
a white stone with a hole in it for luck.

You're not on any of my lists
nor in any of the mounds I make
of the makings of another journey.

The ordinary things come with me anyway –
stray hairs of the cat stuck to my pants
that will become far away memory of cat

demanding supper: tuna. Now.
Some music for the road, some photographs,
and always some of your dust, love.

A stray button that is something of you,
blue as your eyes are,
blue as the sky on a good day in spring is.

This is a dream.

This is not a dream.

The guards are by occupation suspicious.
An oriole is calling in the border strip.

Hills a blue glaze in the rain.
Wild flowers in the upland pastures,
buffalo wallowing in mud.

Wheat that will be bread, poppyseeds
and sunflower that will be husks in the teeth,
grapes that will again be wine's sharp memory.

In the noon glare peasants huddle under trees:
rakes, hoes, scythes, as in Brueghel,
a landscape with Dürer through it.

And by the roadsides so many crucifixions,
blue Jesus hammered into tin, arms spread,
weeping for this grim potholed world.

Thunder through the mountains.
The road snaking up into pine forest.
White horse running through black smoke.

A dream, not a dream. Here and not here.

> *Perhaps this is a fugue, a fog, a fug,*
> *the confusions of another journey*
> *where the languages beat at the brain,*
> *the maps suddenly another tongue.*

It begins in a litany of the many names
of the seven Saxon towns of the Siebenbürgen
that is Erdéli, Ardel, Transylvania, each
a mouthful of argumentative syllables, guttural,
agglutinative, gobstopper names in languages
with knives in their teeth, it depends
who you ask, it depends where you're coming from,
in what irreconcilable tongue
through the passes and the river valleys,
to the lands beyond the forest
forever in dispute and everywhere
as anywhere the neighbours do not like each other.

Each town a scrabble of names: Kolozsvár
that was Klausenberg that is Cluj Napoca,
Kronstadt that is Braşov and Brassó,
Hermannstadt Sibiu to the Romanians
and what the Szeklers call Székelyudvarhely
is their Odorheiu Secuiesc, Roman Apulum
their Alba Iulia a.k.a.Karlsburg and Gyulafehérvár,
Tirgu Mureş Marosvásárhely, Sighişoara
that was Schässburg that was Castrum Sex,
Fort Six, Hungarian Segesvár,
only the ancient names of rivers survive.

In the night cities walking
in the streetlights suddenly
I am a man of two shadows,
one before, the other after,
one hurrying east, the other west,

falling away.

In the hotel of heavy chairs
vodka solo listening to the rain
falling into the town, the traffic
hissing on the streets.

> *I drink to one shadow.*
> *I drink to the other.*

> *In the lobby a million banknotes*
> *switch hand to hand, window*
> *to window, drawer to drawer.*
> *Always the paperwork.*

> *I drink to one shadow.*
> *I drink to the other.*

The TV a hiss of snowy static,
signals from the wrong side of the mountains,
the screen a grey plaza of rainy shadows
shouting in their distant tongues.

Vague shapes running, the soundtrack
a crackle or is it gunfire?

Outside the heavy Transylvanian rain
falling all night into the leaves,
and long after the bars shut the two languages
shout each other down around the square –

proclamations, denunciations,
declarations of ill intent, old wounds
that go on being wounds, chants
of the victors in a game of losers.

Absent from the events of my life,
somewhere I recall little of later
home again in my right self again.

Once again the wrong story
wrong place wrong time.
In my pocket a round white stone.

Think of one who arrives in the square
in Braşov with no history no past
no plan no story at all.

It is the war of the languages
where the neighbours don't agree about history,
too much bloody water, too much misery,
the Vlachs become the Rumanians
kin with Trajan's soldiery
settled on the Dacian frontier
where begins *the East, serfs*
tolerated by grace, banished
from the proud fortified towns, forbidden
chimneys, windows, public office,
embroidery, furs, shoes, boots.

Therefore the wars of the flags that repeat on the wind
Romania Hungaria Romania Hungaria.

Therefore the wars of the tulips along the old ramparts.
Therefore the wars of the chestnuts and the walnuts
each claiming each was here first
and this old frontier their homeland,
the birthplace of the Rumanian
Matthias Corvinus, the greatest **Hungarian** *king.*

It depends who you heard it from.
It depends on the question you ask.
It depends how you ask it.
It depends in which language.

The wars of the statues and the wars
of my dog and of your dog
and each other. Same old.
Same old lebensraum scenario.
A living and somewhere to live it.
Same old poker game in a back room.
Chants of the victors in the game of losers.

> *Whisper of banknotes,*
> *the bad breath of money,*
> *pages in the book of guile.*

> *How limited the sounds of the world:*
> *how limitless, the oriole still singing in my ear*
> *as the radio cuts in.*

In the muddy village of Salt
Mari néni is singing for the lost world
her laments for those who are leaving,
left long ago over the oceans
to Mexico, Australia, Argentina,
their news growing fainter till they vanish.
In her songs the colours of the Székely women
deepen as they age into blood red
into mauve into purple into the black
she wears, she has a tape hereabouts
of when she was famous, she has
no machine she can play it on.

She is singing for those still going away
beyond the border, construction
in Budapest and Balaton and beyond.

> *Everyone, everything, goes away,*
> *one day even the borders*
> *got up and left.*

And in the 7 Csángó villages
set at the mouths of the passes
where they watched for the barbarians –
Pechenegs, Bulgars, Kazars, Huns,
Tatars and Mongols and Turks
arriving in waves of savage unstoppable water –
they recall watchtowers, alarms
they rang, their name Csángó
from the *chang* of a bell, or it means
to go off alone. Solo. They say.

Abandoned villages of the Saxons
gone to Deutschland
falling to crows and Gypsies
and entropy and gravity
and the Second Law of Thermodynamics.

In the Bolyai house a beaker
of the ashes of a poem said to be a love poem.
At Petöfi's monument a boy singing
Flowers in the Spring. The ruins of ruins.

By order of the Minister of Ruins
all the monuments are to be rearranged,
all the junk that tells us who we are
because we were who we were, whoever.

Ceauşescu becomes Chaplin. Some
will be raised a metre, some lowered, names
added or erased, some switched the other way,
shifted to another part of town,

removed indefinitely for renovation
or posing in the statue park of yesterday's heroes,
splattered, greening over, their obituaries
brief entries in the long book of misery.

After the revolution the proof
is in the documents, somewhere hereabouts,
mislaid, lost, burned round the back
of the police station, or the translation
not yet checked, not yet authorised. We have a video
that when we find it is another white
blizzard on the screen, static on the soundtrack.

A revolution. Not a revolution.
The one hand and then the other.
It depends who you ask. The red
has faded from the star, the sickle
come away from the hammer
and the carnival is over.

Not much changed says the professor,
who watches the watchers in next door's
Securitatae yard, *only the names,*
the faces have not changed.

Csaba says *now is better. If now I cannot*
sell a beer, back then I could not find a beer.

> *On the one hand and on the other*
> *says the man of two shadows.*
> *On the one hand on the other.*

> *In the great square in Braşov*
> *the miraculous reappearance*
> *of the children of the Pied Piper*

> *a likely tale.*

And anyway you're out of film
when the procession goes by
and the action starts, the tape run out
the batteries flat, the moment passes
into the history of all moments,
and anyway all the long way up the long hill
you forgot it's Monday and the place is closed,
indefinitely, *closed for restoration.*

Far away now, far away then,
here and not here, messages
written to my fleeing self
in some Transylvania of the mind.

Hung out in the distance
like a lamp, the fading light
of stars fainter and further
in the borderless beyond.

Flowers in the upland pasture.
Pebbles in a yard marbled
into the letters of a word
in some long ago language.

Come back I hear my voice call back
on the long road home.

Bring a few thing to say you were here –
a milkweed pod, a leaf from a walnut tree,
a flower from the upland pasture,
a handful of stones that spell out someone's name.

Night cries startle my heart.
Music dulls me into sleep,
the bird still singing in my brain.

Not the journey but it's recall
fading in the remembrance,
the slow falling into time.

Not the shadow but the other shadow,
death's, falling fore and aft, its agenda
in the swish of time on the watch,

brief as a kiss in passing, voices
shouting down the rainy night street
some name, some message.

Photographs fade. Tapes fade,
the words will come away from the page,
from their meanings, mutters the shadow,

the same that comes with us everywhere
and eclipses us, swallows us whole,
deletes our names in other people's address books.

Think of the snail with a boat on his back
he carries all his days that one day
he will drown in.

Farewell all those I never met,
faces that flit across a mirror,
echoes on the phone, the hiss of stars.

There are the sweet songs of lovers.
There is the wild music of the mountains.
And there is death, suddenly.

There is the chanting among the wild-eyed rag-haired saints,
an unaccompanied singing addressed to eternity.
And there is death.

That knits us all into the ground,
caught up with roots and shards and spent ammunition,
into the names of stones flaked away in the wind.

We live a while in the tales of our children,
their children, gossip and rumour, in the dreams of the sleepless,
the memories of the forgetful.

The knife. Fear of the knife. The cancer
clawing at the guts, or on a narrow mountain road
a fast truck swings onto the wrong side of the road, goodbye.

The land of Cockaigne

South

Picture a city in the mountains,
between one cordillera or another
squeezing the burnt air, like wet moss.

A city of flowers, blossom trees,
exotic fruit and so many beautiful women
the eyes glaze over, everywhere.

Every street a market, chant of
chiclet chiclet, mango mango,
in the street of the watchstrap sellers

a man selling powder singing *cucaracha
cucaracha cucaracha* through the traffic,
every lane a fast lane till it stops.

Zona vehiculo calmado: a joke,
as would be siesta in this city
where the traffic never sleeps.

Bus bus yellow cab bus yellow cab.
Horns brakes whistles backfires. And guns.
Thieves and so many one-legged beggars.

In the doorways of bars squinting
out into the sunlight gnarled old men
wearing machetes. Guns. Guns.

You could just die here in the crossfire.
Yo ya no soy yo. Dead for ever.
Ni mi casa es ya mi casa.

Out beyond the city the dead zone.
You are advised not to travel at night.
You can't get up to the mountains

amongst all that clean air,
but as the light falls sometimes the rain falls,
dry lightning on the high crests.

Paperwork for the Consul

Verde que te quiero verde,
the ship on the sea,
the horse on the mountain.

I'm drinking rum in the Gran Hotel
with Federico García in the dark,
the barman's name is Rubén Darío.

Here the townsfolk call me the Sailor,
Hola marinero, for some reason
I don't understand. Perhaps

the white cottons I wear, the Panama
that blew off in the sudden wind into a pretty girl's fingers
and went off on her pretty girl's head

and who was I to say *es mío*, and gave it
for a sailor's kiss in passing.
Or maybe it's the roll of my walk

wandering the heat struck streets
in *la neblina*, the midday heat-haze,
wary, amused, curious,

mad dog or Englishman,
looking for those two good sisters
Marie and Juana, purveyors of *cigarillos populares*.

Do you want to meet Mr White?
The answer is No. The thought
you could die here anyway marinero,

muerto para siempre, dentro este país quebrado
broken para cocaína, violencia, avaricia.
There'd be no lasting memorial.

Some paperwork for the Honorary Consul,
whose card I carry in my belt. A pointless enquiry.
You had no name anyway, marinero.

Little lost poem

It vanished, that music in the brain,
a few broken bits all that's left of it.
It's like trying to recall rain.

Something about a sailor, wandering
an inland upland city of flowers,
where spring was always the season.

All gone back now into the static,
the sunlight, traffic, music,
the mumblings of an ageing mariner

dried out, marooned adrift ashore,
lost himself, and all he met there
in that hot far away mountain city.

The first note of a melody,
over and over. Beautiful women,
their fleeting loveliness, beguile him.

They smile and lean forward,
pointing to a name in a book, his,
the number of his page,

and oh the deep valleys of their breasts.
a younger man would fall in love
with any one of them. Maybe he did.

Or maybe he died there.
Or maybe he gave his goods to the poor.
We'll never know now.

Bodega de carne

His name is Kovács, the mad Magyar,
drunk, lost again in the foreign tongue.
Where is my passport, my wallet, my hat?

Where did the sky go? Why is the border
never at the border? Please, I have to go
to Playa Bolivar to buy some cheese.

Here you need a ticket for a ticket, a receipt
to get a receipt. Here you hand in your brain,
and don't forget to take the *recibo*.

And what's more, says Kovács in his broken English,
there is a sentence the same in Turkish and Hungarian:
there are too many little apples in my back pocket.

He keeps calling home but all he says is yes, yes, yes.
He calls to say he'll meet me somewhere,
it sounds like Mean Man's Corner, only he's not there.

Only the wind's door slammed in my face
and a voice in my ear saying *You want meat,*
you want the mugger's special? An introduction to eternity?

Lights out. A sudden and anonymous ending
to all these dubious adventures.
It's that live fish swimming underwater business.

Words are dangerous. The government should ban them.
Let me go home now to my imaginary saxaphone.
What I hear is not what anyone would say:

Make way for the Grand Duchess of Alabama.
I was intended for a priest but dodged that one.
The beggars take the coins too small to mention.

But it's OK, we have sent 20 women's horses on ahead,
we have fish, water, apples for the journey
so we'll get there, home wherever home is.

Fields of yellow. I can be calm sometimes,
quiet as the dead are, as sweet as the kiss
of the key in its lock, opening the door.

From Lorca

Verde verde verde, the sailor ashore,
marooned in the mountains.

Death's.

No longer my ship, my house,
no longer I, I.

Death's.

Ayer estrellas azules, yesterday blue stars,
mañana estrellitas blancas, de fuego,
memoría de estrellas.

All death's. The heart, *el corazón*, death's.

And if it's Thursday is it Napoli,
or is it Monday and Medellín, Habana, Nueva York?

Death, that old leveller, traveller, wandering shadow.
If he does not catch me in Bogotá it will be in Bilbão.

Death.

In which the lost sailor and the drunken Hungarian are one,
the dirty old man from Brazil saying *Old horse new grass.*

Death.

In which we are folded, all of us, into the drawers,
the blankets, the white cloths, into the dry uplands,
into the lamps, the dusty corners of our lives,
put away with all the other Christmas toys,
the congratulations of drunken uncles,
forgotten with all the other indiscretions,
things kept in attics, spider holes, coded diaries,
a dog howling in the rain on a distant horizon,
what sound the moon makes on her monthly stations,
the dripping of stalactites, tick of the church beetle,
last gasp of Ferdinand of Austria: *I will have noodles,*
and that's an end to all discussion on the matter.

I am the Emperor. Death.
No more argument, thesis, antithesis, exegesis.

Just death, and his crude stitchery,
his dull music, his black fugues.

Coda: Montezuma's Revenge

Fare thee well, Medellin in the hot south.
Fever, shivers and sweats at once,
too much familiarity with plumbing.

And wherever I lay me down there was always
a madman chained to a table he dragged back and forth
over the floor above, all night long.

An impossible country. Broken. Flowers,
so many flowers, so many guns.

It's the river against the sea.
It's the sea against the river.
And why are the poor always more generous than the rich?

Time to go. On the road to the airport
clouds on the mountains, the watchful infantry.

Checkpoints, TV terror in all the mirrors,
vodka and panic in the departure lounge.

I recall in the rain a great crowd
chanting *poesía poesía poesía*.

Poesía contra la muerte.
Muerte a la muerte.

The Watch

El Pacifico

It seems I've gone grey in here, ageing
into these mirrors, these lights, the chatter
the length of the long varnished bar,
among the tequilas muttering *una más*.

It seems you're far away again. At home
the bed's a mess and I forget to eat
so I'm here again, drinking to health
and good fortune, the long roads you're out on.

The heart beats *be safe, be safe, be safe, my love.*
It's that time again, the mood called *Missing You*
eating down into the bones. *Una más,*
Pablito por favor. Una más, una más.

The wife's sister

She'll say *you know what I can't remember about cucumbers?*
and never tell. She'll say *I know, I look like a dog off the road.*

She'll say *I asked can you play* Wish upon a Star?
But he said Sorry lady our piano player never turned up.

She'll say *I have a friend, she has a house on the Grande Canale,*
but I can never remember her name. It's in the phone book though.

She'll say *We have to go there or we haven't been.*
I can't read a map but I always know where I am.

She'll say *I'll never make horseradish sauce again*
though I'll cry again, again, again.

She'll say *I never loved him, I was blinded by love,*
the only alternative to loneliness, boredom, nothing.

So be it

So that's that, the universe is flat,
and they think now it will go on forever
thinning out into the empire of no light,
into only distance beyond distances.

Question answered. The stars
no more than drifts of smoke
from one of God's occasional cigarettes,
a habit he gave up long ago.

Not a lot to look forward to then:
the death of time, and all the lamps off.
Not much of anything these days: long
interrupted silences, slow afternoons.

My usual limp around the neighbourhood,
a word with the Brothers Fish, home
to the ring doves on the chimney pipes,
the caravan wind in the sawgrass.

Midnight Angst

Was it or was it not all an illusion:
he loved her, she loved him,
they would go dancing, dancing off

into the town & the dawn and the midday,
kids & all, grow old together
into two old beech trees at the lane's end

whose branches nudge each other on the wind
sometimes as in some old school tale,
what they wanted to think of each other.

That world that never was, another propaganda,
another tale written by the victors.
So there were anniversaries, let's say:

there were occasions. Moments.
Some that persist in the memory,
that live in time. That they die with.

Came a time he knew she wasn't listening,
he wasn't listening either, even she
wasn't listening to herself.

Time to go off into the dark weeds
that are always at the edges of all our lives,
time to go off into the shadows & lie down there.

Asleep

Came home late on the last train,
shot the bolts home. Slept,
dreaming of missed trains, missed planes,
lost tickets, failed connections.

I hear you whisper in your sleep
in the soft feather of your voice
blessed be the rain, and wake again,
or dream again but you're not here.

The night: rainless, moonless,
endless, I could lose myself easily,
asking *Are we nearly there yet?*
How long is this road?

Nothing between cause & effect,
nothing saves us. I'm getting old
with my pussycat, still a kid
cheering for the Indians.

Still rooting for the cowboy
in the black hat. I make it all up
as I go, spinning some thread
from all these journeys.

I am the Sultan of Reflections.
I am the consort of the Queen of Spain.
I am king of all the snows.
See how everything melts all around me.

The story so far

The house on the hill, no one knows
who lives there, what they do there
with each other, praying and scrubbing
night and day but it does no-one any good.

Fields of yellow kale, sky, to the left
a stand of trees, scrub, sharp briars,
what happened there thirty years ago is never spoken of,
but the birds and the other wild life never go there.

The sharp spurs of the teazels, weaving on the wind,
landscape of innocence and childhood, pushy clouds.
Who knows where the bodies and the knives are?
Look to your right: the gravel ponds.

Reflections, shaving

Getting old, wearing out, boring,
nobody fancies any of it, the body
for ever rudely introducing new pains
from parts I'd never thought about.

All I want for Christmas, really all I want,
is a plastic gorilla in a cage, this high,
that yells *Help. Hey you. You.*
I'm trapped in here. Get me out.

Over and over till the battery runs out.
It's a long way from the Land of Green Ginger,
where my beery adolescence was misspent.
Let this be a warning to the rest of you.

The neighbour

He reviews his territory, all forty foot of it,
mapped, a general planning his campaign,
Napoleon next door in his massive
vomit-green shorts. Him and his wife.

In his own little corner of his own Third Reich.
He identifies neglect, waste, labour requirements
for the next grand project in concrete,
the next five-year plan. Him and his dog.

His enemies are the slugs and the snails,
they die by the dozen and still they keep coming,
he stamps them, clubs them, salts them,
watching them foam into nothing at all.

Him and his dog in his flagstone empire.
Not that anything grows there these days.
He knows: under the paving the worms writhe,
and they're every one of them enemies too.

The shed in question

Nobody out here but us spiders,
grown fat through the summer,
in early September hanging out
in all their glittering tiger-striped menace,
bloodsuckers, warriors in the endless wars,
gladiators in the arenas of their nets.

This is the empire of the vampire,
the Republic of Bad Manners.

In here I'm merely tolerated, the delegate
from Out There among the stars. In here
I have no friends, relatives, lovers, offspring, antecedents,
no language to know anything, I know nothing.
I am alone in my brief season out here

wondering this that the other, whether
we're far enough back from the river
to withstand the tsunami.
                              We could end up
with a beachside residence in our old age,
our days spent beachcombing and renting deckchairs,
soon there'd be a promenade and a bandstand,
a stick of rock with EAST HAM-ON-SEA right through it.

After the storm

Milly, ten years dead now. I recall
her saying such odd things:
I'm worried about the dog in the rhubarb.

The rain a catspaw at the window,
outside the wind another game in the weeds,
the storm over at last. Night coming.

I'd like to write to her to say the blackcurrant bush
cut from her garden has filled with fruit this year,
the first in fifteen, black pearls, enough to make a pie.

Eventually the stereo will turn itself off,
the phone will not ring, no one will call. It's OK.
The captain's sober and the ship sails at midnight.

Mail from the Campania

'I write from Amalfi, a white
winding bee's nest, jewels cleft between
mountains falling seaward.

Too hot for my slow northern blood,
too claustrophobic, too many tourists
in baggy shorts, the only shade

beneath the blue plastic umbrella
of the tour guide calling over and over
I'll be right here, right here.

Always something to be done, forms
to fill, applications in by due date
in triplicate, signed, witnessed.

Though I'm busy doing nothing
I keep busy anyway, what with the compass
to invent, my *Parsifal* to write.

Always curiosities, gossip, love affairs
around the back streets of Salerno.
Just sitting watching everyone go by.
In the slow afternoons the old city
whispers to itself in doorways. I fancy
those conceived in the hours of siesta,

they are born clever and grow up
to be lawyers, loansharks, politicians
who steal from all the rest of us. Ciao.'

The afternoon

Gone into white mist, the way it is in the movies,
into states whose names we don't know yet,
borders not yet thought of. Gone anyway. Dust.

So many centuries just getting up to go.
And it rains and rains. My love,
my life is turning into a list of things I used to do.

My love consoles me. Sometimes I think of her,
a bird high in the tree of the house, a river
of sunlight warm on her cheeks.

So much patience with paint, silk, *the least gap
and it bleeds.* In the end it's a scarf in the wind, love,
beads of water scattered into sunlight.

Midday, Anna

The phone rings, it's Anna, she says
I'm under a restraint order,
they can keep me here as long as they like,
they can do what they want with me.

But she doesn't say where, there's bugger all
I can do for Anna, lost daughter of my lost friend
Duncan the Drunken. She says *only two of us*
in here are ambient and all the rest are chairs.

And hangs up. The wires buzz in the ear,
all the way to Bristol and beyond. What was it
I was doing before Anna rang?
What to do now with the afternoon?

Interim

A Bloody Mary sort of Friday,
all the way on that long slide
into Monday, Tuesday, Thursday,
when the liver fails, the pump quits.

Prague, Amsterdam, Bilbão. Some place
you least expect, all around you
the big people in expensive suits
leaving footprints all over the maps.

Out amongst the scatter of languages and stars,
part of the world's chatter that's all of us,
in some distant place where even a fruitstand
by the tramstop *glazed with rain* is significant.

Allah il Allah. Father forgive.
O Israel. O mane padme hum. A man
running shouting into fire to any God that listens.
Faethere oure, the tho eart in heofene.

Evening primrose

Every moment itself, at dusk the many greens
of the darkening garden, background to the sheer
white sheets of the hydrangea, the yellow cups
St John's wort offers to the deepening blue.

The opening of the hour of the evening primrose,
last homeward chatter of the blackbird,
that moment the city's traffic stills. Music,
perhaps, a little night music on the FM,

Bach's Staccato in B Minor, a little Mozart,
Relax relax natters the DJ, a plane drills
a hole in the horizon, a siren wails its urgent mission,
and the world's with us again. Nag. Nag.

Still, there were moments, yellow flowers
closing in the last of the light, musk
of lavender and woodruff and a cool breeze
in the long half-light that becomes no light at all.

Wall dreams

Wind, cloud, rain gullied slopes.
Border country, lawless by habit,
nature, habitat, ungovernable.

Snores from the corner. Someone
scratching his itch. A ripe fart, a groan.
Oh for the blessing of sleep and forgetfulness.

Outside a nightbird, nightingale, robin?
They say in sleep we travel,
talking in another time.

Messages rise from the muck:
Lydia, please come to my birthday.
I send you Flavius a gift of woollen socks.

Part of the world's mundane chatter
to itself. Men drinking after work,
embellishing stories that become legends.

Voices behind voices; behind each thought
the ghost of another thought, travellers
arriving with their dogs and sandwiches,
cameras, backpacks, their own preoccupations.

Ghosts, drifting through, out for the day, here
to say they've been and gone. By the south gate
a loud woman describing the dress from was it
C&A or M&S, or is or is not that out there
the 3rd cohort *ala I Pannoniorum* glittering
in the long sunlight over the fell side,
come to relieve us at last?

Me, I'd abandon this place
to the wild beasts howling all night
and the painted men skulking
in the bruised hills, the dumb
contradictory panorama of the north
from which cries come: *Go home Rome.*

Watching north where I'd rather turn south.

I praise the horned god of the hunt
Lord of all the Animals
I praise the three hooded ones
in their stitchery of stone
I praise the blood red calling of the rooster
I praise the black beak of the raven
I praise him as the lightning
I praise him as the courier of the sun
I praise him as the lion
I praise him as the stag
I praise him as the eagle
I praise him as the bear
I praise him as the snake
I praise him as the ring dove
I praise him as the swan
I praise him as the owl
I praise him in the language of all the birds
I praise the hawthorn's pink bloom
I praise the purple on the blue hills
and the gorse that is always in season.
I praise the hare and the spider and the wolf.

By day by night I stare over the blank space
we call landscape, my share of the watch
my share of the world. Some days
a messenger, others a sulky sentry,
on a bad day skiving in the shithouse.
I make all sharp and bright burnished,
my watchword in whatever tongue, my password,
motto muttered in the wind's mouth
           don't mess with me,
my chorus and my long refrain:
           we're here because we're here because...

My brother is to be the man bride
of the evening star. Think of that.
It is a secret, a mystery among others.

I praise the old ones and all
that come in threes, what
can be devised from the flight of birds,
glimpsed in the whorlings of water
in the fast upland streams.

My brother will be *Miles* the soldier
under Mars. He will kneel, naked,
blindfold, his hands' bounds
cut at a stroke, he will step up
to be crowned and refuse the crown.

In this half lit theatre there will be
scorpion, raven, dog, snake,
the sun and the moon, brass, drumming.

He is crowned, then he is free,
he can see at last in so much smokey gloom,
declaring *Mithras is my only crown.*

Words put into the mouth of a god,
words that get men killed.
I praise the sun and the sun's rays.

I praise all that lives and struggles,
and those that have power over water,
appearing at the crossing wearing
the armour of those to die that day.

So what can he see now that not before?

So what is he? – a soldier or a bird,
or does he think himself a god in feathers,
the corpse bird speaking from the other world
in all his colours that are all of them black?

He will be the sun runner, dressed
in the colours of fire and blood and the sun,
his cape the star map of the night sky,
his pointed cap, he will straddle the bull,
yanking his nostrils back, he will slit
the bull's throat and scatter his blood
glittering like the constellations down the sky.

I am in praise, especially of Orion.
I am in praise, especially of the raven,
battle bird, bird of foreknowing and forgetting.

The raven says time for a new dispensation,
there is a wobble in the constellations,
a long slow shift among the stars
and therefore some shift in the complex
arrangements of the gods, therefore
the long war between the dark and the light,
between chaos and order, therefore war
and therefore men will die for this.

We're here because.

Because.

Because the Wall.

Because because.

Because we do what we're told.

Go where we're sent.

Because the commandant.

Because the Emperor.

Because it's here.

Because the government.

The government says so.

Because.

There would otherwise be barbary.

So we're here because it's here.

And it's here because we're here.

Because.

Because.

Iberia, Dacia, Pannonia, Gaul, Syria,
from the watery lands at the mouths
of the great rivers, some from Africa,
some from these parts, how I envy
that for them is no country of childhood
to long for, or I despise them this vacancy.

As well envy another man his prick.
Our lives a dice game in the crapper.

My world is not much though my life
is filled with it, its tune the same
over and over, *quick march, halt,*
at ease, attention, present arms,
in my head counting the arithmetic:
2 steps equals one pace, one mile
a thousand paces, a wall one sea
to the other sea. Mine is a world
all in the wind and the wings of birds,
their cries that foretell our deaths.

Of my own I think what women
and what offspring left behind.

There are limits not built of stone.
I am myself a wall, thick,
nothing gets through me. All the walls
have two sides, I could be on the other.
I could get lost and never found,
don't mess with me, wandering
the boglands all my days and after
what life to remember, sent off
abruptly at a sharp edge, drowned
under hooves, choked, dumped in the midden,
forgot, chucked at last into the sharp yellow gorse.

Always in season.

So be it. So it goes. Here.

...because we're here...

There'll always be a big wall,
Big walls keep us free.
Without a wall there'd be bugger all at all,
There'd be nothing here but you and me.

I am that sort of man who bears all
to the last, happy when an old kettle
comes to the boil still, content
with my porridge and hard tack
and share of sour wine, in hopes to live on
with my limbs all in all the right places
and my eyes to see and my strength still,
25 years if I'm lucky enough,
a bit of land somewhere and sons
to work it, living my days out
still tight mouthed, weathered,
scarred, wearing the same tattoo:

don't mess with me.

Scarp. Ditch. Crag. All the north
and the south of it, edge of empire,
blue cap of the sky, cloud splattered.
Sometimes the shadowlands
of the great mountains of mist
shuttering the hills, sliding over
my eye corners as I run, bearing
my message, sheep voicing
their complaints, bull braying
in so much weather. And all the birds.
Voices behind voices. Where was
my beginning, my eyes opening
to the foggy river banks, woods,
wide snakey water lands, glimpse
of my own stranger's face
in the moonlit pool at midnight,
cries of the flayed ox, the stuck pig,
flogged horse, dogs hunting
along the horizon's line, always?

Someone who sang to me,
a woman, milk and tears flowed from her.

Suddenly it all melts inside the head.
According to my base logic there is
water and there is the moon
on the one side, and on the other
fire and the sun. I have seen the sea
rise and fall to the moon's gold mouth,
to the horns of her, new above spring woods,
nameless with all her many names.

I speak from the lost world of all the living.

I am someone becoming someone else,
I have a name somewhere about me.
I am muddy with others, a body
separating itself from the common grave.

I send you Flavius a gift of woollen socks.
I am in praise. Of the sun. Of the bear, the wolf, the deer.
I am in praise of the horned god that hunts them all.
I am in praise of all that breathes.

Transit

A no-bar airport hotel room: bed, mirror, Brueghel print,
toothbrush lonely on its only in the bathroom,
shoes two weary open mouths, nothing to do with each other.
A strange business, to be anywhere, to be anyone.

Today I shall be Ludwig of Bavaria, eating leftover cabbage.

Water, cup, table, evidence of the world's unlikely existence,
tangible. Take the one and pour into the other. Drink,
sitting to the third. Drink, drink the water. A place called *here*,
some vague other country, bedazzled by too many air miles.

Suddenly I remember my black dog, his shadow fading into autumn,
thirty years gone by. Spiro his name was.

It is a room big enough and small enough to write a suicide note
on the little table provided for the purpose, in the little chair

at the little desk where you take the little pencil
and blow your last thoughts all over the fake red flock.

You had nothing to declare. You never had.

As ever too many ifs too many buts. Imaginary conversations
in imaginary English. A narrowing margin.
The parallel lines of rail tracks and jet trails meeting at last,
the distance from here to there closing rapidly.

Objects in the mirror may be closer than you think.

Days weeks months years being invisible, same old tale
the sorry self tells itself, the machinery ticking away
into oblivion, everything designed for the scrapyard,
all the world a theme park, every one a game show.

You can go to bed now you've had your photograph taken.

Here comes a man through the anonymous crowd,
his face bearing his look of permanent urgent enquiry,
eyes staring into everyone, mouth moving into the gift of speech
born in the mouths of distant hunter gatherers, long ago:

have you got ten pence, have you got ten pence?

Incidents along the way. And this is the pretty route,
meandering, roundabout, more interesting for that.
For instance at the Accident & Emergency a man, confused,
an open Stanley knife in his back pocket:

What am I doing here. Where am I anyway?

And in the supermarket suddenly a security alert
will a member of management go to the security panel
over and over, again and again, sometimes *this is a secu*
this is a secu a secu a secu secu secu. No one pays any attention.

Anyway it's not my gun. I was never there.

All the whiskers blown suddenly from the dandelion.
Gone over the hills and then some. The book
open to the last words fading in the brain,
the last image a child drinking from a paper cup.

Thé dansant

Nothing in my inbox just now
so you may entertain me. *A pleasure, Sir.*
I hear the Gulf Stream just went south.
How d'you like your pina colada?

What was that music now, a quick
Spanish song, stamp of heels, flare
of a black skirt, flash of white teeth,
lo que el viol se viente. Goodnight Pamplona.

Lighten up Sir. Gone are the days
of the popular Lament for a Penny Cigar
when five farthings was a living wage,
everyone a prince among equals.

According to my stern religion
which is no religion at all, nothing at all
between us and starlight, cause and effect,
between us and our clenched teeth.

And always the mad old bat in the corner
lurking under the fake potted palm
who wants the band to play tango tango
but they won't. Oh no they won't.

Her last tango brought the riot police,
everyone into the vans and off to the caracel,
a week's loss of earnings, scoldings, hungry kids.
That was long ago Sir. We don't speak of it now.

I remember her then, all wild raven hair.
When she left it was for a fortnight.
All I have is this snapshot of her waving,
waving from the boat that took her away.

I see Sir. I see it is taken from the back.
But it is not her and yes she is waving but not to you.
She is waving to someone else, there, that man
in the bow tie, in the black and white of it all. Sir.

Fast forward

one thing then another

one story then another conversation
always interrupted by another conversation

I want the words to barely glaze the page
gone the moment of their utterance

as we are

I want

in back of this a story a man with his face with his name
exile emigrant refugee displaced person outsider offcomerdon stranger suspect
the terms interchangeable politically undesireable
a story of a man who leaves his country

and the woman he loves

and the story of why

and her story

they never meet again
that's it that's all of it

far away she hears in the night street
footsteps footsteps stop
when she stops go on when she goes on
from the dark in back of her she hears

I can see you I can see you
Sammy Sammy Sammy Sammy I can see you
far away she must go on
far away he must go on

*

the middle ages

defeated on all sides
they tire of the games
and become their own gestures

for instance my lords Follejambe
who lie in their armour at Chesterfield
a little mad leg dangling from each helm

the dead and the maimed
already numbered
crows and the old picking women

what happens happens to all
a conclusion that is no consolation
think of silence now

the last message from the buildings
indecipherable over and out
static then the long nothing

the moment the lovers
walk away from each other
the moment the moment

such a sheepish calm on the face of the madonna
look of a man peering through smoke
a man kneeling into the light

who kneels in his own veins
and is alive is alive brooding
the forked branch of his solitude

*

gone the rain falls

the rain renews itself the rain
falling through centuries
columns and forests
oceans the ships nudge into

the house rears through it
its freight of jars bottles boxes
containers for all manner of occasions
assembled just for our amusement

the rabbit enquires of everything
is it good to eat?   is it?
the rain finds the mouths sewn shut
the rain drilling its pits

*

whiteout

think of lovers for whom silence
is all the speech they can bear
become old with nothing to say
but what is unspeakable now

to burst again into language
a thousand years of nothing
then a single cry and again nothing
small talk of the aspens and the stars

at the continent's dead centre
one light on a circle of ground
lighting the sleeve and the face
of a man carrying his lamp

the moment it is blown out

*

the new world

lady you moved me so
I may not be still again

and if I return to my own country
what shall I find there?

grass on the ancient hills
small fields running to smaller fields

the going away of love

and if I walk to the edge of my lands
when shall I see you?

*

here and not here

always among stones stoney places
scuffing the dust's old pedigree
is there nothing it seems nothing

the taken for granted hum of the generator
refrigerator percolator traffic cries
the endless muttering of the machinery

nothing but stars and their stardust
grown upright a little wiser perhaps
from where do the words come

weepings and birthcries
shouts from the tram grunts corner mutterings
sotto voce cacaphony of things left unsaid

the grey tide of everyone
these we call birds
in these we call trees singing singing

the grasses moving under the air's
falling through itself
shadow of hand over hand

voices from rooms I've not been
calls from a country no longer in existence
the wind scribbling the water with letters

*

off message

everybody here on automatic
I'm on the train just leaving Liverpool Street
say hello to Uncle Joe for me
he was always my favourite dictator

lost in the outbox at paperwork.com
a customer at Incarceration Inc
date of birth sign here sign here sign here
all this and a water feature too

I'm out of here off into the twilight
a long way to travel to sit on a bench
listening to the wailing of yet another city
I don't have the language for the language

I need a cup of coffee to get me to a cup of coffee
my next number is called *Accidents While Dancing*,
out in the apocrypha of the world
its dust all over my shoes

*

cape fear

never enough
the sound seeking its silence
all company its farewell

who can't wait for it all to be over
the story the love affair the telephone call
history the message on the tape

at dark I walk by your house
hearing the corn creak
a ship on the sea's nowhere

we have travelled forever without words
I can't bear now to go from your face
forever forever and the distance

*

quickly fading here

huddled cold I woke by a dead elm
looking out over the morning I said
goodbye morning goodbye afternoon

goodbye silence begetting itself
goodbye echo my own footsteps
running away my shadow ashamed of itself

always on the maps where you want to go
is the crease worn away by so many fingers
searching searching goodbye to that

lost in a muddle of egg timers lost
in a labyrinth of assorted cheese sandwiches
signs that say *remember to smile at the customer*

confused by the sign in the video shop
last person out switch perplexed
by the what-does-it-mean of *mind the gap*

so goodbye riddle of the egg in the box
in the Chinese puzzle at the middle
of an infinite succession of nesting dolls

goodbye mouse with an ear of wheat
old drainpipe cluttered with leaves
goodbye rainy country goodbye morning glory

goodbye old drawer of lost keys
blue hills sea glimpse haze on the river
the mulberry shadow circling the yard

goodbye rainy nights in a far off city
the neon shorting at the corner of the eye
on/off orange in the drops on the window

constellations I've not seen a long while
goodbye Big Dipper goodbye Orion
goodbye dodo rain forest caribou

goodbye empire of grass field of wind
hedgeback where no mercy is asked
all the world falling away like a shell

I have seen you step from the house of your flesh
saying *this is it this this is my life*
goodbye is it so it's goodbye so goodbye

*

in the desert

everything lost and the rains gone forever
the rivers and their names the dry stoney riverbeds
the groundwater in the wells falling month by month
the memory of grasslands antelope gazelle

lost as I am on the hot anvil of the desert
under the great shed of stars at last with the wind
without the endless need for explanations
questions to answers I can no longer give

some I met on the brown road to this place
the ant a bag lady with her bundle chamelion scorpion
bells on the wind nets to catch fools
and always some fool's errand to run

I am breaking up into segments of myself
always another chapter in the tale that ends
the clock in my skull out of time in any case
the bones I am becoming walking off into the wind

Just one of you

Sarah, while you were at your keyboard,
online to Japan, on the phone to your boyfriend,
just opening your inbox, scratching your ear,
playing Solitaire while you thought no one was looking,

Flight 175 was homing in on you and all those
you'd shared lunch with, a glass of white wine,
secrets you shared with not many. Ground zero
they call it now. And you, you're in the long queue to heaven.

When you were in diapers he was in his mother,
his father on some road to some Damascus, the desert
sparks flying in his eyes. You were in kindergarten,
he was forming the first words of his language.

He was fluent then, then you were in grade school,
high school, college, he was learning by heart
his holy book, by the time you were no longer a virgin
he knew the insides and the outsides of Kalashnikovs,

M16s, hand helds. He had a licence to fly. There was a plan.
While it was forming you were on vacation in Florida.
You were phoning your mother, getting drunk
for the first time. And so perhaps was he.

Your assassin, who flew in from Boston
on an unscheduled flight, smack into you,
your keyboard, your modem, your coffee,
everyone you loved. Like a huge terrible kiss.

The Donegal Liar

> Far from her nest the lapwing cries away:
> My heart prays for him though my tongue do curse.
>> SHAKESPEARE
>> *A Comedy of Errors*

Magowan the poet, who might have been Irish,
of one sort or another, *Mac an Ghabhann*,
making his way in another disputed borderland,
wearing another mask, north of the south, west of the rain.

A blew in, a run-in, sometimes adrift on a black sea
of sweet black stout, with his companions the captain
and the navigator, whose identitites
may or may not ever be revealed.

A ragged country, the roads under fog,
small towns and their flags of allegiance:
Prod. Taig. *No Bigot Parade. No Pope. No RUC.
No Agreement. Dungevin supports Garvaghey Road.*

No visible border, the miles shift into kilometres,
the signs into script, everywhere stone, stone,
mountains and scree, and the lough suddenly,
a long bolt of blue in the sheer sunlight.

Within him he fancies there was always a Donegal man
butting out from Inishowen, head into the wind
that bears off the Atlantic from the edge of the known world,
northwest corner of the continent of Europe.

Where the neighbours don't like each other much,
here as elsewhere. Ah, the Donegal Liar.
What does he know? He's on the road,
looking for lost uncles, out finding his lost self.

A singer, a fumbling romantic, wanderer,
chickencraw. And in him always the other:
the settler, the stranger, the foreigner,
the blue-eyed English. Thirty years it has taken.

Thirty years before that asking who was that man
who was my father, a man whose life was all
a bad mood, most of that a bad temper,
whose first glimpse of the light was here in Buncrana?

In that town there was a dream night after night
of the wind and a loud knocking at my door,
over and over, and someone calling my name
up the B&B stairs and the rain over the lough.

At this point nothing is certain, little known.
Whether our man comes back changed from a journey
or whether he learns nothing, thereafter sifting
memory's scraps, silence, the blue moody sky.

In Grant's pub they have on the IRA tapes,
just for our benefit: *Have you no homes to go to,*
have you no homes of your own? Oh the English,
they'd steal the crack of the plate and the plate.

I can't argue with you there boys but I'd love to.
Are you a spy? What's your cover?
How long have you been with the British Army?
This with your father and your mother is bollocks anyway.

800 years of this and the rain. The people
you're after are all drunk and have no money.
Our man concludes a pub is a bad place
to begin researching his ancestors. This pub.

What is he with a name like Smith and his granny a McGrory?
Is he a left footer or a right for the sake of Jesus,
Mary and Joseph, not to mention St Bridie
and St Patrick that we thought cast out all the bloody snakes?

Maybe he'll go live in Cool Boy north of Letterkenny
and make fishing the whole of his story. Maybe not.
He could believe all he's told: the rock somewhere there
where the priest's head cut by the redcoat's sword.

Bounced. Three times. To this day where it struck
the grass does not grow, the man swears it,
that and the other stone Wolf Tone was chained to
when he was taken, along the shore there, somewhere.

Somewhere hereabouts by the long lake of shadows,
where the submarines sulk, sunk deep
in radio silence, watching each other. And there's a tree there
cannot be cut down. Men that tried it had sudden bad luck.

All that's certain in my case: a few names, a few dates,
the old man's certificates: birth, marriage, death,
all there is of him. John Patrick. John Smith.
And what manner of a name might that be?

I thought if he was someone else who then might I be?
If he could change I could, I too could be anyone,
anyone at all under the stars, Magowan for instance,
a worker in metal, McGrory, McGroary, McGroy.

His silence was absolute, nothing again nothing,
maybe he knew nothing, shuddered in sleep
in a dream over and over of nuns like angry bees
in a hive he can't get out of, though whether in his sleep

or my own I don't know, never will now,
till he's kicked down the wooden stairs
to the door for the last time, and thereafter
the nothing at all he remembered.

Out on his own. Out on his ear at ten years
one month, from then a working man,
most of his days an itinerant unlettered landless labourer,
a spalpeen in the English north country counting pennies.

Asked, he'd blaze into anger, subside into long silence,
till we buried him, weary, still angry,
angry for ever under the great map of the stars.
Unfinished, as everything is. As this is.

YOU AGAIN

(2004)

Late night call

Discontinued voice from a disconnected number
in distant rainy Seattle, you're sitting on a balcony,
smoking in another no-smoking house, out there
in the time zones. We're out of sync.

Just a faint hum on the horizon of listening,
babble of electronics and the slow hiss of static.

Once upon a time you walked into the room of my life
and changed all the seating arrangements.

You with your blue eyes. My marjoram,
my lumpy gravy. Staring at the rain.

Ancient Lights

Through the shadows and the street cries scribbler Boswell,
as ever in need of a drink and an eye out for the ladies,
limping along beside him old Dictionary Johnson,
as ever in need of a bath. Ghosts in the traffic,
shadows in dim lamplight turning off the Strand,
headed for the lit door of No. 8, there in the Great Room
to attend a lecture on light, and after to the tavern.

Sirs, we are made of light, all of light. And I?
I am the doorkeeper to this house of enlightenment,
though I am long gone into the sunset now, I am but his ghost
among the other ghosts, the company of ancient lights.

Beneath all this noble talk up above of improvement,
I know the other trades thriving underneath
in the tunnels and the arches down below,
down where the river's traffic in wines from the lowlands,
coals from Newcastle, roll up the cobbles on iron wheels
among gulls' cries and women's, rats, dogs,
the odd corpse knocking at the wharfside,

and the black slave boy sneaked by at nightfall, hooded,
lost in the city's night and the fogs of the riverside,
I saw him scurried by just as that moment
Dogood Franklin handing in his coat muttered
to himself liberty, liberty, what is liberty but an engine
that must be fuelled and from which much use comes.

Years go by into centuries. I've met them all.
Reynolds, that toff, I have shaken the rain from his umbrella.
Adam Smith, I have taken his coat and he thanked me.
Marx, never a tipper, nor stood any man a drink.
Stephenson, now there was a gentleman, and the likes
of Isambard Kingdom Brunel we'll not see again,
nor your man Charlie Dickens, forever declaring
Brighten it, brighten it, a man always departing in haste.
And that wee man, the unknown inventor of a writing desk
that in case of shipwreck opens out into a literati,
he gave me the name of a very fine horse once.

So here's to all and all the others anonymous,
may they be blessed and ever of good cheer
who set out to make this world more sensible,
at any rate from where I stand here in the doorframe.

You again

These days of terror I daren't write anything,
or I don't want to, but here you are again,
Sarah, in my waking dreams out in the street
in the midday where suddenly you enter my mind again.

Whispering, your last breath a soft quick *no no*
at my ear, and *Sarah, Sarah, my name was Sarah.*
It seems there's no room in Paradise
or it doesn't exist anyway, so it's you Kenneth John.

In another war I wrote *A fool's work*
to make anything of this, a liar's to make nothing.
And you, you're in the pixels on the screen
bursting with fire. You're in the printout, somewhere.

The sound of you still in the airwaves, on file,
on the web, the net, the desktop, the database,
zipped, unzipped, encrypted, compacted,
but not ever I promise you deleted, erased.

A name in a very long list, beginning with S.
Amongst those names I will find you.
I will go looking for what days are left me, Sarah.
I promise. I promise you.

The 72 virgins question

As I understand it, those who die as martyrs for the great mad cause of the Believers go immediately to Paradise, there to gawp at the angels and the fine plumage of the birds and eat delicious foods, where for eternity they will have the tender and erotic attentions of 72 virgins. What I've not been able to discover is who originated this theory, now resident in the minds of so many testosterone-and-fundamentalism filled young Muslim men. Is it in the Koran? For them, this is the reward for flying aeroplanes into tall buildings, and slaughtering thousands at their work stations.

I have a few questions, however:

How was the figure of 72 arrived at? Why 72? Does 72 hold any particular significance, like Douglas Adams' 42, the answer to everything? Any connection with the tradition that only the camel knows the 72 names of God?

Given the recent sudden influx of martyrs into Paradise, is the supply of virgins sufficient to the purpose? Is there, in Paradise, an infinite supply of virgins?

Are any of them boy virgins? What proportion, if any?

Given the length of eternity, how long, and how, do they remain virgins?

Given the length of eternity, I would think even 72 virgins would get tedious. Are they all dropdead gorgeous? Do they grow old, or, if they stay forever young, what would there be to talk about after the event? How long before the martyrs start straying, coveting their neighbours' virgins? And think of all that bickering and scheming.

What if the martyr is a woman? Does she get the same privileges. and how does that go down with the lads back at the base?

Another question. The investigators think not all of the 19 hijackers knew they were going to die, and only six left letters behind them, so far as they know. The others just thought they were going on a jolly hijacking spree, and weren't in the full loop. So: If the martyr doesn't know he's about to die, is he eligible for the same rewards as the one who does?

And then another question. At the chemical plant that blew up on the same day in Toulouse, now thought to have been a terrorist act also, they say they found the body of a Tunisian who worked there, wearing four pairs of underpants. This is then said to have something to do with preparations for paradise, and the aforesaid virgins?

What does it have to do with it?

Where in Holy Writ does it say one pair of underpants per 18 virgins?

Bin Laden is Ken Smith

This is from the wilder shores of cyberspace, from a site called Terrorist Watch. This bit of the conspiracy theory centres on a place called New Era in Portland, Oregon that acted as a cover for a terror base whereat many of the infamous heros of Hamas, Hizbollah, al Qaeda, etc etc appeared from time to time, including bin Laden. That's what it says here, anyway. It says:

Usama bin Laden initially showed himself at New Era under the guise of a nondescript backyard mechanic type named 'Mike'. His chosen cover for the late hours in which he worked over a handmade forge, and the huge volume of propane he used while melting down his precious plutonium was that he was recycling aluminium transmissions. At the rate of over 500 gallons of propane every week, that would have made for some very valuable aluminium.

However, it was Usama's characterization of himself as that of a tall, lanky Missouri man called Ken Smith that allowed him to appear natural... ...the only difference between bin Laden and Ken Smith is the color change of his hair, and the fact that Ken Smith had no accent.

My name has been hijacked. I expect the CIA to come knocking at my door. And what about the plutonium? Should I see a doctor? Should I turn myself in?

From semtex to anthrax

Semtex: you blow up and burst, causing collateral damage.

Smallpox: you shrink from it, you shrink away to nothing.

Pox: you don't want it, whatever it is. See Durex below.

Pax: yes indeedy brothers and sisters and mad dogs, peace, dammit.

Prolix: you just keep banging on the way I am. So I've got it. Look out here it
　　　　comes.

Hoax: you believe every rumour and spread it.

Perspex: you're invisible. People see right through you.

Pyrex: you get very hot, and people can still see through you.

Syntax: first the pleasure, then you get to pay for it.

Durex: no more offspring.

Bisquix: this is safe. Make pancakes for breakfast.

Detox: a period of being very dry and edgy. Don't drink, don't smoke.

Tux: an eternity of tuxedos, high school proms, virgins, 72 in number.

Box: you get brain damage from this. Then you're in one. Forever.

Lax: you don't care any more, roll another one, just like the other one.

Wax: you turn into a masochist. Forty of these is enough.

Latex: you go all rubbery and inert.

Aertex: you're full of holes. Your're a string vest.

Ilex: you turn into a tree, a very fine tree.

Playtex: you turn into a girl in a girdle.

Essex: you turn into a girl in a big bra.

Middlesex: you can work this one out for yourself.

Wessex: your location is imaginary, but absolutely real.

Kotex: you start to bleed once a month.

Lurex: you shine in the dark but you have great legs.

Redsox: your spelling goes haywire. Three strikes and you're out. Or in.

Rollodex: you've got it, all of it, right there, but you just can't find it right now.

Remix (1): you say the same things in different order, like the President does.

Remix (2): you think you're the Prime Minister, and say the same things as

Remix (1) (above), playing an imaginary concertina with your hands, saying over
　　　　and over *you see you see…*

Affix: you stick close to tactile surfaces.

Rolex: you get mugged.

Complex: don't go there. Just don't bother.

Reflex: see above.

Styx: there neither. Don't cross that river.

Pandora's Box: don't open it.

Halifax: don't go there. Hull, Hell, and Halifax, avoid these.

ExLax: come again?

Amex: you turn into a Mexican.

Tex: you turn into a Texan and get to be President.

Texmex: get out of there fast fat boy, stop singing those cowboy songs.

Lox: you can only eat Kosher.

Four X: you turn into an Australian, and don't give a XXXX for anything.

Max, as in Bigmax: problems with spelling again. Don't go there either.

Matrix: uh oh, lifetime hallucination, don't go there.

Tyrannosaurus rex: don't mess with him. He'll have you for breakfast.

Rex: you think you're the king, and master of all you survey.

Dux: now you think you're Mussolini. It's just the quacking of the crowd you
    hear.

Lex: so now you're a lawyer?

Pontifex: so now you think you're the Pope. All together now *Pax in urbe et orbi*.

Cicatrix: well you're sick anyway.

Moulinex: mixes you up completely. You're either a mess or a good mayonnaise.

Fedex: expect unexpected packages, rapidly delivered, contents unknown.
    Don't open.

Fax: few of these these days I find. Fog of war etc, first casualty etc etc.

Tax: you give a lot more money to the government to pay for all this.

X: unknown, too terrible to name. Marks the spot. His mark.

X-ray: people can see through you.

My ex: here's one I made earlier. What was her name?

Anthrax: was that really her name?

Vortex: you just go down and down and down.

Subtext: one way or another, I fear we're exed, four exed. Banjaxed.

The Ring

Scenes from a Civil War, Exeter, 1640s

She threw her wedding ring high in the air,
far into the night grass of the graveyard.

And I, one eye on her, one eye on its quick glint
spinning in moonlight, followed and found it.

Gold, thought I to myself, solid gold:
hot dinners, a bed, a warm winter jacket.

There we parted, the wife of those days and I.
She went her way. I went nowhere

*

I looked for a grave and found none.
Wind, rain, moss, lichen
had wiped even their names from their stones.

All faces are soon erased: neighbours,
friends, lovers, not one of all these
in the town I once knew I know now.

Kings and saints on the battered face
the cathedral presents to the west wind,
sandstone wearing away in the rain,

slowly down time, their gestures
making some fine point of doctrine
in the centuries of their long discussions.

And within there the saint's nose kissed away,
the bishop's effigy slashed,
hacked, arms, face, feet, gone.

Children who are long away
into the oncoming cannonade,
their cries that are long lost.

Townsmen I knew, scattered now, fled,
dead some, one who was my sworn enemy
whose grave I swore to piss on.

But I can't be doing with that now,
and where is it anyway?

*

Late at night as in the old times,
the last drink poured and the tabaccy low,
the clock's tick and the rain's drumming,
and I sit pondering my fortune, or lack of it.

Maybe I should not have come back here
to this town of my defeats and betrayals.
I should have passed by on the other side.
I should have kept to my wanderer's track.

Yet I am always connecting up the dots,
stitching up the tears in my coat sleeve.
In all this rattle of traffic I can easily forget
there was once something called silence.

Here it was that I as I was then,
just coming into being, knowing myself
numbered among the quick, there came
trouble and turbulence. Here I fled from.

And all fell apart. Wandering the town
and its rainy alleys, I met lads tooting pipes
that were the organ flutes of the great church,
and they jeered me, out of all command.

Years gone, I'm drawn back, into old doorways,
staring to the hill's line, the leaning
of one house on another, and the western wind
again on my cheeks, and always the rain.

Here in a lit doorway a man steps away
into his own shadow and is never seen again.
Here in an early window another lights his taper
and takes down his books of close scrutiny.

615

At the bar suspect conversations: money & property.
As ever. Always money to be made from grief.
I observe preachers and lawyers sow war's seeds.
Lawyers and preachers gather its whirlwind.

*

And I thinke those that crie Goddes worde
to bee lawe absolute, suche wordes
ever subject to variation and errore
in translation from tongue to tongue;

subject to sundrie interpretation thereof,
depending which way downwind they drift,
subject to weather, the mood on the high road;

subject to primers' error, faint hearing, bile,
bad eyesight, bad temper, indigestion,
the sudden sputter of the early morning candle.

Those I say who cry out Goddes goodness to all,
commanding obedience to the Boke's command
they do not sleep in a windy hedgeback
I have observed them doe the most harm.

*

That evening in the cathedral,
the notes of the organ's flutes
rippling over the high arches,
the great pillars rising into gloom
and the choir's voice fading out
into silence, the night forming
into a solid as the sun went down
beyond the coloured glass saints,
and as the dark and the music
flooded God's great barn
stacked with so many prayers
for so many centuries, then when
a single candle was lit on the altar,
I at that moment as the great world
turned into night and the fear of it,
would have believed anything.

*

All day then I stood barking wares on the market,
and at night in my fair hand transcribed
lists of ordnance, and the new regulations.
Aye and many a long crawl through the taverns,

In these fragments my life is, somewhere.
I recall one who died here on the quays,
crushed under a boat's keel, lightning
took another, others went under wheels.

Had I siblings, predecessors, antecedents,
a line all the way to Adam and the apple?
Will there be offspring of my offspring,
some of my own blood to wander the future?

Here on this bench, long ago in summer,
as I sank a slow cider, my youngest daughter
sweet Kate, was discovering the writing of her hand
its confident slopes and downsweeps, its cursives.

Adapted from my hand as mine was from Milly
my mother's as hers from her father's
copperplate entries in the history of calligraphy,
that elegant style they used then.

*

Someone whistling on the corner.
Voices outside the window,
if there is a window, when in these times
someone is always listening.

For what?

For private thoughts in late night cups
mutterings against God and the godly
damn Parliament and God damn the King.
For that fined or sent to the jailhouse.

For what?

All talk then was munitions and the price of meat,
Neighbour cast a curious eye on neighbour.
No joy was to be had in those times to come
only worse in the savage toing and froing

Sometime they locked the cathedral,
God they said, needs no such room but the heart
nor the great bells they melted into bullets.
They had other uses for such vast spaces.

Then it was divided between two parties,
and a wall set over the middle, a new door cut.
Then it was storehouse, stables, stalls,
a jakes for the beastly exonerating of natures.

That last winter they pulled down the thatch
against fire, and for fire to warm themselves
took everything else: doors, lintels, floors,
a fine chair I had from my grandfather.

*

No question ever answered,
no thought ever finished.

I think we just fade out
across whatever borderland we come to.

A while we go on, buying milk,
bread, wine, filling the shaker with salt.

Good morning a fine morning,
crossing the bridge into the city.

We do the same things in the same order,
in summer's heat imagining winter's cold.

And vice versa. So this is the after life
of my life. Already this is it.

*

Our world over, we withdraw into the wind,
into the throaty susurration of pigeons,
chitter of birdsong, chatter of the high grass.

We are a flicker of light in the shadows,
breath of a sudden breeze on a still afternoon,
something glimpsed at the eye's corner

that when looked at is merely imaginary,
a fiction, an invention in the air, what the eye
wants to see, as it does, days out on the ocean.

Always on the cusp of some thought
that evaporates, the verbs falling from the nouns,
the sentence running out of sense.

To both sides I went for an ill paid soldier,
cut, shot at, wounded, slept in snowy ditches
without a warm coat, at the end without shoes.

At the last caught on the wrong side sent away.
Land and sea then were all my adventures.
Here only the exile of he who returns.

Fragments. My life's bits.
Scraps of memory. Disconnections.
I say this and I say no more.

*

She threw her wedding ring high in the air,
far into the night grass of the graveyard.

And I, one eye on her, one eye on its quick glint
spinning in moonlight, followed and found it.

Gold, thought I to myself, solid gold:
hot dinners, a bed, a warm winter jacket.

Thus we parted, the wife of those days and I.
She went her way. I went nowhere

Almost

IM Izet Sarajlić

Izet, Izet, I regret
I have not written my words
to your words, to your courage,
to your love, to your pain,
to your child's mysterious smile
in your old man's face
under its wild white hair.

To your wounds.

And Sarajevo's,

Not yet.

*

Everything, almost

A slow life in the fast lane
what with everyone in a hurry,
boring, boring my grandchildren say
of almost everything.

Everything is moving away, waving,
waving, flags, stars, flowers in the wind,
handkerchiefs from the boat's rail,
the signal fading as the land falls off,
a far window glinting in the sunlight
a single gull riding the air's weight.

Goodbye, goodbye. Everything
in its sudden intensity, the blue cup,
the black bench, the empty bottle,
the white stairs going up.

*

Begins like this

This is the almost poem, the not yet poem,
maybe the never to be poem. Perhaps.

It begins over beer with the Polish girl,
already bedded with one of three at the table.

To me she says *Ken, I could almost be in love with you.*
Here we go. Almost? Only almost? So then:

we almost could go to bed, almost make love,
by the morning you could be almost pregnant.

By the morning you would almost have forgotten me
By the same token I'd have forgotten you, almost.

Or. We could almost have a love affair,
you could almost have our children, and I,

I could almost go to Warsaw, a flat almost in Stari Grad.
One day I might almost forget the wife I had.

The life I live already, the one I'm not waiting
any more to start beginning one day but now.

Her Indoors we call her in my lingua franca,
Miss Peaches I call her still, almost this moment

of the same evening gathering tomatoes, planted
months ago in our garden at the house back,

quieter just now without my heavy footsteps.
She'd never forgive me nor forget me. Almost,

I would most certainly have a fight with your husband.
He might almost kill me, I almost him.

And you, you'd almost come to see me, one Sunday,
in the hospital or in the jail or in the cemetery.

Almost you might bring flowers. You might
almost remember me. Otherwise I'd almost kill you

for your endless infidelities. Almost.
For your carelessness with what love is.

*

Nema problema

Doesn't work. Nothing works.
Almost everything lost in translation.
The wrong word in the wrong sentence,
wrong coin in the wrong pocket,
by the omission of a letter,
the variation of a constant, said Vishnu.

And you're stuck here forever perhaps
among the unknown alphabets
between the mountains and the sea
waiting for the ship that never sails,
the office never open, the phone not picked up,
the recorded voice far away offering options
in umpteen languages, none of them your own.

And it's your own fault, dummy, waving your arms about.
What time is the bus? What time is the bus?

You may be this way again o mi amigo,
so behave yourself, you with a stick
you like to think is a gun.

OK amigo, you got me scared now.

Nema problema.
No problem.
Niet problem.
Kein Problem.
Es neme probleme.
Pas de problème.
No hay problema.
Mish mushkila.

They say. Tell that to the marines blacking up
for yet another war, tell that to the gunmen in the hills.

Kindly inform the poor kneeling at the roadside,
palms up, eyes fixed on the almost endless empty distance forever.

*

Nightbird

At midnight the full moon over Lake Orhid,
its full light scattered over sheer still water,
tiny waves sifting the pebbles of the shoreline
with a *shush now* sound, hard to find a word for.

As is the sudden soft throaty cry of a nightbird,
just overhead, its wings soughing the balmy air
in a splash of feathers, like a passing prayer:
Let there be peace in this land. Peace, now.

*

Listening

to the last ashes of any sound at all,
a vague music fading in the courtyards,
the announcement of twilight in the mouths of birds,
in the bus stations the destinations to distant cities,
Mostar, Vukovar, Sarajevo, Banja Luka,
in all their names in all their tongues,
with all their bloody histories, and all this
only the immediate neighbourhood,
and whatever lies further out beyond the last lights
along the Albanian shore we've not yet figured out.

All this to the last breath you take anywhere. Almost,

Oh and there was something else:
what would anyone want beyond food enough,
warmth, some promise, some love
on this mean miserable planet, anything at all
that is your gift to your children and to theirs,
some shelter from almost all of the above.

*

Split interlude at deadmouse.com

Ok the keyboard is differently configured.
Ok there's no sign for infinity, but you get there,
you write over and over *I love you love you,*
I'm not in jail, I'm alive, I'm not sick.

Hit Send. For what we are about to send and receive
may the Lord make us truly thankful. Doesn't work.
Must enter identity the man says. *Make password.*
Any word will do. Almost any word almost.

But the mouse is dead. *Dead mouse* he says,
fiddling at the back, *very old late ex mouse.*
And no spare. *Nema problema.* So my message
I love you won't arrive in your inbox. Ever.

*

Night coming

Travel torn, sitting on a balcony
watching the heavy Dalmatian rain
lash the streets, boats tossing on the swell,
thunder rolling in, lightning's swift stitchery
in the steep bowls of the hills
when all the lights go out.
                              Suddenly
I am content, not almost but utterly,
soon to fall asleep alone in white sheets
rocking in the windy cradle of the harbour,
the sleep of an angel that is once in ten thousand years
to wake as if born again almost, still dreaming.

How tentative our lives, how short a time in the sunlight,
and most of it imaginary elsewheres, Dubrovnik for instance.

*

Things

The way they have their own particularities,
left alone long enough, their solitude, silence,
fullness and emptiness, their togetherness and
their autonomies, their connection to everything else.

The stone.

The rusty horse shoe and one nail.

The abandoned suitcase.

The lost doll on the roadside.

The rake the saw the hammer, tools that were his tools.

The empty Coca Cola can in a half-built house in Sobra,
the rope coiled on the quayside, a one spit, one shoe,
one shot, one last cigarette port call if ever I saw one.

The spent police bullet found in the gravel at Castle Stanjel.

The fallen chestnut.

The fallen leaf from a gingko tree
by the old synagogue in Sarajevo.

The bone.

Everything.

*

Seafarer

landward mountains and mountains, upended strata
tipped all the way up the coastline of what was
an almost country, almost Yugoslavia. Islands
that are mountains in the sea, the same in the same
dark blue waters the ancient wanderer spread sail on,
ten years lost, the waves cresting the same, bright

sunlight's swift jewellery forming and fast fading,
wind never willing enough, always far from home.
Not even almost there, the boat's wake always behind him.
So if not home then some haven beyond the next headland,
round the next cape almost, sunlight striding the sea
receding always into sea haize and more distance.

Home to his ancient dog and the wife's endless weaving,
not to mention the slaughterhouse he soon made of it.
Tales told round fires, late night yarns over alcohol,
trying some sense to this endless confusion of water.
Waves, tentative, foam crests soon falling, seamen
staring the sea down for some place looks like home
and the stars above in the right configurations,
wind whipped and sea blind, he sees in the sea's skin
forever on the move sight of the sun through pines
in the bright sea's reflections as it once was on land,
the motion the same as the same wind's back home,
almost. The endless immensity of longing for home.

Almost. Rocks, trees, beasts, faces of the familiar,
rearing from stone, out of water, wood, smoke, rock, clouds
out of yesterday's brisk trade in the town, flash ahead of him
gone. And below where light strikes, snakes, almost,
creatures writhing away into seaspray and light shine.
Words on the sea. Light's brief brilliant reflections,
languages never learned, cuneiform, glagolitic, Hebrew,
Arabic, glyphs, runes, living almost into letters, tongues,
alphabets, lost in the quick calligraphy of wind and water.
The almost everything almost always is, or boils down to:
it was or it will be, could be, may be, might be, perhaps,
though doubtful. Uncertain. World on the brink of itself.

Always almost always making it, becoming itself,
being or not being, uncertain of itself. Potential, say.
Out on the sea for instance where our seafarer
almost always is. Off the bitter coast. Off Hvar
and Korcula, birthplace it says here im Deutsch
of Antenor of Troy, and of Marco the Polo, wanderer
by land to the earth's ends and limits. Or by Ogygia,
Mijet now, a long lumpy island wherein seven
of ten lost years went by: cloudy light, forest,
a single road looping the gaps. *Ah Ithaca, where*

are my olives, my olive trees? Ogygia: upright rocks,
stoney warriors armed to the teeth, no landing there.

All this, blind, long after. Homer saw.

*

On the other hand

Given a compass, Racal Decca,
geostat positioning and a decent map
there'd have been none of these adventures
and no tales to tell the grandchildren.

He'd have been tucked up night after night
with Penelope dreaming one eyed giants,
men turned to pigs. On the wind off the sea
the singing women calling him in to his ruin.

And for her none of these tapestries,
done and every night undone again.
An ordinary life, long forgotten now.
Wine in the evening. His olives.

Almost

*

Old man's advice

War: the worst dialogue there is,
all the nouns scattered body parts,
all the verbs fire. No sentence
ever gets finished. Just the abrupt
chatter of bullets, punctuation of artillery,
cluster bombs translated into collateral damage.

The wailing long after.
There's no future tense.
And never enough adjectives. A language
only of lamentation.

But they're talking it up again.
It's show time folks. Take my advice:

you go on whittling that same piece of wood
you end up out of stick, a bunch of shavings
at your feet and a blunt knife in your hand.

*

For Jan Morris

Long ago before the war we haven't had yet
there was I in Trieste. Someone had written
on a wall just off Unita in Cats' Alley
No stars for me this night.

All laughter with its edge of sorrow.
All regret with some punchline of its own.

Too many tears falling,
like the cold light from the stars.
Here. Everywhere.

*

A night of many dreams

none of which I now remember. Trumpets
perhaps, blown in some deep cave in the karst
slow water has carved into figures and faces,
the white columns of some ancient cathedral.

Almost.

Or maybe the white trotting horses of Lipica,
glimpsed in an autumn country runny with fruit,
orchards heavy with apples, pomegranate, grapes,
sticky on the fingers, the wind's songs.

Almost.

By day's end a host of faces flash by,
coming on fast as if out of rock and wood,
out of water and iron and fire, their voices
in so many languages keeping me from sleep.

Almost.

*

Almost not a sonnet

You can be the king of England and be happy, almost.
You can win the state lottery and almost be a millionaire.
You can be almost famous. You can almost die, over and over.
You can almost live. You can almost go to war with the neighbours,
or almost live in peace with them. Some days almost
you can walk on water, you can fly, you can dance the kolo again.
You can almost be in love with that girl you glimpsed in Zagreb.
A white dress, yellow braids, high heel shoes, almost evening,
the light rain almost over. Or was that Ljubljana? Almost
you could go and go forever over the landscape, always
a new town with its new adventures, its women almost
holding on to you, almost every night a different bed.
Unlimited possibilities are not given to man, saith the I Ching.
If they were his life would dissolve in the boundless.

*

I rest my case

Lizard.
Scorpion.
Pine cone.
Water falling. Wind.

I was making my way between mountains and islands,
all on my ownio, o solo mio, almost at last a bona fide grown up,
just getting there, wherever there was. Tomorrow
I could go to Hvar and wander in its woods. Or tomorrow
I could bugger off to Rijeka and get drunk. Almost.
As ever I do neither. Watch the sun come up, go down.
Sleep. Split for Split and a late night beer with Ante,

who builds ships in the yards but would rather sail them,
elsewhere, anywhere, the girl in the tourist office
who envies those she sells the tickets to: another life,
another world than this, any place almost. Some place
she'll be someone else completely. America for instance.

Wind. Water falling.
Pine cone.
Scorpion
Lizard.

I rest my case.

Poverty's prayer

Poverty's shoes, if any.
Poverty's house, falling down.
Poverty's hard bed. Poverty's sticks,

Poverty's thin cat,
poverty's dog and its fleas,
its leg in a dirty grey bandage.

Poverty's bread. Poverty's dust
Poverty's mice and cucarachas.
Poverty's rice, poverty's beans.

Por favor
bring me the head of an American president
on the green platter of a dollar bill.

[*Havana, 2003*]

The white chair

The man whose seat this is,
heavy iron, white paint, that he dragged out
one day into a corner of the rattling leaves
in the seawind, he is not here today.

He went off some place, some business,
and just now he is standing perhaps
amongst other leaves drummed on the same wind
Coming in fast off a different sea.

But he has no seat to sit in, and here
it's as if his chair was waiting for me,
among the dropped brown leaves scurrying
like small animals, like birds into flight.

So therefore I will sit here thinking of him,
someone very like me perhaps, a solitary
who likes company, wherever he is and in what language
he listens to the wind, and what it says to him.

I will disturb nothing. Back again,
he will not know I have been here,
stepping down into the evening to sit
in his chosen spot, lighting his cigar.

[*Havana, 2003*]

APPENDICES

SELECTED BIBLIOGRAPHY

POETRY TITLES

Eleven Poems (Leeds: Northern House, 1964).

The Pity (London: Jonathan Cape, 1967).

Academic Board Poems (Exeter: Peeks Press, 1968)

Arc Pamphlets 4 & 5 (Gillingham: Arc Publications, 1969)

Work, distances/poems (Chicago, IL: Swallow Press, 1972).

The Wild Rose (Memphis, TN: Stinktree Press, 1973)

Hawk Wolf (Knotting, Bedfordshire: Sceptre Press, 1974)

Wasichi (New York: Aloes Books/Spanner, 1975)

Tristan Crazy (Newcastle upon Tyne: Bloodaxe Books, 1978).

Tales of the Hunter (Boston, MA: Night House, 1979)

What I'm Doing Now (London: Oasis Books, 1980)

Fox Running (London: Rolling Moss Press, 1980; Newcastle upon Tyne: Bloodaxe Books, 1981).

Between the Dancers, with John Christie (Guildford, Circle Press, 1980)

Grainy pictures of the rain (Arkansas: Truedog Press, 1981)

Abel Baker Charlie Delta Epic Sonnets (Newcastle upon Tyne: Bloodaxe Books, 1981).

Burned Books (Newcastle upon Tyne: Bloodaxe Books, 1981).

The Poet Reclining: Selected Poems 1962-1980 (Newcastle upon Tyne: Bloodaxe Books, 1982).

Terra (Newcastle upon Tyne: Bloodaxe Books, 1986).

Wormwood (Newcastle upon Tyne: Bloodaxe Books, 1987).

The heart, the border (Newcastle upon Tyne: Bloodaxe Books, 1990).

Tender to the Queen of Spain (Newcastle upon Tyne: Bloodaxe Books, 1993).

Wild Root (Newcastle upon Tyne: Bloodaxe Books, 1998).

Wire through the Heart (Budapest: Ister, 2001)

Shed: Poems 1980-2001 (Tarset: Bloodaxe Books, 2002).

You Again: Last Poems & Other Words (Tarset: Bloodaxe Books, 2004).

Collected Poems (Hexham: Bloodaxe Books, 2018).

PROSE & NON-FICTION

Frontwards in a Backwards Movie (Todmorden: Arc, 1975).

Anus Mundi (Ware, MA: Four Zoas Press, 1976)

Island called Henry the Navigator (Oak Park, IL: Cat's Pajamas, 1976)

the joined-up writing (London: X Press, 1980)

The Queen's Dreams: a short story (Harry Novak Books, 1986).

A Book of Chinese Whispers (Newcastle upon Tyne: Bloodaxe Books, 1987).

Inside Time, with Dave Wait (London: Harrap, 1989; Mandarin, 1990).

Berlin: Coming in from the Cold (London: Hamish Hamilton, 1990; Penguin, 1991).

ANTHOLOGIES

Klaonica: poems for Bosnia, with Judi Benson (Newcastle upon Tyne: Bloodaxe Books, 1993; with *The Independent*).

Beyond Bedlam, with Matthew Sweeney (London: Anvil Press, 1997).

MAJOR ESSAYS ON KEN SMITH'S WORK

Sean O'Brien: 'Ken Smith: I Am Always Lost in It', in *The Deregulated Muse: Essays on Contemporary British & Irish Poetry* (Newcastle upon Tyne: Bloodaxe Books, 1998).

Stan Smith: 'Salvaged from the Ruins: Ken Smith's Constellations', in *British Poetry from the 1950s to the 1990s: Politics and Art*, ed. Gary Day & Brian Docherty (Basingstoke: Macmillan, 1997).

Colin Raw: '"Best, Ken": Letters and an Interview', in Ken Smith, *You Again: Last Words & Other Words* (Tarset: Bloodaxe Books, 2004). This consists of a full-length essay, a series of long extracts from letters by Ken Smith and an interview, and is the most comprehensive critical resource on Ken Smith's work. It is followed by second interview with Ken Smith, by David Crystal and Tim Cumming.

COLLECTED POEMS

This edition draws on all the poetry titles listed in the bibliography, including all the poems from Ken Smith's two previous retrospectives, *The Poet Reclining: Selected Poems 1962-1980* (Bloodaxe Books, 1982) and *Shed: Poems 1980-2001* (Bloodaxe Books, 2002), the latter including all the poetry which he wished to keep in print from that period, from his Bloodaxe collections *Burned Books* (1981), *Abel Baker Charlie Delta Epic Sonnets* (1981), *Terra* (1986), *Wormwood* (1987), *The heart, the border* (1990), *Tender to the Queen of Spain* (1993) and *Wild Root* (1998), together with a new collection, *Shed* (2001).

Fast forward was commissioned and broadcast for the 2001 Poetry Proms by BBC Radio 3, while *Wall dreams* and *The other shadow* were commissioned and broadcast by BBC Radio 4 and Radio 3. *Hungarian quartet, The other shadow, The Shadow of God* and *Wire through the heart* were published in book form by Ister (Budapest), together with a CD of the BBC programmes of the last three poem sequences.

The eponymous painting referred to in 'Countryside around Dixon Manor' hangs in the Cheltenham City Art Gallery; the verse prefix in the poem is from *Five Hundred Points of Good Husbandry* by Tusser Thomas (OUP). Ken Smith acknowledged the chapter on Sir John Hawkwood in Geoffrey Trease's *The Condottiere* for his *Hawkwood* sequence, and Andrew Wheatcroft's *The Ottomans* for the prologue to *The Shadow of God*, which is the content of a letter sent by Suleyman the Magnificent to the King of France, proposing an alliance.

The poems from *Work, distances / poems* (Swallow Press, Chicago, 1972) in *Collected Poems* are included in their original order but with later revised texts or revised titles taken from *The Poet Reclining* in some cases, and with some other poems from the same period added where they appear in the selection he made for *The Poet Reclining*.

The publication history of Ken Smith's later work included in *Shed* is well documented in the bibliography. However, *The Poet Reclining* included poems drawn from a variety of small press publications in the US and UK, some of these appearing in more than one previous title, marked in the following list with an asterisk*:

Eleven Poems: Family group*; Grass*; The pity*.

The Pity: Family group*; The street; Country: Keld to Reeth; Grass*; The pity*; The hunter; Water; A fragment.

Academic Board Poems: The boss*.

Arc Pamphlets 4 & 5: The child's version*; The son; Gravedigger; Bitter*.

Work, distances/poems: Exiles; Dream journeys; She speaks; The child's version*; The boss*; Bitter*; Where winter begins; In Pennsylvania, winter's end; After a journey; Little Notes; Persistent narrative; Crying woman; Song for the whites; From the Nahua; The Sioux cleared from Minnesota; Ghost songs; Ghost dances; Where did I learn such quiet [as *Untitled*]. The Wild Turkey [as *Calling the Wild Turkey*]: Wild Turkey One; Wild Turkey Two; Living in the Danelaw [as *The Danelaw*]; Another part of his childhood; A description of the lichway; Wild Turkey Six; A farewell to the city of Exeter; In the Americas, so the tale goes; The author, a teacher of petomania; A journey through part of western Pennsylvania. The Eli poems [as *The dead orchestra*]: The marsh; The third month; Eli's poem; The rooming house; His lament; The obsession; What was done.

Hawk Wolf: Wolf vision; Hawk vision.

Wasichi: Valley*; The clearing.

Tristan Crazy: One for sorrow; Two for nobody; Three: tales of the hunter*; Four, being a prayer to the western wind*; Five, which is here by the river; Six: the wife's complaint; Seven: when he can't sleep for thinking; Eight. The singer; Nine: Shorty's advice to the players*; Ten: the tale unfinished*.

Tales of the Hunter: Tales of Urias the shape-shifter; Old postcards of the river; The Swan; Reports from the east; From the southern river; At the western beacon, the second of the songs of Urias [as *Among the dancers, being the second of the songs of Urias*]; *Tristan Crazy* three [as *Tales of the Hunter*]*, four [as *The fourth song of Urias, a prayer to the western wind*]*, nine [as *Shorty's advice to the players*]*, and ten [as *The message*]*.

What I'm Doing Now: Playing field observations; Caesar Caesar; A right curse on the enemy; Spartan communiqué; From the vale of White Horse; Being the third song of Urias [as *'Lives ago...'*]; In transit; Huneus the shoemaker; Operations undertaken at or near the surface; Transcription of the crying woman; Planting aloes; Mouth; Tongue.

Fox Running: This was revised and extended from its first printing with Rolling Moss Press in 1980 to the 1981 and 1982 Bloodaxe texts.

Between the Dancers: Moiré effect*.

Grainy pictures of the rain: My father fading out; Valley*; Childhood in the lowlands; Sunk Island, that winter; The Tivoli Bar; Federico; Maria the thief; The veterans; Peasant; Duck at Haldon Ponds; Moiré effect*.

Uncollected poems: these poems appeared in the following magazines and anthologies: *Boston Phoenix*, 'Remembering when he was a wolf; *London Magazine*, 'Old business: the drowned bride'; *New Poems 1972-73*, ed. Douglas Dunn (PEN/Hutchinson, 1973), 'To survive'; *Not Poetry*, 'Six items heard in three locations', 'At the college des beaux arts', and 'Some unfinished movements'; *Perfect Bound*, 'Fun City Winter' sequence; *Poems for Shakespeare 4*, ed. Anthony Rudolf (Globe House Publications, 1976), 'Winter occasions'; *Seizure* (Eugene, Oregon), 'Half songs, 1790'; *Stand*, 'To survive', 'Bowl', 'Wants', 'Fly', and 'Lake'; *Surviving in America* (Tucson, Arizona), 'The door'; *Telegram*, 'The poet reclining' and 'The night music'; *23 Modern British Poets*, ed. by John Matthias (Swallow Press, Chicago, 1971), also published as issue 21 of *Triquarterly* (Evanston, Illinois), 'The stone poems'.

Previously unpublished: 'Another night of muttering'; 'Crocus'; 'Surprised again beside the river'; 'Shallow dreaming'; 'Old movies'; 'The Ubi Sunt variations'; 'Fox in October'.

INDEX OF TITLES & SUB-TITLES

BIOGRAPHICAL NOTE

Ken Smith (1938-2003) was a major voice in world poetry, a writer whose work shifted territory with time, from land to city, from Yorkshire, America and London to war-ravaged Eastern Europe. He was called 'the godfather of the new poetry' because his politically edgy, cuttingly colloquial, muscular poetry influenced a whole generation of younger British poets.

Ken Smith was born in Rudston, East Yorkshire, the son of an itinerant farm labourer. He worked in Britain and America as a teacher, freelance writer, barman, magazine editor, potato picker, BBC reader and creative writing fellow, and was writer-in-residence at Wormwood Scrubs prison in 1985-87. He received America's highly prestigious Lannan Literary Award for Poetry in 1997, followed by a Cholmondeley Award in 1998.

Ken Smith was the first poet to be published by Bloodaxe, with his pamphlet *Tristan Crazy* in 1978. Smith's first book, *The Pity*, was published by Jonathan Cape in 1967, and his second, *Work, distances/ poems*, by Swallow Press, Chicago, in 1972. His early books span a transition from his preoccupation with land and myth (when he lived in Yorkshire, Devon and America) to his later engagement with urban Britain and the politics of radical disaffection (when he lived in East London). His first retrospective, *The Poet Reclining: Selected Poems 1962-1980* (Bloodaxe Books, 1982) covered the first half of his writing career.

In 1986 Ken Smith's collection *Terra* was shortlisted for the Whitbread Poetry Award. In 1987 Bloodaxe published his collected prose, *A Book of Chinese Whispers*. Four of his collections, *Terra* (1986), *Wormwood* (1987), *The heart, the border* (1990) and *Tender to the Queen of Spain* (1993), were Poetry Book Society Recommendations. His last separate collection, *Wild Root* (1998), a Poetry Book Society Choice, was shortlisted for the T.S. Eliot Prize. All these collections were included in his second Bloodaxe retrospective, *Shed: Poems 1980-2001* (2002).

In 1989 Harrap published *Inside Time*, Ken Smith's book about imprisonment, about Wormwood Scrubs and the men he met there. This was published in paperback by Mandarin in 1990. Ken Smith was working in Berlin when the Wall came down, writing a book about East and West Berlin: this turned into *Berlin: Coming in from the Cold* (Hamish Hamilton, 1990; Penguin paperback, 1991). He edited *Klaonica: poems for Bosnia* (Bloodaxe Books/ *The Independent*, 1993) with Judi Benson, and with Matthew Sweeney co-edited *Beyond Bedlam* (Anvil Press Poetry, 1997), a book of poems by mentally ill people.

He died on 27 June 2003 from a hospital infection caught while being treated for Legionnaires' Disease, which he had contracted months earlier in Cuba. His last poems were published in *You Again: last poems & other words* (Bloodaxe Books, 2004) along with other uncollected work, tributes from other poets, photographs, a biographical portrait, an essay by Colin Raw with extracts from letters, and interviews covering the whole range of his life and work; this is the most comprehensive source of critical writings on his poetry. His *Collected Poems* was published by Bloodaxe in October 2018, coinciding with his 80th birthday and with the 40th anniversary of the publication of Bloodaxe's first title, Ken Smith's *Tristan Crazy* (1978).